Enchanted Community

Enchanted Community
Journey Into the Mystery of the Church

Robert Thornton Henderson

Wipf & Stock Publishers
Eugene, Oregon

ENCHANTED COMMUNITY: JOURNEY INTO THE MYSTERY OF THE CHURCH

Copyright © 2006 Robert Thornton Henderson. All rights reserved. Except for brief quotations in critical publications or reviews, no part of this book may be reproduced in any manner without prior written permission from the publisher. Write: Permissions, Wipf & Stock, 199 W. 8th Ave., Suite 3, Eugene, OR 97401.

ISBN: 1-59752-665-7

Manufactured in the U.S.A.

ROBERT THORNTON (BOB) HENDERSON

Born: 1928 in Miami, Florida. Education at Davidson College, Westminster and Columbia Theological Seminaries. Pastor for forty years in the Presbyterian Church (USA). Served as Presbyterian campus pastor at North Carolina State; pastor of Blacknall Presbyterian Church of Durham, NC; pastor of Canal Street Presbyterian Church of New Orleans, LA; denominational staff director in the field of evangelism for four years; and pastor of First Presbyterian Church of Hendersonville, NC. After retirement he was Director of Seminary Ministries for Presbyterians For Renewal for ten years. During those years he was a leader in the renewal movements within the Presbyterian Church, served on the former Inter-Varsity Christian Fellowship corporation board; was co-program chair for the Presbyterian Congress on Renewal in Dallas in 1985. He is also the author of: *Of Beans and Philistines* (published by the Division of National Ministry of the Presbyterian Church, 1976); *Joy to the World* (Zondervan, 1980); *Beating the Church-going Blahs* (IVP, 1986); *A Door of Hope* (Herald, 1997); *Blueprint 21* (Providence House, 2000); and *Subversive Jesus, Radical Grace* (NavPress, 2001). Mr. Henderson makes his home in Tucker, GA. with his wife Betty of 52 years.

Table of Contents

Preface
    Beginning of the Journey Into the Church   ix

Journey One
    The Church: Enigmatic and Enchanted   1

Journey Two
    Church: Enchanted Community in the Trinitarian Embrace   19

Journey Three
    Disenchantment: The Groaning Creation   34

Journey Four
    The Enchanted One: Jesus   56

Journey Five
    Jesus Forms the Infant Church   82

Journey Six
    Emergence of the Enchanted Community   111

Journey Seven
    Signs of Authenticity-I   132

Journey Eight
    Signs of Authenticity–II   153

Journey Nine
    You Are Here: What Now?   169

Journey Ten
    Enchanted Community Begins With …   189

Stopping Place
    Enchanted Aliens Between the Ages   209

Preface

Beginnings of My Journey Into the Mystery

Several months ago my wife and I were in Oxford, England for the wedding of two cherished friends. While there several of us took the occasion to go on the C. S. Lewis Tour, which we found advertised on a web site. The irony of the whole event was that the tour guide's only claim to expertise was that he had grown up in the same neighborhood as that of Lewis' home (the Kilns) and had been a playmate of Lewis' stepson. He knew most of the important Lewis academic and social hangouts, favorite pubs, burial site, and general family geography. We were astonished, however, when he confessed that he had never read anything that Lewis wrote, and had no significant understanding (or apparent interest) in what it was that made C. S. Lewis one of the most influential Christians and cultural figures of the 20th century. He knew the neighborhood and that a famous person lived there, but he had no curiosity beyond that.

All of that experience feeds right into the question that has provoked this book. I have often wondered: how many of the people who 'inhabit' our congregations, week by week, have ever wondered what the *church* really is? Or why it exists? Or have any clue as to how it fits into the ultimate missional purpose of God, which is to bless all the nations of the world through his Son? I wonder how many are even curious about the church beyond the borders of their own particular community, parish activities, or tradition?

I, for one, am totally fascinated by the enigma of the Church. This is nothing new, of course. The church has always been an enigma to God's people, from its very beginnings. And it has, not infrequently, also been a stumbling block. The church becomes increasingly confusing to a generation of spiritually hungry folk *outside* of it who don't quite know where it fits into their quest for some understanding of the transcendent.

I am 75 years old, and have spent my adult life as a pastor of congregations in (primarily) cosmopolitan university communities. That means that I am long accustomed to the questions and puzzlements of agnostics and inquirers. But there's something different in the air at the dawn of this new century. And that "something" gives me hope.

My 20-ish friends, on one hand, appear to be those who are not willing to be detached spectators and cynics about the church, but neither are they quite ready to accept uncritically all of the traditions of the church without some searching questions. On the other hand they seem determined to invade the church in all of its enigmatic expressions and to get to the heart of what it is that Jesus intended when he said: "I will build my Church …"

They express both their *need* for the Church-as-community, and their *bewilderment* by it. They are looking, often with fascination, at the multi-faceted traditions and the history of the church back to its beginnings. They candidly state, on one hand, that to them the church is mystifying, embarrassing, and contradictory, … and on the other, that they are intrigued by its history and existence. They also know that somehow they need some kind of community of other believers in Jesus Christ. They know that the Church is somehow involved in that need. This book is written for them, and in many ways in dialogue with them, as we share this journey together. It is, I trust, a book suffused with both honest questioning and with abounding hope.

More recently I have had occasion to be somewhat significantly involved in mentoring seminarians in various theological schools across the nation. There I found men and women engaged in studying to be well-equipped church leaders and pastor-teachers. I also have spent time surveying the curricula of many of these seminaries and found it somewhat mind-boggling that there seems scant attention paid to serious study of the

Preface

essence of the church. When I have raised the question of what the church is all about in student gatherings, I usually got back a puzzled response as to what that question has to do with anything.

There seems to be a dearth of focus on *ecclesiology* (the doctrine of the church), and even less on a *missional ecclesiology*. It is somehow assumed by these theological schools that these men and women have already figured all of that out beforehand. They are being prepared, therefore, to be leaders in church institutions that have quite often not a clue as to why they exist, except to exist (and survive). Now then, if such is true of the church's pastors and teachers, then how much more of the other 98% of the church who are the followers of Jesus, and who are relegated to that dubious category of *laity*?

My own sojourn as a teacher of the Church's missional and evangelistic task has given me occasion to trip over this enigma time and again. My question goes something like this: Is there a *missional ecclesiology* (an understanding of the church) which sees through and beyond the church's institutional traditions and forms to whatever it is that the church is intended to be in the heart and purpose of God? Is there a wholesome *image of the church* that would enable us to see beyond the ecclesial paraphernalia, which so easily consumes us and so often distracts us, to whatever it is that makes the church to be "the dwelling place of God by the Holy Spirit" (Ephesians 2:22)?

Is it possible for us to project ourselves outside of traditional boundaries? Do we have the imagination to think into unthinkable dimensions, to explore into mystery and poetry and into the very heart of God? Is the communal expression of God's great *salvation* a giant piece of God's gospel that has been somehow diminished by seeing it all too familiarly through our merely human eyes?

I look with hope and expectation upon the generations[1] now emerging into adulthood. Someone noted that it was some restless young adults by the name of Madison, Jefferson and Adams who conceived of a form of government which no one had ever before experienced. I also recall from

---

[1] Actually there are at least a couple of generations: the so-called GenX, who are at this writing in their twenties and early thirties, then there is the Millennial Generation (GenY, NetGen, etc.) in their later teens and early twenties. These are two distinct generations, yet the questions with which I want to grapple are, I think, common to both of these.

church history that figures such as Ignatius Loyola as well as John Calvin were both intense young disciples who began their influential role in the church in the restlessness of youth. I have this hope for my young friends in their quest for the essence of the church. I acknowledge the folly of my attempting to jump back fifty years and over the two or three generational cultures to these young friends. God has, however, blessed me with some unique conversation partners from it who keep trying to clue me in.

I need to make several explanations (apologies?) to my readers pertaining to some of the idiosyncrasies of what follows:

- I will use interchangeably the designations *New Creation* and *Kingdom of God*. They are at least near-synonymous in my mind. I tend to use New Creation more often since we moderns don't know what to do with kingdoms! New Creation is used by Paul, though in the New Testament the gospel is most frequently designated the gospel as the "gospel of the kingdom of God."
- You will also be puzzled by my seeming and somewhat arbitrary capitalization of the word *church*. This is purely subjective on my part. I will intentionally use small caps on the word church to speak of those expressions of the community as we experience them and may also be forgetful of their calling. I use small caps to designate that evaluation. But those expressions that have some degree of authenticity in the essence of God's intention I will capitalize as *Church*. You will know that I am making a value judgment here (and maybe forgive me!).
- This book is in the form of something of a dialogue or conversation. Dialogue is always more awkward on the printed page than in audio or video form since you can't see who is speaking or hear the sound of different voices. So you will just register that I ordinarily will put my dialogue partner's (Alan's) questions and comments in quotation marks and will use a different type-font to indicate that it is he (Alan) who is speaking or interrupting or questioning.
- I have already acknowledged my inadequacy in jumping back over several generations and being aware of quite different traditions between these cultures. One of the acknowledged differences is that the Millennials, especially, tend to be unfamiliar with the Biblical story. For this reason at times I will go to some lengths to

retell the Story, so as to bring them up to speed.
- I will acknowledge before the fact that I am consciously challenging some of the church's traditional definitions of itself (with which I am more than familiar) . Perhaps better, I am re-examining the *raison d'etre*, the foundations that have too often gone unnoticed or unexamined beneath the church's life and mission. I expect that this will provoke some defensiveness ... but as the visible and communal expression of God's joyous news it must elicit more than skepticism. There must be some authentic consonance of the church with its message of joyous news in Christ. I will acknowledge those church institutions and such ecclesiastical phenomena as clergy, sacraments, and many of the practices that have accrued over two millennia, and that I personally think need some serious and Biblical rethinking. Enough said. I don't really want to go there!

Finally, I will take the risk of deliberately using something of a dialogical scheme in what follows. I can see no reason why serious engagement with ideas should be some sterile theological treatise laid out in mind-numbing scholarly form. My young conversation partner in this work is actually more of a composite person than a fictitious one. He will be engaging me (probing me?) with the questions that need to be addressed.

I offer these proposals or perspectives in the hope of generating an ongoing dialogue with my young friends emerging into the adventure of adulthood, and hopefully on a journey into the heart of God and the essence of the Church.

So I begin in the Name and for the Glory of Jesus Christ, the Lamb of God.

Journey One
The Church: Enigmatic and Enchanted

"Mind if I ask you a question?" Alan inquired.

You can ask. I don't guarantee answers. Fire away.

"What's your 'take' on the *church*? What's it got to do with anything? Where does it fit into my life as a follower of Jesus? As a disciple?"

In five words, or less? Like, first of all: where does that question come from, and what's behind it? It is a loaded question, you know.

"Before I get into that I'd like to know, just off the top of your head, how you perceive the church. I'm totally confused, and get more so the more I try to find a place for it in my commitment to be a follower of Jesus."

OK. But when you ask that, you've got to begin by sorting out the distinction between your own personal *experiences* of the church, then all of those other *expressions* of the church in past and present, and then, finally, discern whatever it is that is the *essence* of the church in the mind and mission of God.

That can get pretty complicated.

"Maybe so, but let's start with your own experience of the church. How would you describe it to me? Because frankly, I'm pretty confused, maybe even bummed by it all."

(I had to laugh) OK. Try on some descriptions like: *enigmatic, enchanted, confusing, mysterious, awesome, contradictory, uncontrollable, clandestine, impossible, laughable, and unpredictable* – just for starts. These descriptions come to mind. All of the above. Are you still with me?

"Sheesh! Where did you ever come up with a list like that? Especially the 'enchanted' bit? Where'd that one come from? That has to do with something, like, magic. That's about the last thing I would ever connect with any church I ever encountered. Are you serious?"

What Alan didn't know was that our conversation was actually the third such that I had found myself in over the past several months, and in which I had unexpectedly had my nose pushed into someone's dilemma over the church. Those, in turn, had been forcing me to come to grips with my own ambiguous understanding about the church. More than I had realized, I was afraid to face up to a lot of the consequences of what I might discover hidden in the closets of my own heart and mind. I guess I had lived for years in a "lover's quarrel" with the church.

For fifty years my career has been as a pastor and a teacher in the thick of it. I suppose I have accepted its institutional focus and its theological definitions of itself, all the time secretly unconvinced. I have submitted myself to its disciplines and order (such as they were), and found them too sterile to be of any wholesome significance. But the church of my experience was the only one I knew. The voices that secretly whetted my excitement about what the church might be, came from rebel (and controversial) theologians out on the margins.[1]

Alan is twenty-two, blonde, pony-tailed, bespectacled, and a graduate student in bioengineering. His exceptional intellect is obvious. His questioning is relentless. His insatiable spiritual appetite is often in conflict with a brutal honesty (which is not always well received in "comfort-zone" christian communities). I found him to be a true gift of God to me. He provoked me to climb out of my own jaded acceptance of the normal ecclesiastical ruts which I had come to accept. But he also made me stretch to see into his generational culture, which is so radically *other* than mine. We had initially met on several occasions after worship with the large

---

[1] Leonardo Boff, Jacques Ellul, Miguez Bonino, and more recently Gerhard Lohfink, Lesslie Newbigin, Orlando Costas and many others.

congregation which I attended and which he attended, occasionally, on his search. He was a winsome guy. I came to love him.

But, as I said, he was the third such of similarly insistent provocations.[2]

David: The Disconnect Between Life and the Church

The first encounter with such a probing inquiry came at the end of a long day of a weekend conference. The two of us were sitting in the lounge of a lovely resort looking through the rain-spattered plate glass windows across Boundary Bay to the distant lights on the Canadian shore. I was a septuagenarian interloper into a conference of about 150 younger (GenX) adults who had come together from across the country for a weekend to explore the question of how it is that the true Life and Light that was theirs in Christ was to express itself in the transformation of church and society.[3]

The make-up and leadership of that conference was, to understate it, absolutely awesome. These folk came from their own responsible involvements in the church. They represented most of the traditions: Roman, Orthodox, mainline Protestant, evangelical, Pentecostal, and independent. A few were pastors or priests. All would have identified with a broad Christian orthodoxy (in contrast with theological liberalism, or ecclesiastical trendiness), though designations such as "orthodox" or "evangelical" were seldom evoked. It was a new experience for me to be in such a setting where the richness and diversity of all of these traditions were warmly and wholesomely celebrated.

At the same time, all had come with an unfulfilled spiritual and vocational hungering – a questing for something beyond, and more than what they were realizing in their own local incarnations and church experiences. Theirs was a mutual persuasion that the true Life, that was ours in Christ, was to be a creative and transforming presence in the world.

---

[2] Alan is more a composite than a fictitious person. He represents real persons with whom I am in conversation. It is easier for me to hear and respond to a real person than to engage in abstract propositions.
[3] I use the setting of the Vine conference, in Blaine, WA in February of 2002, and this is an actual conversation which I had with a friend.

Yet, there were so many discouragements and constricting traditions which were inimical to that vision. There were so many narrow perspectives and limiting horizons. Their own church communities seemed, for the most part, hardly aware of much beyond their own ecclesiastical self-perpetuation (which seems a harsh judgment, but was a common disappointment among them).

It was a creatively planned weekend. Its setting was at a conducively lovely resort. The design was to explore, primarily in panel discussions, something like twenty-nine different areas of Christian presence, transformation, and creativity. All of the participants were assigned to be presenters in panels of their special interests, discerned in pre-registration forms. The spiritual and intellectual energy generated was both thrilling and exhausting.

Gathered in that place were musicians, lawyers, journalists, medical personnel, research scientists, community organizers, authors, environmentalists, plus the leader of an international youth movement, to name but a few. This whole spectrum of thoughtful folk was gathered, and included a very small handful of us elder interlopers. The energy washed over round tables at mealtime, into small assigned discussion and prayer groups, intensified in the panel discussions, and was all brought back together before God in beautiful and profound worship times.

It was after an evening of such worship that David asked if we could have some time together to talk. I had no idea why he singled me out for this, but I liked the idea, and so we had wandered off to the lounge, settled into this table overlooking the bay, ordered drinks, and plugged-in to one another. David, I found, was coordinator of company strategies for a growing start-up, and quite successful, software company. He had progressed rapidly up through the ranks. He was modest in relating this to me, but it became obvious that his rise was because he was incredibly gifted at what he was doing. He was, professionally, well accepted and respected, and even sought out by competitors in the industry. He had a happy marriage to a similarly gifted wife, and they were expecting their first child.

"This conference totally freaks me out!" was his opening salvo when I asked how he was responding to the day we had been through. "And I love it!" he added. So, curious and amused, all I could say was: "Alright, fill me in."

"It's like this conference speaks to my whole sense of what Jesus' call to me to be the light and salt of the world is all about. It does it in such a compelling way. These are sounds that I never, never hear in my church in Portland. And that's precisely where my frustration lies here. I really love my church. I love the people. I'm really attached to my pastor. It has always been affirmative of Christian and Biblical orthodoxy. This is all important to me.

"But this is precisely where my frustration enters. I could be totally consumed with the inner life of our church. Yet, … always lurking in the back of my mind is how it all relates to my work, my neighborhood, my life outside the church institution. That subject seldom comes up. Hey, I'm into strategies, and about thinking into the future, for at least fifty hours a week. But the strategy of my church seems to go no further than the happy maintenance of our existence and programs. On the few occasions that I have raised questions about our ministry outside the four walls of church meetings, or of how we support each other in this ministry, … the only responses I got were either non-comprehension of what I was suggesting, … or a lame: 'You ought to go into the ministry.'

"Bob, do you catch my frustration? I *am* in a very real ministry every day of my life. That's where I live. What I know, and what you know, and what this conference is underscoring 'in spades' is that Jesus lives in us by the Spirit so that we can be redemptive, creative, and transforming forces wherever we are. Every panel here,[4] every discussion I've been in today, was an immersion into a community of others excited about such a calling. The others in my discussion and prayer group have shared my frustration, and have prayed for me. They all sense the same tensions.

"And Monday I fly back to Portland. I go back to a church in its own little 'churchy' world. I go back to my daily life and calling in a totally other competitive 'kick butt' world with no discernable moral or spiritual framework.

---

[4] There were something like 29 different panels with such themes as: "Personal Tales of …" with stories of a holocaust survivor's encounter with a Nazi general's daughter and the forgiveness: or "Rising Protest v. Sound Business" with one presentation on the negative effect of globalization on the developing world; or "A Culture Readjusting" with such presentations on what it means to be a free society, or will this transform out consumer culture? Or "The Church's Role In the Changing Face of America" that dealt with the multi-culturalism, and the need for intercultural engagement. I was a presenter in a panel on the environment. There were panels for writers on the necessity of community in the writing process, and a panel for the aficionados of Tolkien and C. S. Lewis. Nearly everyone could find a panel that dealt with issues that he or she met in their daily life and work, which was the purpose of it all.

If I were honest, I think I'd chuck the church as a distraction to Christ's calling. But that calls forth my second frustration in being here, and that is how much I need others on this same pilgrimage as I, and how much I need the rich traditions of the larger church which has struggled in this same pilgrimage over all of these centuries. I'm being stretched. How about you?"

I could only resonate with his frustration. Then he plied me with questions about how I had coped with this in my career of pastoral leadership. Actually, it was my own sense of this all-too-frequent dichotomy that caused me to perk up when I read the announcement of this very conference. But here, David had focused me again on the issue of the essence of the church and its design in the mind and heart of God.

A Bible Study Discussion in Galatians

Several months later, it came up again. Our Sunday morning Bible discussion bunch had been studying, and processing, Paul's letter to the infant Christian community in Galatia for many weeks. We were digesting some of the implications of it for ourselves. There was a pause in the discussion while we all pondered it, when Ann (who is a lawyer and who has a gift of keeping the discussions honest) broke the silence and verbalized her question: "Something here troubles me, or doesn't fit. Paul is warning these Galatians about those Jewish believers who were teaching the Gentile believers the necessity of Torah, and especially of circumcision for true Christian faith. OK? And Paul has been exalting the total sufficiency of Christ as the one who has fulfilled that law for us, and through whom we are, therefore, justified by our faith in him. OK? But there's something else more subtle here that leaves me with a big question.

"Look at the contrast he draws: over against all of the rules and rites of temple and Torah, what does Paul offer? He offers something that is a bit 'off the chart' of my own experience. He talks as though these Galatians all had experienced the *reality* of some kind of a dynamic Spirit-inhabited community. Look at how often he refers to their *experience* of the Spirit. Those repetitive references to life in the Spirit portray lives and relationships and behavior which were all being dynamically formed and animated into newness by that Power. The experience he seems to be describing is not some external and impersonal and institutional religion. It sounds like something transformational and intimate and authentic in Christ. Words such as *love, joy, patience,* and *longsuffering* all speak of some unique kind of community not in my experience here! Are you with me?

"OK. So what's my problem?

"I don't see much difference between what those troublesome Judaizing people were representing, and my own experience in this thousand member church institution we belong to here. You get baptized, you join the church, you give your tithes, you serve on a committee, you attend the church programs. ... All OK, maybe even fun, but all external and impersonal. Whatever the Galatians experience of community dynamic in the Spirit is all about, all sounds good to me—but I've missed it. We've got a very congenial church institution here, but it surely doesn't fit the Spirit dimensions we're looking at here in our Galatians study. Or have I missed something?"

Phil picked it up. Our discussion group had been together long enough and were comfortable enough to challenge easy assumptions. Phil sharpened Ann's question. "If the temple and the priesthood, and the external rites, and the keeping of the law are so inimical to the Spirit, then what is so different about that from our 'doing church' here in a congregation (if we are to be honest) of basic strangers. We all accept baptism and observe the Eucharist with the other strangers. We all give our tithes, ... all of these without any significant relationships formed out of love and grace in our mutual pilgrimage, and without the mutual exercise of our gifts? Paul's instructions here all have to do with *relationships* within the community. Hey! apart from this discussion group I hardly know anybody in this large congregation more than superficially. So how is our 'doing church' different from 'doing Temple' for the Jews?"

Needless to say, that provoked an interesting discussion of what the church was intended to be in God's redemptive plan, and then what it actually was in our experiences. We never got to any resolution, since time ran out on us. But the question lingered in my mind. The question also kept cropping up in our discussions over the following weeks. How is the church more than an acceptable and comfortable religious institution? The problem with such discussions is that you just get 'on a roll' and it's time to quit and go to the next activity (sometimes called "worship").

Most of us agreed that the bonds and relationships we had developed with each other over those months of discussion and study were probably closer to the kind of Spirit community described by Paul in Galatians than most of our other church associations. But ... it still left something incomplete and unfulfilled. The alternative realities of *institutional religion* (Jewish or Christian) by way of contrast with some kind of community which is dynamically created *in Christ* and *through the Spirit* were clearly on the table for us, ... and uncomfortably so. After all, we were all quite responsibly involved in this particular vibrant church institution. But it was time to go.

Alan's Dilemma

All this was in my recent experience when Alan raised the question again that morning in the coffee shop.

I need to explain again something of this conversation, but more particularly of my relationship to Alan. In many ways it is a strange and unlikely friendship. We are three generations apart. We are formed by distinctly different, even disparate, cultures. First impressions can be very deceptive. My first impression of Alan certainly was. Here was this ponytailed guy in casual dress. Another typical university student (whatever "typical" defines)? There wasn't anything about his quiet demeanor to suggest the profound and surging inquiry within. I had first met him one Sunday morning at a gathering of the church with which I was affiliated. After that I did not see him again for several months until this chance meeting at the coffee shop. It was one of those "where have I seen you before?" situations in which you know you've met the other somewhere, but can't immediately put your finger on when or where. So we recollected our initial meeting (after a few false starts). Then we put aside what we had been doing and spent nearly an hour getting acquainted.

We implicitly liked each other. I have never quite understood the chemistry between persons which produces that kind of bonding. It was unmistakably there between Alan and me from the beginning. It is still remarkable to me that it should be so, since we are such totally different types of personality. Alan is twenty-two, something of a prodigy and, as I have noted, at the beginning his doctoral program in bioengineering. That means that right from the get-go our minds operate on different tracks (planets?) because I have only the vaguest notion of what bioengineering is all about. He, likewise, doesn't have a clue as to where my mind roams.

The Church: Enigmatic and Enchanted

His story is that he grew up nominally and marginally identified with the Christian faith and the church. It was for him only a cultural identification, and only on the outer fringes of his priorities. He was never knowledgeable about, or convinced of, the Christian position or worldview. He was an Information Age product with a vast curiosity. Whatever he knew or had experienced of the church had certainly not impressed him in the slightest. It seemed to him not to have much of anything to do with anything that was of significance to him.

In the university world he found the outlet for his immense curiosity. He wasn't at all a party-animal. He simply pursued knowledge relentlessly, and found his social companions with those of mutual intellectual interests. Secular? Probably. Postmodern? That's a bit too facile, but that certainly was a factor. Irreligious? No, not intentionally. He was simply at that point where he was fascinated by the data, and every new idea, but had not seriously contemplated the larger picture of reality.

Late in his junior year he somehow became aware of the questions behind the questions. His professors seemed to avoid the questions that Alan was asking. Why is all of this so? Where does this obvious design come from? What precedes observable data? What does it all mean? What is my life all about? And is my life significant in anything of ultimate value? All of this triggered a subliminal restlessness and a growing conviction that there was some huge piece missing in his picture of reality. To say, then, that a spiritual quest was begun at that point which ultimately brought him to a point of awakening, and then to the awesome reality of Jesus Christ. This "conversion" as you can easily imagine was not in any way superficial or sudden. It was certainly not mindless. It came after some rather agonizing and soul-searching inquiry. It was not without multiple doubts and cynical responses along the way. His puzzlement about the church was simply another piece of that process.

It follows that what I encountered in him that day in the coffee shop also severely disturbed my own comfort-zone—my own repeated attempts to escape facing this question. Sitting across from me was a person with a wholesomely reckless and insistent mind. Alan was, first of all, dead-serious on following Jesus and allowing God to live in him. But he was also on a quest to satisfy his moral and intellectual integrity. He was delightfully honest and candid. But then again he was restive with many of the mindless assumptions of so much of the *church culture* that he had experienced thus far.

On the other hand, one of the components that had precipitated his new life was the sheer cynicism, the numbing secularism, and the meaningless hedonism of the guys he lived around. In the midst of all those currents, Alan was also not intimidated at complexity, with seeming contradictions and ambiguity, or with any of the other challenges of the "secular whitewater" he was experiencing. After all, the *chaos theory* is familiar territory to most of the scientific community.

But the church was obviously a subject that was very much of an enigma to him.

That's Alan. Then there's me. I am a somewhat typical expression of my own generation, which is almost the opposite of Alan's. Notwithstanding that I have prided myself in keeping somewhat abreast and informed of the changing and emerging cultural and contextual realities of his generation (at least more than most of my generation keep abreast), I was hardly prepared for what these next months would produce.

After all, as I have said, I've been around for a quite a while and I have walked as a follower of Jesus for most of that time. I have spent my whole adult life as a teacher and a writer and a leader within the Christian community. I am too jaded and conditioned by the unquestioning sameness of my experiences within the ecclesiastical traditions. I am, likewise, probably too accepting of the definitions of the church produced by academic theologians to think with any freshness unless provoked.

OK, so Alan provoked me. He uncorked a bottle and let out the *genie* of my own unresolved restlessness with the church. In a real sense my engagement with him was tantamount to a converting experience for me. It was an awakening to a more awesome contemplation of the Church[5] than I ever imagined before that time.

Back to the Conversation with Alan

"Get real! Enchanted? Right. Like, that implies something *magic*."

---

[5] A word of explanation here: I will attempt henceforth to use the capitalized "Church" for what I consider the essence of God's design for it, the reality of the Spirit Community which Jesus is building, and conversely, the small-caps "church" for the institutional

The Church: Enigmatic and Enchanted

Of course it does. This whole God-created and God-occupied world is *enchanted*. We're not alone here, you know. So why should it seem so strange that the community of folk who somehow relate to God as daughters and sons through Jesus should have some aura of *magic* about them, something *enchanted* about their life together? Does that seem so strange? After all, one of the Biblical writers actually defines the church as the *dwellingplace of God by the Holy Spirit.*[6] So is the church *enchanted,* or what?

"No, when you put it that way, it's pretty awesome."

He processed that for a few moments, swirling his coffee around in his cup. I was glad for the time because, frankly, that was an image that even surprised me. I had come up with it unpremeditated and "out of the blue" some months before. I had never taken time to clearly define it in my own mind. In a sense, I was running to keep ahead of him (or even up with) in this conversation.

"Are you going to leave me dangling out here with that outrageous description, or are we going somewhere with it?"

I told him that to be honest I didn't really know. I didn't even know where that description had come from, … it certainly wasn't premeditated. It had just passed through my mind at some point as having potential for further reflection. Maybe our meeting was expressive of the very *enchantment* that it pointed to, like, to something *mysteriously other* that takes charge of conversations and thoughts from time to time. First of all, I needed to know where *his* question came from. What was the story behind it? What had provoked it? I asked him to fill me in on the background.

Alan's Story

"I guess that you deserve that. Look, Bob, I'm not always certain of where such questions come from, but this one won't go away. I know I am influenced, maybe formed, on the one hand by the *church sub-culture* that has always been a small piece of the landscape of my life even if it was only on the margins. I know, too, that I am influenced, or

---

expressions that pass for the Church, but which are probably less than … (My spell-checker has a hard time with this usage!)
[6] Ephesians 2:22

formed, probably much more by my total immersion in the somewhat hostile rejection of that same god-thing in the circles I've operated in here in the university. I've got about as robust a cynical streak in me as anybody.

"But for these past couple of years, since 'the lights went on' for me, and since I became persuaded of Jesus and all the new awareness of Reality and of Truth and of Meaning that came along with that, ... I've been looking at everything, like *everything*, with a new set of eyes. But somehow this has precipitated as many questions as it has answers. And primary among those unanswered questions is the one that has to do with the church. I'm having a really tough time making a 'connect' between the *church sub-culture* that I have experienced, and the message of Jesus that I have been studying in the New Testament.

"What has made it an issue for me was when the pastor of West Park Church (where I met you) figured out that I had been hanging around long enough and was a 'hot prospect' and so asked me if I had ever considered *joining*? I asked him: 'What does 'joining' mean? Why should I join?' His answers were *non-answers*. They were like: it was what Christians did. Or, I would meet a lot of wonderful people. And that the Bible expected God's people to come together. Plus: there were a whole lot of wonderful activities that I would enjoy, ... stuff along that line. None of it seemed to have much (if anything) to do with my desire to follow Jesus, or to be faithful in obeying him. It was almost like they needed more participants for the activities of their religious club. I told the pastor I needed some time to think that one over.

"So I've been thinking about it, ... and the enigma only gets worse. For these past months I've been researching it. I've been making the rounds of a bunch of the other churches to see what was going on. I checked out churches like Antiochan Orthodox, Roman Catholic, Southern Baptist, Pentecostal, plus some others like the Vineyard, and one neighborhood church. It's been interesting, to say the least, and helpful I guess. All of them point to something, to transcendence, to God, to Jesus. I have at times really been deeply moved and blessed in those experiences. Yet somehow so much of it all seems so depersonalized and coldly institutional, so consumed with their own inner life. What I saw was mostly a comfortable 'in house' religious society with a lot of assumptions and activities that didn't seem to have a lot to do with anything, but which are obviously presumed to be an important part of the Christian 'shtick'.

"Is that cruel?

"Not only that, but I've been reading my Bible with a focus on the church. I read a history of the church. I even read a missional history[7] of the church and of the Christian faith. Fascinating. The missional history exacerbates my dilemma even more. But that's, like, a whole other story.

"Bob. I am just having trouble seeing where the church fits into the gospel. I really don't see it. I know it's assumed as a *given* with Christians. I know that somehow it has got to be a critical part of what Jesus came to accomplish. It's all over the New Testament. I know that the church has had an enormous impact on history and culture. I know, too, that the whole thing is complicated even more by being made up of such a scruffy collection of imperfect people – me for instance. I know that the reality of God's generous forgiveness is critical to its existence. All that being so, somehow what I've experienced of it on one hand, and what I understand of the Biblical message of Jesus and of the kingdom of God on the other … just don't connect in my mind. Is there somehow a Church behind the church? Is there a Reality behind the *institutional* phenomenon? Or is this just some unreal illusion that I have?

"What's missing in my picture? All of my encouragement and nurture come from a small bunch of us on campus. We get together every week to study the Bible, to pray for each other, then eat together, laugh, and process our lives with each other. We're really bonded. It's really helpful to have some friends like them with whom to share the realities, and the crap, that are part of daily life. It's simple. Oh, sometimes we could wish for some kind of a mentor to sit with us, a person with more maturity than we possess, but where do we even begin look to find such a person? Still that little gang of us guys know and relate and care about each other.

"What I'm saying to you is that the pastor's proposal about 'joining' his large enterprise called 'the church' looks like a major distraction to my attempt to follow Christ. How can all of that vast institutional stuff be 'the dwelling place of God by the Spirit?'

---

[7] He had been reading David Bosch, *Transforming Mission* (Orbis Press).

"I don't even know where square #1 is in trying to figure this all out. Do I accept this institution, this phenomenon, which designates itself as 'the church' and then seek to find some justification for it all in the Bible? Or, do I look at what is somewhat discernable and formidable about the church in the Bible first of all, and then draw my definitions out of that? I know the question is much more complex than that. Still, like, it seems to me that there are a whole bunch of assumptions in the church that wouldn't stand Biblical scrutiny (and whenever I have raised them, people get very defensive). Then there are a lot of obvious priorities and practices in the New Testament documents which don't seem to show up very prominently in the present phenomena of the church.

"Is that a valid observation?"

Allow me to sharpen this up a bit more before I go on. Alan wanted and needed some kind of community of fellow sojourners with Jesus. He knew that. That made his quest more poignant. He also had a rather mature sense of *calling* by Christ to be "salt and light." It also meant that his associations with people with whom he interacted daily on campus, with those from other world religions, or with those who were contemptuous of all religions, or with the spiritual "zombies" were very much of a priority with him. He was unavoidably in frequent conversation with such people.

Add to that, also, his sense of stewardship as it pertained to his own career in bioengineering, which was a major focus in his sense of discipleship. He found companionship, mutual calling, thoughtfulness, and encouragement from that small group of believers with whom he met on campus. All of them shared the same Biblical worldview as well as their desire to grow in Christ. They were his community of fellow sojourners. By way of contrast, most of what he experienced "in the church" while it may have been "spiritual" (as he put it) it was at the same time quite distracting, simply because it essentially lacked any of the incarnational earthiness that his own sense of *calling* required. So I continued …

Of course it's valid. But it's not new.

The church has always struggled with its incarnation. It has always been restless with its form and its mission. Every generation has its questioners. It has formed (or packaged) its life together in an endless variety of expressions. One thing is pretty obvious, however, and that is that the church is somehow God's doing and because of that it has survived its fallible human leadership. After all, it is Jesus who is "building" his church. Every time there is some man-made effort to *contain* that church in an institution, … or to *control* it with all kinds of ecclesiastical rules, … it will inevitably break out in some new movement, or in some unpredictable form.

Face it: the church really is not controllable. Or you could probably say that the church is out of control! It is free, … too free for some! It is much more of a communal gospel phenomenon than it is any kind of an ecclesial institution. We're pretty slow to "get it." The more rigidly we seek to impose our order on the church, the more we diminish its true Life, and the more likely we are to see some new missional movement erupt, or some *end run* emerge in some totally unexpected way. It will do this either inside that existing church institution, or outside in some new communal expression.

I remember a Christian author once reporting how resistant her non-believing peers were to even approach the subject of Jesus Christ. She reflected that "Jesus is too wild and free for the timid!"[8] I think the same is true for the church. The true Church, as a missional community, is too wild and free for the timid. Its very being and mission in the heart of God, and the design of God, are absolutely "wild and free." It is happily disrespectful of the best intended human institutions, control, and definitions (or attempts to extinguish it). But for us to say what visible form *is* and what visible form *is not* the Church is likewise perilous. Church *institutions* and *the Church* interact and interweave and somehow interanimate each other all through history. Mystery.

I had been eager to get a little more background out of Alan, however, just so I could be sure we're both on the same page. I asked what else precipitated his question to me about the church. His answer is worth noting here.

---

[8] I think it was Madeline L'Engle.

Enchanted Community

"OK. Right there in the middle of his career Jesus comes to his disciples with this 'I will build my church' statement. So there he is making all of those outlandish metaphorical statements about himself being the Door, the Way, the Truth, the Life, ... that no one comes to the Father but through him, ... about the broad ways that go to destruction, but a small and narrow way that goes to true life, ... stuff like that. They all look like *teasers* to me. Then, this question: 'Who do you guys think I am?' And finally it dawns on them, *ka-zowie*: 'You're the long-awaited Messiah? Wow!'

"So then, what would you expect him to do next? Well, first he lets them know that even that startling revelation isn't something they figured out on their own (and that's a little spooky in itself!). But then what is even more surprising is his response to Peter (and the rest). ... And, Bob, this is probably what is behind my question to you. It almost looks like a *non-sequiter*, like 'I will build my *church*, and nothing will stop it'.[9] Not a temple or a religious institution, but an entrance into something *other* – an assembly or a community—something beyond the religious stuff they were familiar with and surrounded by. Talk about enigmatic!

"OK. Whatever is behind that statement, it reminds me of something maybe like the door in the back of the wardrobe in *The Chonicles of Narnia*. You know, like, an entrance into another reality. Or, maybe it's like Gate 9 ¾ in the Harry Potter stories. Remember that blank wall between platforms 9 and 10 in the railroad station which was really the mysterious entrance into the train for Hogwarts School of Wizardry? You know, like something you're not looking for or don't initially see, but which is the entrance into another reality that is there all the same.[10] That is what Jesus' comment sounds like to me. I find it weirdly enigmatic.

"So I began to wonder what it has to do with all the stuff I see and have experienced but which doesn't seem to be an entrance into much

---

[9] Jesus' use of the word εκκλησια which has to do with an assembly called together for some mutual purpose!
[10] Cf. C. S. Lewis, *The Lion, the Witch and the Wardrobe*, which is his volume one of the *Chronicles of Narnia*, his children's' stories so rich in metaphor. J. K. Rowling's Harry Potter stories are currently in vogue both in print and in cinema, and likewise deal with another occult reality, which is fascinating.

of anything but maybe a pretty tame religious institution. Nice religious activities, but that don't always make much sense to my understanding of discipleship. Not exactly what you'd call an entrance into anything awesome. Just a religious club. Is that too harsh a judgment?"

Alan (as I have indicated) had unwittingly taken the lid off of a whole box of my own personal wonderments and unresolved questions about the church. I had long stored them in the back closet of my psyche. His questions were a catalyst for me. I needed time to pull them out and try to make some sense of some stuff that was just beyond my cognitive fingertips.

What follows here, then, is an account of my quest with him into that mystery. There was a sense in which he didn't primarily want to know *what* the church was, but rather *why* it was? I had no idea how to satisfy my own sense that there was something really out of *synch* between my best understanding of God's design for the church, and my own experience of it, … not to mention the problem of sorting through twenty centuries of data. I knew very well that God had not been passive, nor had God left himself without a witness in all of the vast church institutions. I also knew that ours was not a new or unique quest. We both had to take seriously what God had undoubtedly been doing through this enigmatic thing called *the church*. The Spirit of God has always been at work challenging any *merely human perceptions*. The Spirit reveals: "What no eye has seen, nor ear heard, nor the heart of man imagined, what God has prepared for those who love him …"

Most of the institutions, traditions, liturgical expressions, mission movements, and out-breakings of life which we can observe and study in church history are the result of genuine and godly folk questing for obedience, for clarity in their pilgrimage, and (rightly or wrongly) for *institutional* visibility and permanence. Those brothers and sisters were seeking to be faithful. They did so by creating visible, audible, orderly forms. We have received from them so many *signifiers*, such as a gazillion impressive church buildings and ecclesiastical institutions, not to mention the Roman Mass, beautiful icons and stained glass windows, the Genevan Psalter, chants, hymns, the *lectio divina*, liturgies, the preservation of the historic Christian creeds, … and on and on.

We also have sanctuaries, clergy, liturgical calendars, and a whole body of subconscious expectations of what constitutes an authentic church. At their best, those *signifiers* have been the fruits of the adoring people of God (folk such as we) looking for points of contact with God through the generations. Those are part of our rich tradition and are to be received with gratitude.

I wasn't eager to feed Alan's discontent (nor my own) by becoming just plain cynical. At the same time those rich traditions can and do devolve into ends in themselves. They can become merely human rites and forms, empty icons and without God's Spirit. An even greater grief, however, is when all of those expressions, even at their best, forget or obscure the church's *raison d'etre*. It is heartbreaking when the church forgets what it is called to be as God's agent or missionary community. It is even more so when the church forgets its own message of God's purpose to bless the nations by reconciling all things to himself in and through Jesus Christ. It is a major tragedy when the church actually *hides* the gospel! So I proposed to Alan that maybe it would be interesting to come at this from a whole range of perspectives, if we could hang in there long enough.

He had a different suggestion: "How long do I have to wait to find out where this weird *enchanted community* idea of yours comes from?"

I sat looking at him for a long time before saying anything. Then I could only thank him for including me in on his search. Then I asked if I could have some time to reflect on the question, and could we get together again maybe in a week or so, and maybe from time to time. He didn't hesitate: "Boy, if you have time, I'd love it."

Then, before we got back to what we were doing, he grinned: "Enchanted? Yeah, right. This had better be awesome!"

The *journeys* that follow are my own more reflective responses. They are my perspectives, or proposals, addressed to the issues that Alan and the others have raised concerning the essence of the Church, and of God's design for the Church, of which Jesus Christ is the Chief Head and Cornerstone. He and I continued to meet, and to exchange e-mails, and to challenge each other. These *journeys* are out of my dialogue with him. He is a gift to me, and I would like to be something of gift to him (and to many others).

Journey Two
Church: Enchanted Community in the Trinitarian Embrace

"OK, Bob. I've been reading the stuff you've been e-mailing me. I guess I really did raise more questions than I realized. I guess we've got a lot of avenues to explore. Still, I'm sure you operate on some kind of an overall theory of what the Church is all about. So, off the top of your head, spell it out for me."

Alan had come by the house one Saturday afternoon and we were sitting on the patio doing our coffee thing. And I responded …

No, no, no! Let's not go there right now. Let's "cut to the chase" and get on to your cynicism about my use of the word *enchant*. OK? So, bottom line: I see the Church as the visible demonstration of the human community as God intended it to be. I see it as the communal expression of God's New Creation in Christ. That opens the windows into a whole other realm of reality. That New Creation of God in Christ is not even remotely conceivable in *ordinary* natural or human categories. You were closer than you knew when you invoked those images of the "door in the back of the wardrobe" from C. S. Lewis' Narnia stories, and of "Gate 9 ¾" from the Harry Potter stories. They probably provide us with a good key.

"Spell out that 'new creation' thing for me, can you?"

Sure. Let's just say that it is all about the defining event which was initiated when God invaded his rebellious creation in the flesh and blood person of Jesus Christ. In Christ God came to *rescue* and *reconcile* unto himself both his lost humankind and all of creation with the ultimate design of *recreating* it all into total harmony with himself. I probably need to explain to you also (just so I don't confuse you too much) that I understand the New Testament concepts that are variously called *New Creation, Kingdom of God, salvation, eternal life, age to come,* and frequently the word *righteousness* (and probably a few others) all to be nuanced references to the same ultimate reality which was inaugurated in and by Jesus Christ.[1] I think that may become clearer as we work on our conversation.

"Sounds like a plan."

The New Testament isn't at all subtle in proposing that Jesus came from the Presence of God, that he inaugurated a *supernatural and other reality* into the midst our blighted human scene. It will be described in one place as the *reality* which "no eye has seen, and no ear has heard, and mind has conceived …"[2] You will find all kinds of clues in the Biblical narratives of a *Spirit world* which breaks into (and inhabits) this present world-culture of darkness at unexpected points. I have no problem designating that as the *enchanted world* inaugurated by Christ. This is intended to be especially evident in the Church. Make sense?

"Keep trying."

Listen, our Celtic Christian ancestors had this unique sense that God was everywhere in their daily experience. They understood that God's creation was animated and enchanted with the divine Presence. That perception is so alien to us in the church in the West. The very idea causes much of the present church to raise its *modern* eyebrows, or respond with skepticism to the whole idea. It is more likely to dismiss such an understanding as some kind mystical pantheism. That response has been even more pronounced since the (so-called) "Enlightenment" culture of the 17th century, what with its emphasis on (human) rationality and on

---

[1] In a later journey I will introduce Alan to the technical term *eschatological* to designate the ultimate unfolding of God's search and rescue mission in and through Jesus Christ, and the place the Church has in that mission.

[2] I Corinthians 2:9

scientific method. But then again, the much-revered St. Francis of Assisi had no problem at all with such a sense of the enchanting Presence of God inhabiting in all of creation. One has only to read or sing his lovely hymn *All Creatures of Our God and King* to catch that flavor: " ... burning sun, silver moon, rushing wind, clouds that sail along, rising morn, flowing water, fire, mother earth, flowers and fruits ... O praise him!" Francis talked to trees and animals and birds as his fellow creatures all created for the glory of God.

"Weird!"

Maybe to us, but it shouldn't surprise us since Paul describes the Church as "the dwelling place of God by the Spirit."[3] That description opens the door into the realm of the Spirit that has got to be *supra*-rational. It is redolent with magic and mystery and new perceptions. Peter reminds the Church that through the power of God, and the promises given by God, it may actually "participate in the divine nature"[4] – which should provoke us to think even more profoundly into fresh dimensions of Reality.

To speak of the Church, then, as an *Enchanted Community* is obviously to say that it is far from being a merely human religion in some institutional form. It is, rather, the *communal form of God's all-encompassing redemption*. It is that redemption's incarnational and communal presence in and through Christ. The Church resides in an awesome and *other* realm of reality in which the Presence of God is both dynamic and normal. New Creation reality resides in a community where relationships with both God and with others are intimate, self-giving, redemptive, loving, and altogether authentic.

Enchant

I can understand your initial and humorous reticence at my use of the adjective *enchanted*. So let's get back to its definition.

Actually, the word *enchant* (and also its counterparts *enchantment* and *enchanted*) is quite fascinating. Let me spell out the definition. There are, understandably, both positive and negative, good and bad, connotations to

---

[3] Ephesians 2:22
[4] II Peter 1:3-4

the word. I intend to use it in its positive (even redemptive) connotation. I want to presume that such is intended to be the *normal* state of God's creation. God's creation, tragically, only lost its magic, obscured its *enchantment*, when God's creatures rebelled and sought autonomous life on their own terms. It was all originally created to fully participate in the Divine Life and it was in that relationship that it was fully *enchanted*. Apart from that *enchanting* Divine Life, then, "disenchantment" became the norm. So we, here and now, have a very difficult time even imagining what God fully intends. But that much will inform the thrust of what follows in our conversation.

Enchant's Latin roots (in+cantare) mean to "sing in" or to "sing against" something. It has the flavor of *delighting*, or *endowing* with magical powers and properties, or of *imbuing* with fascination and attraction so as to call forth a song.[5] It can mean to *charm*, to *delight*, to *enrapture*, … or to infuse, permeate, or transfix with *allure*.[6]

Don't you think that's a fascinating word picture?

"And you're going to tell me that this *church* I'm struggling with is *enchanted*? Boy, have you ever got your work cut out for you!"

I'd sure like to explore the possibility that God had something like that in mind. But that's down the road a bit. We need to start at the beginning.

Just look at God's creation in the opening chapters of Genesis. Look at God's delight when "the morning stars sang together for joy" over such creation. Look at the sheer joy when "the trees of the field clapped their hands together," and when "the heavens declared the glory of God." All you can do is respond: Why, of course! Makes sense. Why didn't I ever see it before?

Leaping ahead over the centuries and into the New Testament, you find that something of this was also true of the infant Church. It was awesomely God-inhabited. It's hard to miss that fact. There was an all-animating and dynamic Presence written all over it! Such a community of ordinary (and often obtuse) persons, who had responded to the apostle's preaching of

---

[5] This definition is a composite from both Webster's Unabridged Dictionary, and the Oxford English Dictionary. There is of course the "bad sense" of the word, which means to delude or befool.
[6] From Oxford English Dictionary.

Jesus, would become in reality the dwelling place of God. That was not in some sterile theological proposition for them. Not at all. They lived by, and they depended upon, *the enchanting Spirit Presence.*[7] Power! There was something about what was happening to them that defied human explanation. Think about the report of those early disciples who walked "in the awe of the Lord and in the comfort of the Holy Spirit."[8] It's difficult to explain that away or to get around it. That early church community actually expected those continual demonstrations of the Spirit and power to be displayed through all kinds of totally irrational and *impossible* signs and wonders and miracles and transformed lives. And it was visible!

The populace in Jerusalem didn't miss the message either! There was something tangibly and humanly quite intimidating about such a bunch of otherwise ordinary men and women being so endowed with the awesome Presence of God. It became public knowledge. It is even recorded in one place that no one would even dare identify with them who was not one in heart and mind with them. Why? Because of that inexplicable Presence of something or *Someone* that (quite beyond their comprehension) created the "fear of the Lord" in the whole city.[9]

Pagan observers were astounded at the depths of love that the followers of Jesus had for each other. Such costly self-giving was so alien to their own spirit and experience. But then, those outsiders were still captive to the disenchanted powers of this age. They couldn't explain it. They didn't even believe it, … but they could see the living, breathing demonstration of a different kind of community. It just didn't fit their merely human categories.

If words have any meaning at all, then, we would do well to reclaim that word *enchant* and then deliberately invest it with our own understanding of all that it implies. Words are, after all, simply *signifiers*. This word *signifies* the flavor of the Church community that is inhabited by the Spirit of the Triune God. The Church, then, becomes a visible *sign* of God's *New Creation*.

"You're getting my attention. Let me see if I'm following you. You're proposing then that such a notion gets us back to the very nature and

---

[7] Ephesians 2:22
[8] Acts 9:31
[9] Acts. 5:13

purpose of God. Like, it drives us back to creation's beginnings as it was intended in the heart and mind of God. Right?"

Absolutely. But that isn't quite as easy as you make it sound. It will require that we not only invoke our *gift of imagination,* but it will require that we take into account the contributions of the brothers and sisters *over the centuries* who have grappled with these same questions. It will help us as well to look *internationally* to those in other cultures who today see into the Biblical story perhaps with clearer eyes.

"Carry on."

In the Beginning: Trinity, Community, Perichoresis

A case in point: Miguez Bonino. Bonino is a gifted Latin American brother and Biblical scholar who has beautifully stated that we (the Church) are included in "the missionary dialogue of the Trinity."[10] Taking his insight one step further, I can only reflect that it is also in the Trinity that we discover not only a "missionary dialogue" but also our very real *paradigm community of Persons.* It is out of that Trinitarian community that I, at least, begin to understand the relationships and dynamics as they are designed to express themselves within the Church—as they are designed in the heart and mind and plan of God. I do not think this to be at all theoretical or idealistic. I don't think it's wishful thinking. Quite the contrary. I think it flows quite easily out of the Biblical narratives. Our problem is that we are so blinded or distorted in our perceptions by a *false paradigm of the church.*

Look at the Biblical story, Alan. As we have it recorded, it begins with a scene of primordial nothingness, … nothing except for the uncreated God. It is only as that same God chooses to make himself and the awesome mystery of his being known to us that we begin to sense something of the wonder and awe of *Who* God is. Right away we are plunged into the depths of the mystery of One God who eternally *is.* But it gets even more

---

[10] Jose Miguez Bonino. *Faces of Latin American Protestantism* (Grand Rapids, MI: Wm. B. Eerdmans, 1995) 141. I am indebted in many ways to Bonino for giving voice to many of the inarticulate thoughts rambling around in my mind as I have struggled with this theme.

fascinating since this One God will begin to make known to us that within himself there exists a *community* of three Divine Persons.

Are you still with me?

"Sorta."

Just look at it. The God at whom we are looking in the Biblical story is the God who reveals himself as Creator. For our purposes it is essential that we come to grips with something of the flavor and color and character of the Divine Community, the Trinitarian Community who creates. I may be jumping-the-gun to introduce it now, but our understanding of this Trinitarian Community will unfold along the way in the Biblical narrative. If you can accept that much, stick with me. This Divine Community has been given interpretation by the Church's theological reflection over these two millennia, so I'm not introducing some off-the-wall new idea to you. As the Biblical narratives unfold, the Creator God of Genesis reveals himself as Father, Son, and Holy Spirit

If you're ready for this, then let me risk something else with you.

"You're so far out in space already that nothing else you can 'risk' is going to come as a surprise to me. Fire away!"

I want to retrieve a wonderful concept out of the earlier Church's grappling with this same Trinitarian mystery.[11] The teachers of the Church came up with a beautifully descriptive concept. They used the word **perichoresis**. Isn't that a cool word?

"Don't press your luck."

OK. *Perichoresis* is the concept that the Church came up with way back there. It is used to signify for us that very unique and beautiful and indescribable harmony which exists between the Persons of the Trinitarian community. Our problem is that we find it so very tough (if not impossible) to even begin to humanly imagine such harmony. We are so captive to our own broken and blinded perceptions, to our human proclivities to autonomy, to jealously, to self-interest, to individualism, to my "rights," to suspicions, to competitiveness, to turf-guarding, and the like. It all makes us unable to grasp the concept at all.

But it is in the picture of that Trinitarian *perichoresis* that we discover our very model and paradigm for true and holistic community. Our

---

[11] I hasten to remind my readers that the doctrine of Trinity is a theological formulation of the Church, and is not a term found in scriptures.

predecessors in the early Church used this word extensively to attempt to signify the utterly unique *relationship* which eternally exists between the persons of the Trinity: Father, Son, and Holy Spirit.

I like it!

"Well, at least one of us does."

Listen up. In the New Testament you catch glimpses of this intimacy, especially in John's writings. It is obvious in places like Jesus' prayer in John 17. The relationships among the persons of the Trinity are of pure, self-giving love for each other. I want to propose for the sake of our conversation here that this *perichoresis concept* become our paradigm for relationships within the community of Christ's disciples, or … more to the point, within the Church!

Perichoresis conveys the picture of divine love expressing itself as those three Persons are *in* each other, *making room* for each other, *interpenetrating* and *interanimating* each other, *drawing life from* and *pouring life into* each other, *rejoicing in* each other, and *seeking the glory of* each other. "… in eternity Father, Son, and Spirit share a dynamic and mutual reciprocity."[12]

For my part, I don't think that the New Testament teachings about relational life within the Church make a whole lot of sense *unless* we can embrace this concept. It is there that we observe the Triune God living out his own *perichoretic* Life within the community called the Church.[13] Those teachings don't make a lot of sense unless we see Jesus making his habitation within and among his followers by his own Spirit. In so doing, Jesus forms them into his New Creation community—human community as it is intended. Those persons living within that community are to be so animated by the Spirit of the Father and the Son that they give themselves to each other in love. The community is then to give itself back to God in adoration and in missional obedience.

Most of us stumble here because of our own experiences in a broken and alienated (often sterile and flawed) human community which fails to realize that the Church's life and relationships begin within the Triune God!

---

[12] Colin Gunton. *The One and the Three and the Many* (New York, NY: Cambridge Univ. Press, 1993) 163.

[13] I think I just invented that word *perichoretic* as the adjectival counterpart of *perichoresis* – I confess.

"That's a stretch. You're assuming that the Trinitarian God created the human community with the capacity for, and with the intention of it being interactive within the Trinitarian Community."

Bingo! Check out this definition which spells that out. It really gets even more thrilling:

> "The Father is not properly Father apart from the Son and the Spirit, and the Son is not properly Son apart from the Father and the Spirit, and the Spirit is not properly Spirit apart from the Father and the Son, for by their individual characteristics or distinctive properties as Father, Son and Holy Spirit, they exist in and through one Another and belong to and even live for each Other. Each person is intrinsically who he is for the other two. They coinhere in one another by virtue of the dynamic Communion which they constitute in their belonging to one Another. **Hence in establishing communion with us through the Son and in his Spirit, God wants us to participate in this living Communion which as Father, Son and Holy Spirit he eternally is, and it is thus that the nature of the divine Being is disclosed to us as Communion, ...**"[14]

I just find that absolutely fascinating! (Alan was just staring at me.)

Don't look at me that way. That really has some awesome implications for our journey here. Our orthodox faith[15] is quite familiar with the affirmation that we are not "authentically human" without God. But *here* ... here is the less familiar discovery that *I* also am not authentically human without *you*, and that we are not authentically human without the *others* in the intimate community of God's family in Christ. Here is the discovery that there is no *authentic human community* apart from Jesus Christ.

Just look at Jesus' statements: "I in you, you in me; ... The Father and I will come to you; ... We will send (our) Spirit; ... As the Father has loved

---

[14] Thomas Torrance. *The Christian Doctrine of God: One Being, Three Persons* (Edinburgh, T. & T. Clark, 1996) 132.

[15] Given the overload of obscuring baggage that go along with designations such as 'evangelical' or 'catholic' I am choosing to use the word 'orthodox' to convey that consensus that the mainstream of the Church (Roman Catholic, Protestant, Orthodox, Pentecostal, etc.) has held concerning its mutual understanding of the Biblical and apostolic tradition.

me, so have I loved you; ... Love one another as I have loved you."[16] Or think of Paul's descriptions: "The Church ... the dwelling place of God by the Spirit." Or: "By the power at work in us, ... glory in the Church and in Christ Jesus."[17] Or again, Peter's awesome word that through [God's promises] you [the Church] may participate in the divine nature.[18]

If you look at these, you begin to pick up on what the above quoted theologian was getting at, namely that the Church, as it is authentically the Church, lives out of the *perichoretic* interanimation of Father, Son, and Spirit. How's that for starts?

"I'm listening."

If we take this seriously, then, what it means is that the Triune God's love and grace and good purpose for *you* and for *me* ... empowers and flows through each of *us* toward each other. That is because of God's own supernatural and recreative Presence through the Spirit whom God has given to us in Church. And that is reciprocal. That is all about the Church as the *Community of Glory and of God.* That is all about the community through which God accomplishes and demonstrates his own missional purpose in flesh and blood to our confused world. That is all about the demonstration of his New Creation.

How can I say it more plainly? Through the Church, as it now exists in Christ and by the Spirit, *Enchantment* once again enters communally into this present *disenchanted* age. The *disenchantment* is the result of humankind's rebellion against the Creator. It is ultimately the abnormal state of things.

"Like, are you telling me that the Church is intended to be embraced within this *perichoresis* thing?"

That's exactly what I think I'm trying to tell you.

We need to explore that. But for the moment, just underscore in your mind that such a community *only authentically becomes itself* as it lives out those intimate, self-giving, interanimating relationships of love between persons. Such love only comes from God and then returns to God by the Spirit's empowering, by our participating in the Divine Nature. Such an authentic community is not likely to be ecclesiastically controlled by, or

---

[16] Sel. From John 14-17.
[17] Ephesians 2:20-21.
[18] II Peter 1:4.

exclusively contained in, any church institution. That would be like trying to "catch a moonbeam in a jar."

The Trinity and the Human Community in Creation

"Hold it! You're doing an amazing job of confusing me. All that stuff about some alternative Reality and about relationships sounds to me like you're on another planet. I'm still stuck back here on earth with my original question about some church lost in a bunch of activities, programs, and other stuff that doesn't remotely resemble anything we're talking about here! Are we going to get back there?"

Hopefully, but you've got to be patient with me. I want to explore the foundations some more. Because if the origins of the Church are really to be found in the Trinitarian *perichoresis* (which is the thesis I'm proposing) then we will need to look all the way back behind and before your problematic church which is lost in inconsequential stuff. We'll need to look (insofar as we can) at the beginnings of the human community in the mind of the Trinitarian community.

Humankind in the Image and Likeness of God

Back there in the early chapters of Genesis (and out of the divine community of Father, Son and Holy Spirit) comes the initiating word: *"Let us make man in our own image and likeness."*

If our Biblically formed imaginations can only *listen* to that intention, then we've got to hear that the Triune God's intention was to create for Himself specific other *persons* who were made to share in (and somehow participate reciprocally within) the community which exists between Father, Son and Holy Spirit. Essentially, such created persons (in God's image and likeness) would be embraced within the Divine *perichoresis*. Isn't that wild? The human creatures would actually commune with the Divine Community of their Creator.[19]

Doesn't that blow you away?

---

[19] Ibid.

Those would be God's very unique persons created with the capacity and for the purpose of interacting with their Creator. They would be created able to love and will, to have the intelligence and creativity of their Creator (though with the limitations of created beings, not as Uncreated God). Even more so, they were to be *persons* who could respond and communicate and interact with, and give themselves *to the Divine Person* and to *one another* in profound love and intimacy.

"Once again, you have my full attention. It's getting a bit more focused. Keep going."

Look at it. Our first clue is the creation of those first persons "in the image and likeness" of God. Then follows the second clue: *It is not good for adam (the human) that he should be alone. He needs a companion!* Those clues introduce us into another created reality, namely, that humankind is created to be *social*. Persons do not ultimately prosper in alone-ness. Isolation is not what they are created for. God's all-knowing sensitivity, therefore, created for *adam* an intimate and complementary other: *woman*. So now we're looking at the beginnings of the primordial human community.

We're looking at those two creatures and their Creator living together intimately in an *enchanted* community. It was out of their community with their Creator that our primordial human parents would then pour themselves into one another out of love. Out of their mutual love they would then pour themselves back into the Trinitarian community out of sheer adoration and worship. That, to my eyes, would indicate that they were created in and for just such participation.[20] That is all part of what it means to be *truly human*.

Alan laughed and tossed the remnants of his cold coffee out on the lawn: "OK. I'm beginning to tune-in to the implications. It's fun. But I hope I get to see where this leads in our ultimate quest into the Church. But I must admit, it *is* beginning to emerge as a pretty exciting paradigm."

I don't personally have any problem with letting our imaginations run free. I think imagination is a gift of God! I would only be jealous that our imaginations be formed by, and in harmony with, the Biblical data. That's the "orthodox" in me.

---

[20] This is what lies behind the first question of the Westminster Larger Catechism: What is the chief and highest end of man? And the answer: "The chief and highest end of man is to glorify and fully enjoy God forever.

Church: Enchanted Community in the Trinitarian Embrace

Think through the implications of God's verdict after the creation: "Very good!" In God's garden nothing would be imperfect or incomplete. There would be fullness of joy, unhindered communication, and adoration. There would be consuming delight in God the Creator, and in the stewardship of his creation. There would be delight in one another. Adam and Eve would have a reverence for, and a harmony with, all of God's creation along with a God-given curiosity and creativity and expectation. There would be no doubts, no uncertainties, no suspicion. In God's garden there would be complete freedom of spirit. There would be adventure.

Stir into that mix a rapturous and sensuous delight in each day's experiences: sights, smells, feelings, sounds, tastes, bodily life and sensations …

"Sex?"

… Yes, Alan, beautiful sex and all!. They would hear the music of God's creation. There would be a holy innocence that for us is totally unimaginable. No fear would blight their existence. They would have no shame, and nothing would need to be hidden. They were naked and unashamed. There would be, between Creator and creatures, all of that reciprocity and interanimation, and mutual joy in one another that would make their humanity all that it was designed and intended to be. We see something of this portrayed in the "peaceable kingdom" vision in Isaiah (11:6-9).

In painting such an imaginary portrait of the enchantment of that created garden, and of the human community, don't forget to underline the *joy note.* It needs to be there. It keeps emerging in all of the Biblical narratives. The *joy note* takes away the pallor of sterile doctrinal formulation. The *joy note* also says to us worlds about our image of God. And it will say worlds to us about how we 'image' (or conceive) the community which God creates and inhabits. For starts, try these:

- "The morning stars sang together and all the heavenly beings shouted for joy …" (Job 38:7.
- "… you will fill me with joy in your presence, with eternal pleasures at your right hand." Psalm 16:11.
- "Then I will go … to God, my joy and my delight." Psalm 43:4.
- "… you believe in him and are filled with an inexpressible and glorious joy, …" I Peter 1:8.

- "... so that they may have the full measure of my joy within them." John 17:13.

That *joy note* is replete in all of the Biblical documents describing the Presence of God. I sometimes wonder why is it is so foreign to the sort of somber ecclesiastical heaviness, and inhospitality, and sterile relationships which blight so much of our church experience?

"Now you're asking my questions."

OK, so I'm leaping ahead into New Testament territory. But as you and I consider the *what* and *why* of the Church, we've got to remember that the very word *gospel* carries with it the thrilling note of a *joyous* announcement about Christ. That would mean that somehow that same joy should be an essential piece of that Church whose builder and maker is Jesus Christ the joy-Giver! Whatever else we discover the Church to be, it must be a community of joy in God, of joy in each other, and of joy in all of God's creation. That has to be a dominant note in the beginnings of it all.

"Then the Church should also be *gospel?* Is that where you're going?"

I have no problem with that. That picture, which I have painted, had to be the *normal* state of the Community of the Triune God. I had to be the created nature of the human community which was created in God's likeness and image. If you look ahead to the advent of Jesus, the Son of God in human flesh, ... and at the same time refer back to your original questions to me (about the *what* and *why* of the Church), it is thrilling to extrapolate the answer. It is precisely such a community of persons within the Trinitarian Community that is in view when Jesus says: "I in you, you in me ... Make your dwelling in me ... my word dwelling in you ... By this shall all men know that you are mine, in that you love one another."

"Or 'I will build my Church' maybe?"

Absolutely.

The embrace of the human community within the Divine Community gives us our direction for this journey we're on. But more: I have to believe that the community of the New Creation will be that and even more than that because of God's great redemption in Christ.

"Am I Missing Something?"

"Sounds too good. Somewhere there's a whopping-big 'disconnect' between your 'perichoretic' dream world and all that, … and then the stuff I'm dealing with in the church. Am I missing something? Are we going to get to any conclusions that I can make sense out of before dark?

"Frankly, I'm on overload. All this is fun, but its still a little 'off the chart' in terms of what I was looking for from you.

"Name a time. I got you into this, so I'll stick with you. But I'm getting a bit restless to see where we're going."

It was getting on in the afternoon. And Alan was not the only one on overload. We agreed that we would put a bookmark here, and get back to the "what happened next" when we got together again. I could only explain that "what happened next" was the cosmic tragedy. It was (however one seeks to explain it) the rebellious act of that primordial community exercising their God-given capacity of will or of their moral choice to attempt life on their own (and apart from the Divine Life). Autonomy. Death.

Our whole journey back into the beginnings of the human community (as it was designed by God) is really quite necessary *if* we are to get to the heart of Alan's dilemma and that of all of my conversation partners (as in Journey One). The two of us wound up our afternoon still having all kinds of unresolved questions racing around in our minds. We both knew that we were undoubtedly raising far more questions than we could ever answer. But Alan was insistent that he was with me (though I'm not sure he was really convinced that I would ever come close to answering his initial question).

Journey Three
Disenchantment: The Groaning Creation

Orphaned.
Suddenly alone.
Lost from their heart's True Home.
Intimates became strangers.
Silence replaced the song.
Sadness eclipsed joy.
Darkness descended. Hope faded.
The magic, the enchantment, … but a memory.
Fear replaced trust.
"You will be as God" they were told, … but … it didn't happen!
Not the way it's supposed to be!
Death.
Dissonance.
Disenchantment.
"All creation groans, … waiting …"

Alan and I had finished our next conversation (which follows here). These descriptions were our reflections at the end of a very sad exploration into what had violated the *Shalom* of God's creation. Our focus this time together had been on the sheer and unimaginable tragedy that resulted

Disenchantment: The Groaning Creation

in a fractured human community We pondered the haunting aloneness and the *disenchantment* which had followed that tragedy. That subject was the next critical component in our pursuit of the "essence of the Church" which he and I were tracking.

Most *apropos*.

When the Abnormal Becomes the Normal

We keep running into a problem, which is a critical one. That problem is that the *abnormal* (or the *disenchantment*) of this present age has disguised itself as being the *normal* state of things. The church itself gets sucked into that abnormality (that disenchantment) so that the very idea of *enchantment* is hardly even a category for us.

"Say what?"

Maybe if I can unpack that. It's like when our lives, or when all of creation and the whole human community, are without any *enchantment* – when there's no magic. It's life without the joy which comes from Life in God's Presence. It's when all that sort of thing becomes the "normal" state of things for us – or "the way things are."

God's paradise (or more specifically the infant God-created community) was authentic and *enchanted* as all of its life flowed out of the Triune God, and as it all flowed back into God through adoration. *It was only authentic and enchanted as it was what it was created to be.* For us, that means that the human community can only truly authentic as that same community embraces and is embraced by and within the *perichoretic* community of Father, Son, and Holy Spirit.[1] It is paradise only so long as those within the human community relate to each other animated by, and embraced within, that same Trinitarian Life.

Can we make that concept an axiom for our future reflections?

"We can make it an axiom. But what happened that would so totally screw it all up?

"Why in the world is such *authentic* community so totally alien to us?

---

[1] One notes that many of the hymns on the afterlife try to conceive of heaven without even any mention of God and of the Lamb, who are the focus of heaven. Christian communities, likewise, that are not focused in adoration are also less than Church!

"And, by the way, what does it all have to do with the Church?" Precisely the question.

The story related early in Genesis gives us the clue with such a skillful economy of words. The word picture it paints *suggests* far more than it ever *defines*. The wonder and enchantment of that primordial garden, and of the human community ... included a couple of realities both of which are still very profound mysteries to us.

One reality was that those two persons were created in God's "image and likeness." Their true humanity was to participate in the fellowship of the Trinitarian community. They had (in that "image and likeness") the capacity of *will*, the gift of *moral choice*, the responsibility of *intelligent decision*. But, then, we must consider that those capacities (or gifts and responsibilities) were, in fact, also *innocent* in that they were *untested*.[2]

The other reality was that there were awesome dimensions of God's own nature and character, of God's unfathomable love, which would only begin to unfold in time. The later Biblical writers could only describe all of that as the mystery kept hidden for ages which was only revealed in the advent of Christ.[3] Something of that mystery is revealed in the passion of God for his own glory to be demonstrated in all of his creation – every artist understands this. The unimaginable love of God, the patience, the longsuffering, the grace and mercy of God would only unfold as God would redeem what was lost. It would only be revealed as God comes in Christ to rescue his *disenchanted* creation.

God's unfathomable caring, his loving kindness, his mercy, his patience, his infinite self-giving ... would only be set forth in all of their splendor because of the tragedy that took place when these human parents violated their true being and sought equality with God, when they sought their own autonomy, when they rebelled against their Creator. They had violated their own authentic humanity by *choosing other than what God*

---

[2] I really do not want to get into the whole area of the origins of evil, of theodicy, and the like. They are wonderfully investigated in such books as the science fiction trilogy of C. S. Lewis, especially **Perelandra**, and more recently in **Not the Way It's Supposed to Be**, by Cornelius Plantinga. My concern is to pursue how this reality has been destructive of true community, which is to be restored in Christ, and hence demonstrated in the Church.

[3] Ephesians 3:5, 9.

had designed for them, which was communion with each other and within the Trinitarian Community.[4]

Can you begin to "connect the dots?"

"Downloading."

However it all came about, there was a tragic choice made by that original community. In the garden story at the beginning of Genesis there is portrayed an alien serpentine voice that enticed and lied to them. It was a demonic voice, if you will.[5] That voice planted a huge question-mark in their minds. It had to do with the nature and the intentions and the integrity of their God. It also inserted into their thinking a false concept (a lie) of what constituted their true humanity. It proposed to them that their true humanity was to be found in autonomy, that somehow they could be their own gods. That serpentine voice provoked those two naïve persons to question the nature of their relationship with the Creator. It provoked them to doubt the veracity of God and his word of prohibition which surrounded the mysterious tree of the knowledge of good and evil.

The reality of good and evil along with the fruits of experiencing that reality are brought into question. Like, is it really *good* to dwell in an intimate relationship of obedient adoration with their Creator? Is it really essential to their best interest to dwell in fellowship with God within the *unity* of the Trinitarian Community? Or is it maybe *more good* to assume that this divine Being who is their Creator may have some ulterior motives? Could it be that it might be better to leave God out of the equation? If that were the direction, then might it be possible to create their own better human community? Might their true *good* really be in autonomy—could life be richer and more free on our own? Possibly, after all, God was really their *equal* and so would be of the same essence as they. Perhaps God was to be respected but not necessarily adored. That serpentine voice impugned the motives of God. Could it be? (Don't you love mysteries?)

---

[4] It is interesting to speculate that when these two, Adam and Eve, became *conscious* of their being (and even the best of scientists cannot define consciousness!) they were aware of *the Being* who was there before them, who was revealed as their Creator, and with whom they had access and communication. But they were innocent as to who *the Being* really was, and what went on within his own consciousness and purpose.

[5] A voice disgruntled, rebellious, supernatural, non-creative, and sowing discord. This personality is also is a mystery, portrayed on one point as walking with the sons of God (Job 1), and at other times as an angel of light, as a liar, a murderer, etc. This is a study in itself.

Enchanted Community

"Would you like for me to provide some ominous background music to heighten the tension?"

It would be fitting. Remember that those persons were created in the divine image and likeness with all the potential of that. And that meant that they had been given the (shall we say "dangerous") capacity to make just such a critical decision.[6]

"And they blew it! Right?"

Exactly. They chose to do what God out of genuine love had warned them never to do. And so the tragedy of life "without hope and without God" intruded into the human scene.[7] The *abnormal* became the *normal*. Darkness descended. Their human community became just that: *merely human*. It had lost its true authenticity. It had lost the true *enchantment* with which it had been endowed. They were now without the Spirit. They were "lost in the cosmos."[8] They entered into a *disenchanted world* which they had never imagined could even exist.

On the surface the whole scene appeared to be quite the same. In so many ways it was not changed visibly at all. It was only that the whole *Enchanting Presence* had ceased to be a part of their conscious experience. That broken and violated creation in which they now lived (and in which we now live, and accept, and conceive to be *normal*) was not normal at all. It was, rather, very very *abnormal*. They were alone! Some poet said it so poignantly: "It's been lonely in the world since God died!"

The immediate evidence of their *merely human*[9] existence was the introduction of a series of tragic consequences. Those who had previously lived and walked in the sweet fellowship and in unity with their the Creator—now hid from him. Those who had been so delightfully intimate were now ashamed of their own nakedness as estrangement entered their relationship. More than that, as soon as their "screw-up" was exposed by God (who was still walking in the midst of the garden), they were called out of their attempts to hide from him. Their loss of innocence was made

---

[6] C. S. Lewis has written an incredibly beautiful counterpart to this temptation and its consequences in his science fiction novel **Perelandra.**
[7] Ephesians 2:12
[8] **Lost in the Cosmos**, is the title of a wonderfully provocative book by Walker Percy.
[9] One of the Greek words which the New Testament translates as 'flesh' or 'carnal' actually means 'without Spirit'. Cf. Ψυχικοσ.

obvious. In lame attempts at self-justification they began to cast suspicion on each other. They made excuses for their guilt. They blamed the serpent (the seductive voice) as their fall-guy: "he made us do it." The erosion of all authentic human community was immediate and obvious and tragically demonstrated.

"Come on. How do you explain such stupidity and dissonance in that setting of such perfection? Like, how did this happen? Why did God allow it to happen? How do you explain it?"

You don't!

The Creator's continuing engagement in and with his creation is one of those mysteries of God's being that we have to look at in wonder. We can only know that "the foolishness of God is wiser than men."[10]

"Hmm. If you say so ..."

Tragic Consequence: The Loss of Authentic Community

A major component of the created design was their human need for intimate and loving community. Now they found themselves incomplete and living with a scarred version of that community because they had violated God's very design for their welfare. In their grab for autonomy they had essentially destroyed what God had provided. It was *still* not good for them to be alone, yet now the first evidences of a pathological alienation and aloneness began to show themselves. That deserves a bit more attention.

As Alan and I got to this point, I nudged him to think back to his initial question about the Church and to begin to make the connections.

A frightening new and different kind of relationship was suddenly present: *strangers, competitors, enemies*! Not only did God become a competitor to his human creatures, he became the enemy to their autonomy. They not only became estranged from each other but they became the accusers of each other. Even more subliminally, they became

---

[10] I Corinthians 1:25.

confused as to who they themselves were as persons (with all of the emotional and psychological tangles of that confusion). The story is so sad. The distortion of all of the possible relationships: God, each other, self, and even nature. All now became part of that strange new condition of (what I have called) *disenchantment. Enemies* replaced intimate others. True (authentic) community became only a receding memory and an unrealized longing in their human spirits. True community actually became an impossibility when all others were competitors with, and even threats to, their own autonomy!

"Keep it up. I think I'm beginning to get your focus."

Enter the Virus: Violation and Distortion

The Biblical narratives as well as our human history are a dismal record of the consequences of that violation of God's design. And it's still our history. God's design was that his own glory was to be wonderfully demonstrated in all that he had created. His glory was to be exhibited in the human community which was to be lived and embraced within the Trinitarian Life and Community (*perichoresis*). It was that very glory of God which was so tragically violated in the act of attempted autonomy by those first parents. But you will note that it would also (in due time) reveal the depths and lengths to which God would go to rescue his own rebellious and irresponsible and destructive community.

We need to remember: "This is [still] my Father's world." God does not abandon that which he created for his own glory. The Biblical story is replete with evidences that God has continued to relentlessly break into, and cause his voice to be heard, even within the most dismal scenes of this human rebellion. God intends (sovereignly) to be known. God speaks. God continues to reveal his glory in unexpected and wonderful (left-handed?) ways. But the scene is now one of *disenchantment*. It is absolutely "not the way it's supposed to be."[11]

Disenchantment has a whole array of dimensions to it. It would also be a mistake to overlook the element of the *demonic* in all of this. There is

---

[11] Cf. Cornelius Plantinga, **Not the Way It's Supposed to Be**. Wm. B. Eerdmans Publishing Co., Grand Rapids, MI. 1995.

a supernatural being or influence which has personality involved here (as incredible as that sounds to our modern ears). Just note that this personality is one who is malignant and who inhabits the disenchantment.[12] The New Testament will refer to this disenchanted (and abnormal) realm not only as "this age" but also as "the dominion of Satan" and the "dominion of darkness." It refers to one Satan as "the god of this age." Make of that what you will, but don't underestimate it.[13]

Alan looked a bit dubious.

"You mean that Voldemort in the Harry Potter stories is not so far-fetched after all? Some malignant figure lurking out there?"

Precisely.

The interplay between that serpentine figure and our primordial parents only *suggests* to us something of the wonder of their creation. To use a contemporary figure, their act of *will* and *choice* was like the introducing of a *virus* into the computer program. Anyone who has experienced a computer virus knows that the hardware may appear quite the same – but nothing works as it should. What should be communication comes out in a bunch of garbled symbols. Something like that expresses that alien factor which entered into the good creation of God. The *Shalom* was shattered. Created beauty withered. The song ceased. The human community fragmented almost immediately.

It is the essence of that *truly human community* which we need to pursue as it relates to our quest for the "*why?*" of the Church.

Lost

The human community lost its *raison d'etre*, ...

"*Raison d'etre?* Say what?"

Sure. It's a fancy way of speaking about the *reason for existence*. That is exactly why we need to pursue the word *lost*. It's that awareness of its essential purpose (in the design of God) which the human community lost. And the word *lost* ... is a haunting word. It should elicit our tears.

---

[12] Cf. Ephesians 2:1-2 as a statement of this.
[13] I refer my readers to both Walter Wink's three volumes on the "Powers" (Fortress Press), and Gregory Boyd's **God At War** (Inter-Varsity Press) 1997.

The Church has probably (and most often) used the word *lost* to speak about our individual human condition of being *lost from God,* like *lost* sheep, or *lost* children. We speak of those who have *lost* their "heart's true home." The Biblical story paints the image of our emptiness and of our longing for that "something" which we can't even define. Lostness carries with it the horrible baggage of guilt, and self-destruction, and meaninglessness, and broken community. But it also speaks of the loss of humankind's true humanity. In the Biblical stories we see the origins of our lost capacity to see with God's eyes, or to hear with God's ears, or to conceive with God's heart and mind.

But then, ... if we were but able to look through the eyes and heart of the Creator, then we would also see something else. We would also see that the God who created humankind for himself in love ... also *lost* us. God *lost* those whom he loves and whom he created to dwell with him, to be blessed and to be authentic within the community of Father, Son and Holy Spirit.

Remember that it was out of love that the Triune God created humankind in his own image and likeness. That's critical to remember. God, out of love, purposed for these daughters and sons to dwell in the very joy of God's own Presence and Community. We need to be aware that it is the same God who has *lost* that which he created. God lost what he loves and longs for. We must consider what God lost when his much-loved creatures, his glory, chose to leave him out of their equation.

We need to keep in mind what it was that God lost when those whom God loved violated their intimacy and relationship with the very One for whom and by whom they (we) were created. If we do that, then we will begin to sense something of the unimaginable depths behind John's affirmation that "God so loved the world that he gave his well-beloved Son." We might even begin to think about God as "the broken-hearted God."

But germane to our *church quest* is that we also need to be reminded of the *loss of true community* which is also a tragic dimension of our own lostness. Underscore that one. It is a dimension that is quite too seldom addressed. Not only do our human hearts have a longing for their true home in God personally and individually, but equally we also have a built-in longing for authentic human community *in God* by virtue of our creation. We have created in (maybe deeply buried) a need for intimacy

Disenchantment: The Groaning Creation

and for relationships with one another. We are created for ministry to one another because we are created in the image and likeness of God. We are created to have God's Life in us and flowing through us in our communion with each other.

Listen up! It's right here that we have a most essential clue to what is behind Jesus' statement: "I will build my Church." His declaration there at Caesarea Philippi speaks of the critical communal dimension of God's New Creation in Christ. It finds its roots when we look all the way back to that dimension which was lost in the tragedy of the rebellion, in the *disenchantment* and fragmentation of the human community as it was intended to be.

We need to hold in juxtaposition two things: 1) the nightmarish emptiness and separation that is ours apart from the Triune God who created us on one hand, and 2) at the same time, the kind of God who with infinite love and mercy comes seeking to bring us again to himself in the fullness of his purpose. That *mission of God* grows out of *the missionary dialogue of the Trinity* (as our Latin American brother quoted in the previous chapter notes).[14] The Biblical records early on include the "teaser" that the seed of the woman would crush the serpent's head, but that the serpent would also bruise the heel of that seed (Genesis 3:15).

Only a few chapters later in the Biblical story God mysteriously and wonderfully (in an *enchanted* moment) intrudes into the life of an oriental sheik by the name of Abram (later Abraham). God announces to the astounded and god-fearing Abram that "all the nations of the earth" were going to be blessed through his offspring (Genesis 12:1-3). Enter *anticipation* and *mystery*.

"And I'm supposed to see some 'clue' here? This all has something to do with the Church?"

Absolutely. How else would you explain Abraham? As the Biblical story unfolds there is a whole succession of interesting individuals who respond to God. Their hearts responded to someone or something that was *other*, some *enchanted reality*, as being the key to life's meaning. God has a delightful way of breaking into our human scene quite unexpectedly in just such *enchanted* moments. God continues to remind us that he is not at all indifferent to his human community. God reminds us that he

---

[14] Miguez Bonino.

created us to live in relationship with himself. That unexplained promise to Abraham begins to unfold before us. All the people groups of the earth are in view with this promise.

What we're looking at is the *unchanging mission of God* to recreate God's original and designed intent, and that includes the created human community dwelling in unity with (and as the glory of) the Uncreated God. Only ... God's *New Creation community* will be *more than* the original because it will be rescued, reconciled and recreated out of the sheer and infinite love and mercy of God. As the Biblical narrative unfolds the expectation grows upon us as there are promises given to David about his endless kingdom. Later it unfolds through the prophets as they look into God's future, into the *eschaton*. They would see a day that would come in which God brings all things together again in his unimaginable New Creation.

"And you're still talking about something that has to do with the Church?"

The Church is right at the very heart of that whole New Creation design!

"The Law of Sin and Death"

The setting in which God works out this New Creation design, however, is right in the middle of the pathological darkness and autonomy and blindness of this very real and rebellious and *disenchanted* human community. It's far more serious than we can fathom.

Humankind may choose to leave God out of its equation, ... but God never reciprocates in kind. His love has been violated to be sure. Our guilt is real. There *is* such a thing as divine wrath! No question. But God's anger is never without redemptive purpose. Rather it grows out of God's infinite love and justice. God continually (and early on) makes known that he purposes and earnestly desires to dwell right in the midst of his people. The *people of God* theme begins to catch our attention very early in the Biblical story. God would choose a particular people to be his instrument. He selected an extended family in the form of the people of Israel (Abraham's heirs) to be his priestly nation. That nation's calling and purpose was to be the witness of the True God before the whole earth

– of who God is, of God's character, and of God's will for the human community.

Those children of Jacob (or the people of Israel) were preserved, blessed, and given a covenant by God. Their covenant with God was called "Torah." It was given in order that they should have a holistic pattern for their life in relationship to God. Within that Torah you will find the pattern for their communal responsibility to, and practical care for, each other (and even to strangers). The intent was that each person be God's personal instrument of God's caring for each other. The Torah spoke eloquently and holistically of God's heart and mind and will for the people who would bear his Name before the world. It was to be their guide into a life that was totally God-focused, as well as expressive of God's caring and nurturing of the human community of Israel.

Listen up. The *clue* for us in all of this is easily overlooked.

"I think I'm overlooking it. I'm not even sure I'm following you, but I'm trying to keep up. Get to the point."

Patience, my friend. Just look at it. In the giving of such a covenant, God instructed his people that there be a "tent of meeting" which should always be squarely in the middle of their encampments so that God could visibly *dwell in their midst*. The life of God's chosen community was to be focused in and motivated by his gracious Presence among them. The design for their life as his people was very complete. It included rhythms of work as well as specific times of reflection on and with God. It let them know that God wants his Being to be honored and cherished among them. The Torah also taught them about their relationships with each other which was to reflect God's own character and purpose in the realistic dimensions of life. It included such things as the sanctity of property, of sex, of truth, of contentment, and of human life. It is God's *enchanting* Breath showing them his design in a very unlikely setting.

"Problem here. So I've read that stuff. I remember the story. But I don't get the picture that anything like what the Torah required was ever implemented. Where was the breakdown? Did the Israelites ever do that stuff?"

You do come up with good questions. But you're very observant. "Loving your neighbor" is a cool concept in the abstract but it comes with a price-tag that has costs in both possessions and in discipline. Loving God, likewise, sounds great in the abstract. The whole design for the

God-centered community with all of its networks of compassion built-in sounds like an OK design when you read it. Like who can fault taking care of the helpless of society? The problem with the Torah was that caring for each other came with that high price tag! God's provision for those who had fallen on hard times, those who had sold themselves into servitude to pay off debts, those who were homeless and hungry – all of that has a warm feeling to it in the abstract or on a printed page.

But the reality is that these requirements do not lend themselves to selfish or non-costly responses. They don't come free of costs. They come with demands that can include a significant price tag. When you factor in that the homeless poor were to be given a place to stay in *your* home, or that the edges of *your* field were to be left to be harvested by the poor, … or even more costly, that debtors were to be forgiven their debts in the jubilee year and their original land returned to them *by you*, … that could get downright expensive! Add to that the patience needed, the demands on time and emotions, the intrusions upon your privacy, all in addition to the economic costs, … then it was probably more "convenient" to equivocate on what the Torah required of them. (Keep all of this in mind when we get to the New Testament teachings about the nature of the gospel and the responsibilities and behavior and gifts within Church!)

The problem was and continues to be that the *disenchantment* (which we have been talking about) produced in human lives and in the human community what can only be portrayed as *vast filters of misunderstanding and darkness*. The glory of the Triune God was no longer the dynamic reality in the lives of those Israelites – even when they knew that God had spoken to them. Something *demonic* was pervasive. There was a brute self-interest that lurked everywhere. A worldview existed in which God probably was unquestioned, but at the same time existed only as one outside of their primary areas of self-concern (themselves and their own well-being). Sound familiar?

Paul would later describe such self-focus as "another law" at work in our human lives. It was and is the *law of this present disenchanted age*. It is "the law of sin and death."[15] That being so, even though those Israelites (and we) could admire God's law, and could know that keeping God's law (the Torah) was probably good for them, and could know that it is given for

---

[15] Romans 8:2

their welfare, … still … that other *law of sin and death* kept kicking-in and keeping them (and us) in bondage to their more self-centered interests.

There is something in our *disenchanted* human natures that sees God and sees my neighbor as competitors. That "something" in us is resistant to any intrusion made upon my autonomy, my stuff, my space, no matter how good the cause. That autonomous, self-focused "power of sin" in the Israelite community, and in the human community-at-large, has a built-in resistance to anything that would make demands upon its autonomous self.

Still, the need for true human community is always there. *Loneliness* is precisely that. It is the absence of community which God designed for our good. From time to time, unselfishness, and true love triumph. But face it: the economic provisions in the Torah such the as the Jubilee Law (through which periodically the whole of the economy would return to Square #1, and to redistribution) was probably never practiced much because it was too demanding and too costly for me and mine. The "gleaning law" may have been practiced only at times because it made demands on the owners' profit.

What becomes obvious to us is that whatever *costs* me and mine; whatever becomes an intrusion upon, or a competitor to self-interest, and whatever makes demands upon our possessions seems always to have been resisted. It all demonstrates what a vigorous hold the "law of sin and death" has on the human person and on the human community – especially economically. God's law was "holy and just and good"[16] *in theory*. But something else, some pathology runs much deeper in the human spirit in this disenchanted age.

The Torah was to give form and content to the community of those who held God in awe. But it ultimately could only serve as a "guardian" (to use Paul's term)[17] or a tutor to show those of us in the human community starkly (Israel and the rest of us) how captive we all are to that other "law of sin and death." It shows us how profoundly we need something dramatically and divinely *other* power than the external laws written on tablets of stone. "O wretched man that I am," cries Paul. "Who will deliver me from this body of death? In my mind I serve the law, but another law

---

[16] Romans 7:12
[17] Galatians 3:24,25.

in my members wars against such."[18] Only God can redeem and recreate. Only God give us a new nature and so re-enchant his rebel creation.

That "law of sin and death" is perhaps most graphically visible before us in the continual and tragic deterioration of the human community!

Parenthetically, just lest all of this sound to totally cynical and negative, let me remind my readers that God has a wonderfully gracious way of providing for us those gifts that keep the human community from self-destruction. He sends the rain upon the just and the unjust. He gives beauty and generosity. He provides artists and humanitarians and neighbors. He gives persons skill in medicine and he gives those who have a heart for justice. He raises up public servants and environmentalists. How does this happen in such a scene of disenchantment? The Church has simply acknowledged that it is by God's common grace, or God's preserving grace, through which God evidences of his love for, care for, and preservation of humanity, even in its rebellion and undeservedness.

Back to Alan's Question: The Church

Periodically, as we proceeded through all of this background, Alan would ask me: "Are we there yet?" with a smirk or a twinkle in his eye. At the risk of being laborious, there are some rather generally held misconceptions that need to be clarified as we go along.

We, who are the followers of Christ, have frequently and conveniently focused only on our own individual guilt and separation from God which require atonement, forgiveness, and reconciliation with God. We rightfully look to Christ and to his death as God's provision for dealing with our personal estrangement from God and with our guilt – which well we should. Such an awesome expression of God's unimaginable love stands at the threshold of the newness.

At the same time … we really must never forget that it is not only our personal reconciliation with God that is necessary good news for us. We also must always remember that God intends to reconcile the

---

[18] Romans 7:24 ff.

human community and recreate it into his New Creation community. That is what the Church is all about. The Church is the New Creation community. Such recreated community is the other most necessary (and too often overlooked) dimension of God's good news (*gospel*) to us. It is in the New Creation Community that the gospel just may have its most visible and powerful expression to those who are still outside. The Church is the community of those "called out" to demonstrate to this disenchanted human scene what God intends *authentic human community* to be.[19]

The Church is the human community as it is recreated and reconciled through Christ Jesus live into its true nature and intent. It is the Church that is the community indwelt by the Spirit. It is the Spirit who recreates the community so that reconciled sisters and brothers are enabled to dynamically live lives of loving, self-giving responsibility for each other *in God*. They are enabled to live such reconciled life together with spontaneity out of the Life of the Triune God who lives within and among them by the Spirit. The Church thus becomes the reconciled community now embraced again into the *perichoretic* love and intimacy of the Triune God. The Church becomes the communal dimension of New Creation in which God's gospel is displayed most clearly.

Enchanted Community indeed.

That's where we're going with this journey.

But I'm jumping to the end of the story. There's more to the landscape before we get to the *Church as gospel*.

The Dilemma of Disenchanted Religion

The thirty-nine books of the Old Testament are a heartbreaking narrative of the communal display of *disenchantment*. Paul would later lament:

> "So I find this law at work: When I want to do good, evil is right there with me. For in my inner being I delight in God's law, but I see another law at work in the members of my body, waging war against the law of my mind and making me a prisoner of the law of sin at work with my

---

[19] It could be added that this New Creation community could be termed the *eschatological* community, or God's ultimate purpose in the human community.

members. What a wretched man I am! Who will rescue me from this body of death? Thanks be to God – through Jesus Christ our Lord." (Romans 7:21-25)

The mystery and wonder of God and the mind of God! Who could ever plumb the depths of such? That God loves his lost creation, and pursues it relentlessly, patiently, long-sufferingly, mercifully, persistently despite all of its stubbornness, fickleness, and rebelliousness ... is a marvel beyond our comprehension. The story of Abraham, Isaac, Jacob, the captivity of the children of Israel in Egypt, and God's deliverance cover generations and centuries, but God was never absent (though he may often have seemed to be to them). When God revealed himself and his plan, or intervened dramatically (as in the Exodus), their awe of God was rekindled, ... but only temporarily. That memory soon faded and the "other law" kicked-in.

A high point of the Biblical drama took place when God gathered this rescued nation of former slaves before himself at Mount Sinai. Through Moses God made known to them (again) that they were heirs of his promise given to Abraham. Only on that occasion they were given a covenant and a calling. That calling was (they were reminded) was that they should be a community in dynamic relationship with God which, in turn, was to be visible before all the nations of the earth:

> "This is what you are to say to the house of Jacob and what you are to tell the people of Israel: You yourselves have seen what I did to Egypt, and how I carried you on eagles' wings and brought you to myself. Now if you obey me fully and keep my covenant, then out of all nations you will be my treasured possession. Although the whole earth is mine, you will be for me a kingdom of priests, and a holy nation." (Exodus 19:3-6)

"I carried you, ... I brought you to myself, ... my treasured possession. ... a kingdom of priests, ... a holy nation." *Priests* communicate God to the community and represent the community before God. *Holiness* is the demonstration of the character and will of God in the lives of God's people. So it was that in the midst of the nations of the world Israel received a calling from God's to be so unique that all of those other ethnic groups of the earth should see and glorify God because of them. To put it another

Disenchantment: The Groaning Creation

way, they (all the other people groups) were to find God *awesome* through the life and character of that nation of Israel.

What followed that calling has become one of the unique documents of human history: the *Torah* (mentioned above). Far from being a dull ancient manuscript, the Torah is, rather, a fascinating constitution of community life in relationship both to God and to each other – even to strangers. It incorporates relational principles, hygienic and environmental guidelines, property laws, economic guidelines, and much more. All are given to them in the context of that primary relationship which they are to have with the one God who insisted that, above all, they should have no other *gods* before him. That was all etched visibly for them on tablets of stone. It reflects the intent and design of God for the human community. It reflects for us, as well, the self-giving love and interanimation of the Persons within the Trinitarian community toward each other. The Israelite community was to reflect the heart and mind and intent of God in the context of human relationships.

God had spoken. Those tablets of the law were a constant reminder. The tablets were *taberncled* in the midst of the camp of the people of Israel. But then we mustn't forget that the "other law" was there as well. That "other law" would keep them in bondage to their *disenchanted worldview* in which God is surely real, but somehow external to their (as it is with our) primary self-interests. There was a physical *place* provided where Israel was to meet God. There were provisions given so that even their worst failures could be forgiven and made right. There were special persons set apart to mediate between the people and God. There was *religion* aplenty. There were regular festivals and feasts given to be physical and temporal reminders of who they were and Who was their God.

With all of that, ... Israel kept repeatedly reverting to being like the other nations around it. They were religious. Yet they were anything *but* holy. They were anything *but* a sign to the nations. Even their interpersonal relationships within the community of Israel were fraught with injustices, absence of mercy, slavery, greed, sexual exploitation, indifference to human need, and gross idolatry.

Sound familiar?

Still, ... In the Midst of Such Disenchantment ...

In the midst of such a dismal catalogue of those evidences of the *disenchantment* ... there inexplicably and occasionally appeared *enchanted* figures who responded to God. There were those *enchanting moments* when responsive persons responded to the *Enchanting Presence* and so became signs of hope. It was not only the ancient patriarchs (father figures), but there were also the poets and the prophets who came onto Israel's scene. One has only to think of such persons as Abraham, Isaac, Jacob, Samuel, and especially of David. They were somehow God-awed and alert to the *Enchanting Presence*. There were all of those *enchanted* women such as Deborah, Rahab, Ruth and Esther, who were significant keys to Israel's story. Please don't ask me to explain this.

Then there were those prophets who spoke from God to Israel's default of its holy calling. Prophets were a unique breed. They often took the brunt of the destructive darkness within Israel and Judah. They were frequently beaten. They were sometimes killed. They were thrown into dungeons and they were ridiculed. Yet for all of this, they spoke faithfully from God.

God never left himself without a witness. Centuries later one of the New Testament writers would catalog a whole list of those persons of faith, those *enchanted persons* who inhabit the pages of Israel's history. They were unlikely people. They were ordinary people, sometimes outsiders, as well as Israel's patriarchs, judges, poets, and prophets. God was always their heart's true home. God has always been revealing his glory in his creation. God has always responded to the supplications of his believing (and semi-believing) saints.

Yet there was always an incompleteness.

There was always that "law of sin and death."

There was always that fractured human community.

There was always the deception of external and disenchanted religion. What was the use? Where was the hope?

"Are we there yet? Like, Bob, I'm enjoying the history lesson, but I sure hope it's going to get us to the Church on time!"

Disenchantment: The Groaning Creation

Hints of Things to Come: "I Have Plans for You ..."

Alan, you may not believe this, but we are actually getting closer. But all this history is pretty foundational for us if we are to come close to understanding that statement of Jesus about "building his Church" that tripped you up.

So stick with me, I'm going somewhere here.

"Do I get bonus points for sticking?"

Don't complain. You got us started on this journey.

"I confess. I did. Proceed"

In the darkest night of Israel's history the anointing Spirit of God came upon persons who were often eccentric to the core. Those persons responded and were able to see the present and the future out of God's own eyes and heart. They saw not only Israel's present disobedience and rebellion, but they also saw its future. They delivered words of hope. Consider the word spoken to a hopeless situation many centuries before Christ:

> "For I know the plans I have for you," declares the Lord, "plans to give you hope and a future." (Jeremiah 29:11)

Those prophets gave intriguing and enticing references to how (at some future time) God would gather his people for a feast and would eat with them. There was the vision of some kind of a recreated community. There was the vision of a new creation where God's compassion, God's justice, God's peace would be so exhibited as to make it the essence of joy. There would be no more fear, no more guilt, no more alienation, no more dismal religion. Rather, God was seen as dwelling in the midst of his own responsive and joyous people. In those prophetic references we catch glimpses of the return of true *Enchanted Community*, ... only that community would be refined, judged, atoned for, chastened, reconciled and infused with God's Spirit. The heart and mind and will of God would be written into the deepest motivations the heart (Ezekiel 36: 24-27). Or:

> "The time is coming," declares the Lord, "when I shall make a new covenant with the house of Israel and with the house of Judah. It will

not be like the covenant I made with their forefathers when I took them by the hand to lead them out of Egypt, because they broke my covenant, though I was a husband to them," declares the Lord.

"This is the covenant I will make with the house of Israel after that time," declares the Lord. I will put my law in their minds and write it on their hearts. I will be their God, and they will be my people. No longer will a man teach his neighbor, or a man his brother, saying, 'Know the Lord', because they will all know me, from the least of them to the greatest, declares the Lord. For I will forgive their wickedness and will remember their sins no more." (Jeremiah 31:31-34)

And the prophet Joel chimes in with:

"And afterward, I will pour out my Spirit on all people. Your sons and daughters will prophesy, your old men will dream dreams, your young men will see visions. Even on my servants, both men and women, I will pour out my Spirit in those days." (Joel 2:28-29)

Ah! There it is.

Enter Enchantment

When God would bring about whatever that *newness* was all about, at that time the (*Enchanting*) Spirit of God is to be dynamically present. God's *Enchanting Presence* will indwell and empower and anoint God's New Creation. It wasn't spelled out, but the vision was there. God would irresistibly create a reconciled human community which would dwell in the intimate embrace of Father, Son, and Holy Spirit. God's heart and mind would be his people's own heart and mind by the Spirit. God's love for them would express itself in that recreated community by their love for each other. His joy over them would be their joy with each other and their joy in God. God's glory would be their glory, and their glory would be God's glory. The nature and character of the Holy God would flow out of and embrace and be demonstrated in a holy nation.

Disenchantment: The Groaning Creation

That unique human community would be a sign among the nations of the reality of God's dominion, of God's New Creation, of God's dwelling place. It was to be the demonstration of authentic human community as God designed it to be.

All of this, and much more.

Now we're talking about the Church!

Are you connecting the dots, my friend?

"I think you're beginning to come through, Bob – finally."

Then let's move on to the next journey.

"Which is …?"

Which is Jesus. In Jesus the *enchantment* breaks into human history once more.

Journey Four
The Enchanted One: Jesus

When we had our first encounter in the bookstore coffee shop, Alan had asked me a theoretical question. Should he should look *first* into the Biblical documents to see what the church was to be and how it was defined there, … or, should he should look *first* at the church which he was experiencing, and then try to justify what he was experiencing from those Biblical documents? In what follows here, Alan will clue me in on how much he (like most of us) is more than a little captive to the second of these approaches, which looks at the paradigm of the typical *church institution* and then tries to read the Bible through that institutional lense.

He had rather eagerly volunteered (to my surprise) to come over one afternoon and help me in some 'hard labor' landscaping that I was doing in my back yard. By that point in our friendship, Alan and I had really created a bond and were enjoying being together enormously. I think he really wanted some time for us to talk some more. In the course of our chatter, he offered this:

"Bob, I think maybe I can anticipate where you are taking me in these conversations. You're proposing that the Creator-God's design for human community got *whacked* when Adam and company declared their autonomy. OK? And then, like, you're going to propose to me that Jesus came along, among other things, to rescue the human community from that disaster and that some kind of new community would be created in the church to fulfill God's intention and design. OK? Am I on target?"

Sounds good to me. Keep going.

"Problem: After Jesus told Peter and the others that he was going to build his church on the foundation of himself, the long-promised Messiah, ... then he died on the cross. OK? He rose from the dead. He spent a few days with them. He did all those things. And then, ... poof! He's gone, ascended into heaven, or wherever. So whatever happened then, he ascended and he didn't leave them any discernable instructions or any strategy, did he? No five-year plan. Nothing. Nothing about building, or organizing the church, or even how to make disciples out there among all the nations. I can't see where he showed them anywhere how to do it. What have I missed?"

Probably what a good part of the church has missed, a very simple pattern that is so obvious that it is difficult to see how so many have missed it.

The Evidences of Lostness Around Us

But hold that question. Before we get into it, I want to go back to something you said in one of our earlier conversations. A while back you spoke of the *superficiality* and *depthlessness* of a lot of the guys are around on campus. Spell that out for me. What does that look like in them?

"Good question. I dunno. I think they hide a whole lot of inner confusion behind some giddiness and compulsive behavior. Some are in overdrive into some entrepreneurial gig or something. Others hide out in endless entertainment and gross regurgitations of all the dumb stuff they've been into. Some even talked in veiled terms about 'ending it all'.

"I think behind that is some inarticulate longing, maybe, to know what's 'out there', or *Who's* 'out there'. Like, some longing to see into the transcendent or whatever. Maybe they're scared of what they may not know. I guess they may be lonely. Maybe even harboring some vague sense of guilt about something they've missed. Or it could be some uncertainty about who they are or what it means to be human. They can get into all kinds of weird faddish religions and occultist stuff.

Maybe hopelessness is part of the mix—they don't seem to have much hope for the future, or even let themselves think about it much. I guess, too, that there is not much discernable framework for their lives, not anything that comes close to a worldview that puts things together into some sense of ultimate reality. So they just go with the immediate.

"And I think that they don't know what to do with other people either, ... with relationships. Some of them have never had much of a healthy family life behind them, not much good communication. So they're intimacy-deprived, or intimacy-challenged. Relationships tend to be really superficial. Chat rooms, web sites, or cell phone trivia and instant messaging don't usually make for much by way of significant conversation.

"It's pretty much momentary gratification. But even in that distraction, they miss any kind of structure, of moral boundaries. They're uncertain about the rules of the game. I'm not even sure that 'guilt' is a category for many of them. Yet, at the same time, there's a longing for something like a good and profound friendship. Even all the group activities turn out to be a bunch of lonely individuals sharing their loneliness by doing depthless stuff.

"Just listen to their music!

"That's one bunch, but there's another bunch ... another bunch who are really achievers, whose family life seems to have motivated them to accomplish something. They're upbeat, motivated and are out to set records. So there's no single pattern. But the whole idea of 'god' and 'religion' doesn't get a whole lot of space, or even any consideration with most that I know.

"That for starts. Is that what you're asking about?"

Exactly. Thanks. And it pertains to what you and I are looking for in our conversations. Now back to your question about Jesus not leaving any plan behind, ... just watch!

The Plan Begins to Unfold

It will help us if we do something like an overlay, like a transparency of what we can clearly see. We need to get a vision of God's intent in Christ to inaugurate his New Creation. That is what the Kingdom of God is all about. God's New Creation in Christ comes with a new pattern of human community which Jesus *calls* into being. That called-out and recreated human community is the *Church*. Once we've got that vision as our overlay then we'll need to superimpose it over of the phenomenon of that church which you and I see and experience. When we do this it will help us to see some of the contradictions with which you and I are wrestling in these conversations.

When we've done all of that, then, maybe then we can see what is *authentically* Christ's church—and what doesn't have much to do with it. We can see some of what is extraneous that Paul designates as "wood and hay and stubble," … stuff that doesn't belong in the true "building" that Jesus was promising. If we can do that, at least, maybe we'll know whether (and if) our involvement in "church" has anything at all to do with *God's mission*. Maybe we'll get some clues about how we can be constructive agents of a healthy and positive kind of focus and authenticity within that mission however and wherever we are involved.

Hey! This is an unending struggle. It's not at all new. We're not the first ones to raise these questions. All you have to do is read the opening chapters of Revelation to realize that the local church communities wandered off and lost their focus within decades of their founding! Now we have two millennia of church history which underscore the reality of how easily the church drifts away from its intended purpose. So please don't get discouraged or impatient yet! We're not alone in this quest.

A Parenthesis: Radical Redefinition ... Then Subversion

(So while Alan and I are digging holes, planting shrubs, tilling a new bed and other stuff, I continued through grunts and panting …)

One of the major, major difficulties that you and I face in looking at these questions has to do with a very early *switch* from the essence of what Jesus was introducing.

This is a very troublesome observation, so stick with me here.

Remember that Jesus' life and teaching were in the context of first century Judaism which was focused on its symbolic Temple. The Jewish people understood that God somehow had his dwelling in their midst through that Temple. The Temple was the geographical and symbolic focus of a people whose behavior was supposed to be formed by their response to the sacred writings of the Torah. Their Jewish story was the story of the chosen people of God who were to live in covenant relation with the God who had called them with a special calling at Mt. Sinai. In the course of time they had allowed that calling to grow dim in their corporate consciousness. They had first forgotten and then misinterpreted who they were and why they had been chosen. And so their story unfolds.

Centuries before Jesus' time they had been taken into captivity as a judgment of God on their disobedience, their forgetfulness, and their unbelief. From their captivity in the Middle East a token group of Jewish exiles had been allowed to return "their land." Jesus came on the scene several centuries after that return. The Jewish people of Jesus' day were more than a little defensive about the sanctity of their Temple, about their identity as Israel, about their land, and about their story. That defensiveness was made even more acute by the occupation of their land by profane outside empires such as Greece and Rome. We need to be alert to those facts as we approach our quest for Christ's intent for the church he would be building.

Why? For the very simple reason that Jesus (in essence) *radically redefined* all of those sacred Jewish identities. Much of the hostility directed toward him was because of that very redefinition. Jesus (both in his parables and his direct statements) identified *himself* as the Anointed One (their long-awaited *Messiah*) who transcended and truly interpreted their Torah. He identified *himself* at the *true temple* in whom God dwelt. And – as if that were not radical enough – he reinterpreted the *true Israel* as being all those who would follow him. He taught in terms (that were not too veiled) that through *himself* the true (eschatological) Israel would now be formed. He taught that through this *true Israel* God would dwell in the world, and through it would bless the nations. That also apparently explains why Jesus never seems to have referred again to the ancient promises about the land of Palestine. The whole world and all its peoples would now be *the land* where God would bring his blessing promised to Abraham. Those nations (*ethne* or "people groups") were all the places where the true Israel of Jesus' followers would be dwelling.[1]

---

[1] Cf. Matthew 28: 19; 24:14.

The Enchanted One: Jesus

It doesn't take much imagination to understand why that didn't go down too easily with the Jewish people considering how possessive they were of their symbols, their Torah praxis and their national story. Case in point: In the very early days of the infant church there was a deacon by the name of Stephen who was actually stoned to death in part because he declared: "God does not dwell in temples made with hands."[2] What you have, then, is the inauguration of a radically new community in which Jesus also redefined the priesthood. The priesthood would from that time be *all* of the people of God, not only a sacralized few. *All* of Jesus' followers were now to have intimate access to the Holy God through him.

Tune-in with me here. Do you remember *perichoresis*? OK. Then look where we are. Jesus was teaching that the calling to be a his follower was, in itself, a calling to be *embraced once again within the Trinitarian community*. It is a calling to be now reconciled, forgiven, adopted as sons and daughters, and in communion with Father, Son and Holy Spirit. It is a calling to be engaged with God in the mission of God. It is a calling into God's ministry of love to and for one another. It is a calling into true priesthood. What that means for us is that there is now no special (or *sacralized*) class of people (called *clergy*!).

There are no *clergy* in the teachings of Jesus, no special class of priests. The incarnation of God in Christ now belongs to all of Christ's followers – he in them and they in him. They are all to be holy men and women. The Holy Spirit (as we shall see) did and does certainly anoint men and women with special *gifts*. The Spirit enables and equips the community to live God's Life, and to obey God's mission. But then, each believer has the Holy Spirit and all are given (by that same Spirit) some Spirit-gift (charisma) for the blessing and equipping of the whole for their calling in the world.

It gets even more serious when we realize that the Temple was also superceded in Christ. The dwelling place of God would now be *wherever his people were together*: "For where two or three come together in my name, there am I with them."[3] No *sacralized* buildings. No stone and mortar would become the sacred precinct since the whole creation was God's. In Christ God would henceforth be with and among his people wherever

---

[2] Acts 7:48 ff.
[3] Matthew 18:20.

they were together in Jesus' name, whether in a home, by the riverside, in a store front, in a Siberian gulag, in a clandestine conventicle, or the ballroom of a Marriott Hotel.

In brief, we simply must register the fact that Jesus as the "great high priest of God" radically redefined Israel's own symbols, its Torah practice, and its own story. He did that by virtue of his own Presence as God's *True Temple*. Jesus, the Lamb of God, is the once-for-all sacrifice for the sins of the world. He is the fulfillment of the Torah. Even more than that, he is the giver of God's *Enchanting* Spirit. He is the long-awaited "Seed of Abraham" coming for the blessing of the nations. He is the long-awaited Messiah. His Church would be the community of that New Creation – it would be *authentic human community*. The Church would, in turn, become the incarnation of the Mission of God in Christ to reconcile the whole world to himself.

"Uh, ... like, did all that disappear into a 'black hole' somewhere? So, how did we get all of these everywhere church buildings that the inhabitants refer to as the 'house of the Lord'? And, man, we've got 'clergy' all over the place. Check out all the people who like to be called 'reverend' or 'father'. So, like, what happened to all of Jesus' redefinitions?"

Do you know what? That is *really* a good question.

The answer would seem to be that it got displaced and forgotten all too soon. I guess it's only human nature that as the church grew it would quest for some kind of security in permanent physical symbols, or to find some kind of guaranteed conservers of the apostolic tradition. My best appraisal would be that it re-invented some of the security patterns of Judaism that Jesus had declared obsolete. As long as the apostolic Church had found its security in God, so long as it prayed and so long as it relied on the power of the Spirit in obedience to Christ's mission, ... as long as all of that was in place the Church and its mission prospered.

"But then ...?"

The evidence would indicate that as the contextual hostility subsided (after a couple of centuries) then the Church tended to 'dig in' in order to conserve its gains but doing so in forgetfulness of its true power. The Church, almost imperceptibly, began to revert to *merely human* religious patterns. As they did so, the Spirit was quenched and the *enchantment* diminished. The Church began to invest in *sacralized* buildings, in physical symbols, and in *sacralized* persons in order to give it permanence and to conserve its gains. But as that happened, the Church lost its primary focus on the *mission of God*. It *subverted* the pattern given by Jesus. In essence, the forgetful followers of Jesus *reverted* to temple, to priesthood, and to patterns of human religion.

We'll come back to that. What is necessary to say here (almost parenthetically) is that such *subversion* continues to cloud all too much of the thinking of the Church right down to this day. That has been so since the early centuries of its history. It has tended to cause the Church, far too much, to focus on institutions and on church authority … rather than on purpose of the Church in the "missionary dialogue of the Trinity."[4]

"I don't think that kind of idea would make you very popular in the kind of christianity I've run into. From what I've seen the church seems so focused on its glitzy buildings, and on its wall-to-wall in-house programs. And that is not to mention those all of those 'clergy' who talk to us about their going into 'full-time Christian service' as if the rest of us guys are a bunch of second-class citizens who are only in 'part-time service' to Christ. I guess you know you're challenging some real 'sacred cows'?"

"Image and Likeness"

I know. But do you remember *why* the Triune God created the human community in the first place? Do you remember *why* God created us in his own image and likeness? Do you remember that the *enchantment* that we used to describe that incredibly beautiful community grew out of the *perichoretic* relationship between Father, Son, and Holy Spirit? Think of what God's design *was* and still *is*. If you can keep that little jewel in your mind, then maybe Jesus' radical redefinitions will make a lot more sense.

If you go all the way back to the beginning of our discussions you will remember that God's intent (or design) was to create *humankind* in God's own "image and likeness." It was obviously God's intent that these humans

---

[4] Cf. reference to Jose Miguez Bonino on page 25.

should have both the capacity and the personality to interact joyfully and fully and intimately with their Creator-God. They were created to be "at home" within the Trinitarian community of Father, Son, and Holy Spirit. Add to that the additional and critical note (for our pursuit of the Church) that the Creator also knew that it was "not good for *man* that he should be alone." That being so, God created a *woman* to share intimacy both with her husband, ... *and* within the Trinitarian Community.

Ah! That was (if we can say it this way) humanity's *raison d'etre*. That was its reason for being, its true and authentic nature. Such intimacy was its *blessedness* (hang on to that word). That was its true *shalom*. That was its true *enchantment*. In that human-divine community, pictured so poetically as the Garden of Eden, those two humans lived and flourished and had their true being within such true community, which was both human and divine. It was only within that community that they had their indescribable joy, hope, caring, adoration, reality, and so much more than we can ever imagine.

"Then we're a long way from home, aren't we?"

You bet. All of that *shalom* was tragically violated and lost, early on, when that primordial pair "got suckered" into making a grab for autonomy, into seeking to become what they were *not* created to be, namely, "like god." It was in that violation that they lost their true humanity and their true human community *in God*. It left a haunting void in them. It is the very same loss that leaves the void in your friends on campus – in all of us, Alan.

That was when the *darkness descended* and when *disenchantment* entered the scene. With it came loneliness and emptiness. With it came the endless and frustrating attempts to realize the false Satanic promise of being their own *god*. Such a fruitless quest is the history of the human community. When men and women know that they aren't really *god*, then they find a need to create something to explain the "out there" and to appease whatever that *reality* was that was lurking somewhere just beyond their senses and their control. The "image and likeness" of God in them becomes captive to the darkness and death of an alien dominion. At the same time ... it longs for Light and Life.

They are still created by God and for God!

Strange as it may sound, even *cynicism* or *atheism* or *secularism* are all (in a very real sense) *faith responses*. They are all attempts to give answer to what is, or what is not – to ultimate reality! You can chew on that one.

The Seeking God

(I'm recording all this after the fact, and digesting a long afternoon's sweating and grunting along with our conversation, but I think that is the gist of how I approached it all with Alan.)

I love the Biblical documents. They are a real gift! They have the *aura of enchantment* all over them. They give us the record of the awesome reality of God who has never hidden himself from his creation. God's creatures may have tried to hide from God, but God always came seeking them. The Biblical documents, mysterious as they are in their formation, are the record in our hands of God's persistent self-revelation – not to mention his continual breaking-into the human story. As such, those documents are God's gift of *light* in the human darkness (even though your friends outside can't comprehend this).

The obvious and primary focus from the very beginning is that *it is our Creator-God who lost us!*

God lost the very human persons whom he created for himself in his own likeness and image. That's pretty awesome. It is God who comes seeking to rescue his human creations from their own folly and captivity. That is what the whole Biblical story is about. That is the wonder and the mystery of the story that ultimately brings us to Jesus. The New Testament writers understood that the focus of Jesus' whole mission was to rescue God's *lost* ones. Jesus was *God's awesome rescue mission*. That mission was initiated before the very foundations of the world. It is God's nature to seek his own glory by bringing these lost ones back to their "heart's True Home." Still, … the profound and pathological darkness and captivity are inescapable in the human community. It is a dominant reality. And that pathological darkness is enormously complex.

The deliverance and healing which God brings will come at a very high price to himself.

"I Will Dwell Among the People"

We can't afford to skip over the long saga of God's engagement with the people of Israel just so we can get to get to our interest in Jesus and the Church. It is tempting for us to want to go directly to God's awesome invasion of the broken human community in the person of Jesus Christ. But to do so would be to miss a vital understanding of how intentionally God wants to be in the company of the human community whom God has created for himself. There are simply too many roots in Jesus' own life and teachings which don't make any sense without some knowledge of the story of God and Israel. The story is both thrilling and depressing.

We've touched on some of this before but stick with me here and don't get too impatient. Don't forget our earlier discussion about the *perichoretic* Trinitarian community, about all of the beauty, the love, and the interanimation among Father, Son, and Holy Spirit displayed in that community. And don't forget that our wondrous God also created humankind in his own image and likeness *in order that* those creatures should have the capacity of intimate communion with their Creator. Especially don't forget what was *lost*. Don't forget what God *lost* when his own first human community (Adam and Eve) made their tragic choice of attempting life on their own!

Here's the story-line. God kept breaking in. God broke in early on (nearly two millennia before Christ) by visiting a *god-fearer* in the Middle East. Abraham was a man who knew and reverenced what understanding he had of the One God. He was open to that God who was somehow very real to him. It was to Abraham that him God sent *enchanted messengers* – angels. Alright, so it's like 'magic' – a couple of angelic visitors and all – but then God's revelation is like that. Through those messengers God made a promise to Abraham that through his natural genetic offspring "blessing" would come to all the nations of the earth.[5] From that *enchanted encounter* the story of Israel unfolds.[6]

"Blessing? What's that all about?"

---

[5] Genesis 12 ff.
[6] Israel: the name God gave to Abraham's grandson Jacob, means "prince with God" and from him came the twelve tribes known as Israel.

The Enchanted One: Jesus

Actually the account doesn't really define it at that point. What I want us to work on is the fascinating thesis that we're pursuing, namely that the "blessing" is the human community once again reconciled into loving and intimate relationship with the God who created it. The Creator God purposes for us to dwell together again in the joy of his own Presence, within the embrace of the Trinitarian community. That's the "blessing." How does that sound?

"Run with it!"

God would continue to break in and to communicate with those Israelite offspring of Abraham. He would often remind them that his special love for them had nothing to do with any virtue that he found in them. His love for them was out of his own gracious nature and for his own glory. He was the *Seeking God* who came in love and grace seeking them. Even after he had supernaturally delivered that whole huge Israelite nation out of their slavery in Egypt with such an unmistakable display of power – they both *believed* – and then they *didn't believe* in God's Presence with them. They were still captive to the darkness and blindness of their *disenchanted worldview*.

God brought them to the foot of Mount Horeb out there in the middle of the desert. There he made his *enchanting* Presence known to them in another dramatic display of his power. You'd think by this time that God would have had their full attention. Not so. Those newly freed people could only beg Moses to keep them away from such a terrifying God: "You go and talk to God. Don't let him near us. He's too scary" (paraphrase). Moses went up on the mountain to commune with God all by himself. There he received from God that amazing covenant that defined their calling along with the patterns of behavior and communal life which were to constitute their Torah.

And just what would you think those people would be doing while Moses was on the mountain? They did what humankind always seems tragically prone to do in their *disenchanted* nature—they set about to construct their own hand-made utilitarian god! They evidently needed to satisfy their appetites for a god, some god, *any* god whom they could see and own and manipulate and control. Contradiction? Unbelievable? Like I have said, the history of Israel is both thrilling and depressing at the same time.

For all of that, however (and in the midst of that history of Israel's faithlessness) there comes through a fascinating glimpse into the heart of God (and into our ultimate quest for the essence of the Church). God asserted to those Israelites that he *absolutely wanted to dwell among his people*. God wanted to be present in the midst of their lives. To make that visible God had them construct the Tent of Meeting to be the symbol of his Presence in the dead center of their pilgrim encampments. "I will dwell among my people."

The Anointed One: Messiah

As one reads the story of Israel as it progressed down through those centuries it certainly does have a familiar ring. God kept breaking in to show his kindness and faithfulness to his people, yet their response was usually to either obey God reluctantly – or not at all. Nevertheless, God kept reminding them that the pathway to true blessing and reminded them through a unique set of God-fearers whom we call *prophets*.

What emerges out of those prophetic writings is God's enigmatic promise of a figure, a unique and anointed person (*messiah*) who was to come. Such an anointed person would be sent with the mission of accomplishing God's ultimate mission among the human community. The mission of *Messiah* would be one of rescuing and recreating God's rebel creation into its true essence, into the glory of God, and into its true communion with its Creator-God. The prophets spoke of a coming "Day of the Lord" and an of such an "Anointed One" out there on the horizon of Israel's expectation. They spoke a promise from God that he would at some point in their future history intervene into the human scene and would "make all things new."[7]

"Persistent, isn't he?"

Who?

"God, of course!

"I know I wouldn't have been nearly so patient if I had been in God's place. I mean, it's like centuries of being patient with Israel, and they keep on screwing it up! I mean, God needs them, and needs us, like he needs a case of hemorrhoids."

---

[7] Isaiah 65:17 et al.

Well then, I'm glad you're not God, Alan! But at least now you're beginning to sense the passion of God for his rebel creation. You begin to see what "infinite love and grace" are all about. God doesn't *need* us, but that all reveals something in his nature that *wants* us, something that *seeks* us. So let's move on …

Jesus: Anointed and *Enchanted*

The stage is now set for the coming of the One who was God's promised *Messiah*. We're talking now about the Anointed One in whom *true enchantment* re-entered this darkened and *disenchanted* human scene. We're talking about the truly *Enchanted One*. We're talking about Jesus. We're talking about that point in human history when God came in Person, came in flesh and blood, came to dwell in the midst of his lost creation.

Humanly non-explainable?

Absolutely.

Smacking of "magic" and "otherworldly manifestation?"

No question about it.

Jesus, the eternal Son of God, entered into human history. Jesus, the Divine Son, took on our human form and entered the very human scene of spiritual blindness and captivity and rebelliousness. Such was the context of God's *lost* human community. That human community was also the habitation of Roman, Greek, Syrian, and Jewish cultures. But with the entrance of Jesus *a radically new and subversive Reality* – an altogether new paradigm – was intruded into the midst of that culture of darkness and death

"So God himself came seeking us in the Person of his Son? Ah, the plot thickens."

You got that right. His coming and his cross have often been described by Christian writers as the *center of time and eternity*. It was in Jesus the Son that God came as the Great Reconciler, and what unfolds is the awesome mystery of God making peace with the world by "the blood of [Christ's] cross."[8] God provided the sin-bearer and so gave us the inestimable gift of sins forgiven. But even more, New Testament writers would communicate

---

[8] Colossians 1:20

their understanding of Jesus as *the Word made flesh*, or as *the firstborn of the New Creation*, or as *the Second Adam*. He was, and he is, God's one and only Son who has come as the *Truly Human One*. He came as the God-sent paradigm of the very *image and likeness of God*. He came as God's demonstration of what that image and likeness are really all about.[9] Jesus is the truly human One. Jesus was the walking, talking, flesh-and-blood perfection of true love for God. He lived both a life of unqualified love for, and obedience to, the Father-God who had sent him. At the same time Jesus demonstrated complete and costly and self-giving love for his neighbors (even when they hated and killed him).

With all of that said, Alan, Jesus was also a major stumbling-block to so many!

"Why?"

Because Jesus simply didn't fit into any of the *human categories* that composed Israel's expectations for their promised Messiah, that's why. He was a contradiction to all of their mistaken anticipations about a human redeemer-king. They were looking for some dramatic figure who would promptly destroy all of their earthly foes, for someone to reinstall the glory of the Davidic monarchy. Their stumbling block was that they simply could not conceive of any Messiah who would have to become "the Lamb of God" slaughtered in order to take away the sin of the world. The very idea of a Messiah who would actually have to die cruelly at the hands of men was to them near blasphemous. After all, God-sent Messiahs weren't supposed to do that!

The Jewish people were unable to realize the depth of their bondage and their blindness to the pathologies of sin and *disenchantment*. It was beyond them to realize that such an offering and at such infinite cost to God was necessary in order to get at the roots of that pathology, to get at the roots of their human rebellion, guilt, and estrangement from the Creator God – not to mention their estrangement from each other. In a word, God *reconciled* heaven and earth through the awesome mystery and the necessary death of Jesus. That is why the cross of Jesus is so central to the story.

---

[9] It is worth inserting here as a footnote what shall become clear as we proceed, namely, that our *predestination* and our *calling* are for the explicit purpose that through Jesus Christ we should be "conformed to the image of (God's) son" (Romans 8:29).

The Enchanted One: Jesus

In order to accomplish that reconciliation Jesus had to reap in himself, totally, the full consequences of humankind's whole tragic rebellion against God. He would have to pay in full the consequences of humankind's sin and death and rebellion. He would have to bear the justice of God's righteous anger and the sentence of death – and at the same time bear all of the human antagonism and resentment toward God, all the fruit of humankind's grasp at autonomy.

It staggers and stumbles all human rationality and imagination. It has often been dismissed as sheer foolishness. But there it stands. In that one awesome, unexpected, almost hidden person, Jesus, ... *Enchantment* **re-entered the human community.**

And with Jesus came all of the fruits of his ministry of reconciliation. With him came the beginnings of a new and reconciled human community. With him came forgiveness, joy, meaning, and hope. In Jesus came reconciled intimacy with both God and the human community. In him came a whole new paradigm of what this world and our existence in it are all about. Ultimately, in him "a new heaven and a new earth" has been inaugurated. With him has come a whole new paradigm that is far, far beyond what any human religion could offer. God's New Creation in Christ is far too radical and uncontrollable to be contained in any religious institution. It was, and is, more like a prairie fire. It is an *enchanted* and divinely-inhabited movement set loose in the world to seek and rescue and transform everything it touches.

Now we're talking about the Church!

Repeat, Alan: *Now we're talking about the Church!*

"Don't shout! I'm beginning to get the message."

Jesus: Builder of the Enchanted Community

"So did Jesus leave a plan? Is that where're your going?"

Just look at it!

Just remember what happened when the human community crashed and eroded. Remember how those first persons became strangers to one another – all that stuff we walked through in our previous conversations. Remember how you described to me the emptiness of your peers, the guys you interact with on campus. Now look at how Jesus came onto this selfsame human scene.

And please take note, that from his very conception in Mary's womb Jesus had that unmistakable aura of *enchantment* all about him.

He was so obviously very human. But then, there was obviously so much more about him that defies human explanation. Somehow there's cosmic music wherever he appears. Angelic visitors from another realm. Visions. Awe. Transcendence had come again into the human scene! To all outward appearances he was just an ordinary guy like you and me, … but there was obviously so very much more to him.

Ever so quietly out there on the margins of the Roman Empire, Jesus began a brief career for which there were (and are) no human religious categories. He faced the same Satanic seductions and temptations as did the first Adam (and the same as we do). Yet unlike that first Adam, Jesus responded out of the true "image and likeness" of God. In so many words, Jesus said to his tempter something like: "You've gotta be out of your mind, Satan! I listen to and obey only God my Father! I live only in and for him. You tried that 'Look out for yourself first' trick once, and look what happened. Go away, Satan."

Actually, the heart of those testings was all about Satan's attempt to provoke Jesus to achieve power and success and self-preservation by forsaking the Cross. It was the most seductive and brute evil ploy of hell. Clever temptations. Satan failed because Jesus knew precisely who he was. Jesus knew why he had come from the Father. He would not violate the will of the Triune God, of whom he was the Son. He was faithful to the "image and likeness of God." Jesus was *true and authentic humanity*.

With that testing behind him Jesus in faithfulness inaugurated his public career. He began with the astounding announcement that in himself "the kingdom of God" (prophesied by Isaiah) was on their threshold! That was the announcement that would introduce the response of the Seeking God to human brokenness and lostness. Jesus candidly and unashamedly told those listeners in his hometown synagogue that he had come to bring joyous news to the poor, liberty to the imprisoned, sight to the blind, liberty to those who are crushed—that he had come to proclaim the year of the Lord's deliverance (Jubilee).[10] Jesus came to be that very joyous

---

[10] Luke 4:18-19; Isaiah 61:1-2 f.

and liberating Person who would be able to rescue real human persons from their existential hopelessness. In that announcement he specifically identified how much God cares for the really helpless and marginalized of human society.

That mission also holds one our primary clues for the authenticity of the Church!

So now comes the question: How did Jesus engage that *disenchanted* human community? How did he begin to reconcile it to God? How would he bring *Enchantment* back into it? What was his own practice? How did he, the *Enchanted One*, relate to all the ordinary individuals with whom he came into contact along the dusty back roads of Palestine? How did Jesus, as the first-born of all Creation, re-establish communication with the Triune God on behalf of the New Creation? How did he demonstrate what it was like to live as an authentic human being? How would he respond to all of this out of the heart and mind of the Seeking God? And most importantly for us is how he would do it all in the midst of a disenchanted society?

Are you ready?

"Do I have any choice?"

OK. Right away Jesus began to *build his Church*.

And, how in the world, you may ask, did he do that?

He began by *calling* a small community. He called persons one by one (and by name) to be *with him*. He called them to be quite intentionally formed by him. He called them to follow him. He called them *to be transformed* into the paradigm New Creation community (the Church). It is not too difficult to figure out that *this is still what the Church is to be about.*

Got it?

"Not really."

When Alan and I stopped our 'grunt work' to have a glass of iced tea, he was looking at me again sidewise with that look of uncertainty and humor, like, where all this stuff was going, and would it ever stop. I had to laugh with him, because I really had become so caught up in researching his basic question that it was quite too easy for me to re-read all of the New Testament with a fresh set of eyes. I had to confess to him that I had really had gotten carried away, but that I really, really was getting to the point.

Here's How It All Began

Just look at what happened. Primarily, Jesus *called* a small bunch of guys to spend significant time with himself. Along the way there was an outer circle of others including some devoted women (such as Mary and Martha) who were also Jesus' followers – but the primary group was the twelve disciples. There's your beginning of the Church![11] It started in those opening days of Jesus' adult and public role. Jesus had obviously created some real curiosity among some of those who had heard John the Baptist speak of him as the "Lamb of God." As a result a couple of those who had heard approached Jesus with a lame sort of question: "Hey teacher! Like, where are you staying?" Notice how Jesus responds: "Come be with me and see."[12] Basically Jesus was asking them to spend the day with him! What do you suppose happened when those two inquirers spent a day with Jesus?

What we have, then, is *Jesus plus two* for a day *in hospitable conversation*. Do you get it? How's that for a *plan*? What resulted was enough conviction engendered in them to convince them that Jesus actually was God's promised and Anointed (Enchanted) One – Jesus was God's messiah. One of them then went off to get his brother and bring him to see Jesus (John 1:42). Jesus read that brother like a book and that brother was Simon Peter. That brother, then, also became part of their little company. So now we have *Jesus plus three*. The *plan* began to unfold.

After the call to Peter and on the very next day Jesus *called out* Philip to become part of his community of disciples.

This gets interesting!

Remember what was going on: "You did not choose me, but I chose you!"[13] Nothing haphazard, nothing "by chance" here.

---

[11] Note: the Greek word for "church" literally means: a people called out, an assembly convened, for some specific purpose.
[12] John 1:39.
[13] John 15:16

The Enchanted One: Jesus

It is worth noting, at this point, that there was a marked difference between Jesus and the ordinary traditional rabbis of Israel . Rabbis were the respected teachers among the Jewish people. They often had exclusive rabbinic schools for those interested in learning how to become rabbis. The difference between those traditional rabbis and Jesus was that with them those who wanted to become rabbis first had to *apply* for permission to be received into the rabbi's very special circle of discipleship in order to be trained.

When Jesus appeared he was quite obviously was an a-typical rabbi. He did just the exact opposite. Rather than candidates applying to him, instead, *Jesus initiated his call to them* with an invitation and command: "Follow me." He summoned them to follow him, to sit under his instruction, to see him in operation, to hear him express the message of the New Creation, to watch him live out true humanity before their eyes, and so they learned from him. Jesus became the initiator of their discipleship and their formation into New Creation community.

After their ever so brief an encounter with this obviously different, obviously *Enchanted* and authentic Person, ... Philip is persuaded enough to go find a mature older local sage by the name of Nathaniel, and to gush on him that they had actually found the *one* "promised by Moses and the prophets." Again, Jesus demonstrated his Enchanted prescience by reading Nathaniel's inner character back to him, and to the others. Nathaniel evidently was not one given to making hasty judgments. But he was instantly overwhelmed by Jesus' understanding. Maybe even intimidated. He knew that he had met someone other than a predictable and merely human rabbi. He was hooked.

So now we have *Jesus plus five*. An infant community on the threshold of many months of transformational and intimate relationships in trust and communication with each other and with this anointed-Enchanted One, Jesus.

Does that begin to ring some bells?

(Alan responded with an unconvinced groan.)

Introduction to Enchanted Community

From that point the *plan* continued to unfold. Jesus summoned a small community of unlikely candidates for his mission. He called upon them to *follow him*. This is like saying: "Come, I want you to be with me. Come spend significant time with me. I want to have some long and profound conversations together with you and let you get close to me. Come, let's learn about each other. I want to know about you and to know your stories. I want to open to you the mysteries of the God's Kingdom, of God's New Creation. Come, I want to show you how to live together in self-giving love. There is a *new reality* now on the scene that I need to explain and make plain to you."

There was that larger group of other followers who would also liked to have been among Jesus' intimates. But Jesus knew that it was necessary to sift it down to just twelve. It was necessary to choose a limited and workable-sized company where intimacy and accountability was possible. We read of Jesus spending a whole night in prayer, in communion with his Father, and out of that prayer he was able to choose twelve of them to constitute his primary band of disciples. With those twelve Jesus created the *paradigm community* around himself. Now take note: Jesus was not only building his Church, ... but he was showing his disciples *how* they were to do it.

Am I coming through?

"Uh-huh. Finally. You're not doing bad at all!"

The number twelve, in itself, is interesting to contemplate as long as we're on the subject and looking for our clues about being the Church. It had all kinds of symbolic meaning to the Jewish people. First off, there were the twelve tribes of Israel, with all the symbolism of that. But more importantly, in the dynamics of community building the number *twelve* is generally recognized as an optimum size for creating intimacy, for creating communication, and for allowing sensitivity to one another in relationships.

Love cannot be lived-out in the abstract, nor can it be lived-out in a large and impersonal group. A large group may be organized into a purposeful society but, at the same time, the larger the group gets, the less the possibility of intimate interaction, communication and mutuality. In a large group it is easily possible to hide, or to be lonely, or even to be

The Enchanted One: Jesus

ignored. In those settings persons can become something like statistics (as so many "church members" actually become!).

Later on we will take note that in the rapidly growing early Church the people met both in larger public gatherings, but also they met "from house to house."[14] That is most significant. It was in the homes that healthy community building was possible.[15] Even though that early Church almost immediately numbered into the thousands in Jerusalem, they maintained home groupings to guarantee that individuals were not lost in the crowd. It was critical that they be formed into communities where the love of "one another" was possible and practiced.

We're looking at the fact that for a couple of years that original group of twelve (that infant Church) essentially lived with Jesus. Jesus began to open their eyes and to reshape their thinking, their behavior, their worldview, their values and their relationships. He began to teach them a new language. What he was announcing was all such a very new and radical and "upside-down" paradigm to them. That new *reality* is the *kingdom of God* (or the *New Creation* as I have chosen to designate it) that Jesus was announcing.

On one occasion he would teach them. Then on another occasion he would take them public and show them how it was done. They could watch him in his conversations with individuals. They observed him as he performed mind-boggling works (like healing some really wracked-out people). He fed a huge crowd out of one man's lunch. He even walked on the water of the Sea of Galilee. Those twelve watched all of this in public and then, obviously, quizzed him about it when they were by themselves. All of those things together were to demonstrate before that infant Church just how the Seeking God would put on flesh and blood, how he would "move into our neighborhood."[16] Jesus demonstrated how God would respond to the human scene. All of that served as a visible exhibition of God coming to deliver his lost ones (us) into freedom, to deliver them from the darkness and death of this present *disenchantment*.

---

[14] Acts 2:46; 20:20.

[15] Acts 2:46, 20:20, et al. It is worth noting that arguably the cutting edge of the Church's growth in the world is in house churches, cf. Wolfgang Simson, *Houses That Change the World* (OM Publishing), or the growing "cell-based church" movement around the world.

[16] Cf. Eugene Peterson's delicious paraphrase here of John 1:14.

Enchanted Community

The authentic "image and likeness" (*Enchantment?*) of God was now being lived out right there in the midst of a disenchanted Judaism. It was being lived under the very nose of the most powerful military government in the world. Jesus did not come with any plans for a grandiose new religious institution (such as the Temple). In fact, Jesus was not too veiled in letting it be known that the old Temple would be destroyed, and that its priesthood, its Torah, its definition of Israel, and even its affinity for the land of Palestine was now being transcended and redefined by himself (which obviously provides us with one compelling reason why the Jewish leaders were not too fond of him!).

Rather, Jesus' *plan* was to create an intentional community of disciples in his own likeness and power. His *New Humanity* would function like leaven functions in a loaf of bread. His community would be mobile, flexible, intimate, versatile, and vulnerable. His community would bring the Light and Life and *Enchantment* of the Seeking God into the daily lives of the people, and onto the backstreets of the "dominion of darkness."

In our journey into the mystery of Jesus' Church it is critical to remember that it was *called out* to bring all of that radical newness right into the grim realities of the present hopelessness, the loneliness, the meaningless, the emptiness of the lives of real people. Jesus brought that not (primarily) to the most gifted and religious and prominent, ... but especially into the lives of the helpless and marginalized in the most remote and unlikely places.

The cry of the human heart reached the heart of God.

"Bob, OK, this is all fascinating, even awesome to play with in our minds, ... but it gets further and further away from everything I have ever experienced in my admittedly brief exposure to church institutions. And it is even further away from that which I have been invited to 'join' by the pastor of West Park Church. Are we on another planet here?"

Hang tough! We'll get back to where we are with that one shortly. I think a huge part of the church enigma is that churches forget to do the very thing that you and I are doing right here. The church often forgets to think through to its roots in the gospel of God. When that is so, then, churches often begin to displace what Jesus intended for them by creating church institutions that can often exist on *merely human* principles – and by doing so they are missing New Creation altogether!

"Yeah, right. But excuse me for changing the subject a bit. It looks to me, reading those New Testament accounts, like what Jesus was teaching was 'off the map' for his disciples too! Like, I'm not the only one confused. They kept reverting to some preconceptions that didn't fit. There are times when it even looks like Jesus got really fed up with their stupidity. Am I reading something into it, or is that true?

"How'd he do it? What did he do to make this happen?"

Foundation for Enchanted Community

Let's just say that Jesus *mentored* his disciples. Does that word register? He engaged them into the heart of the reality of the kingdom of God. He patiently called them forth. He opened their minds in long conversations about the awesomeness and radical otherness of this kingdom, about the New Creation, ... until it began to be 'dinged' into their often-obtuse minds and hearts. That's always the primary discipline of disciplemaking. It takes time to initiate a person into a new and alien *worldview*, especially one that works itself out in power, and in transformed lives – in transformed behavior patterns and thought patterns.

In John's account, Jesus acknowledged to those struggling disciples that he was overloading them. ...

"Like you're doing to me?"

... Probably. He knew that he was telling them more than they could understand or digest at the time. But then he introduced them to the *promise* (and here is where my whole notion of *enchantment* comes in). Listen up! He promised them that when his *Holy Spirit* (translate: his *Enchanting* Spirit) would come to them, then by that Spirit he would open their minds and bring all that he was teaching back into their memory. He would bring it all into focus. John recorded that along the way Jesus progressively revealed himself to them as Light, as Life, as the Door, as the Truth, ... as well as the *One sent by the Father* to "seek and rescue" God's tragically lost and messed up creatures.

In Jesus' final days with his disciples (and just before his execution on the Cross) ... he would give them a set of marching orders that were enough to boggle their minds. "As the Father has sent me, even so do I now send you." It was like: "You have seen who I am. You have seen what I have done. You know what I have taught. You know how I have called you and formed you. Now, it's your turn. Go do the same thing with others until everybody in the world knows the good news of God's reconciling love."

He doesn't allow them to hang around reveling in experiences of "spirituality" either. "You have not chosen me but I have chosen you that you should go and bear much fruit." In plain language Jesus was sending them to live *kingdom-shaped* lives, to make *kingdom-shaped* responses, and to demonstrate *kingdom-shaped* communities – as they were engaging this culture of darkness. That is what would make them (and us) to be Salt and Light in its midst.

Finally Jesus gave them a command: "I have been given all power in heaven and on earth. Your part is now to go among all the people groups, every kindred and tribe and nation of the world and to make disciples among them just like I have done with you. That's the *plan*. You will initiate the disciples you make into the community of my followers by baptism. You will teach them to be *doers* of all of the teachings that I have given you. And make no mistake about it, as you do this I will be with you to the very end of the age."[17]

(I remember that at this point in our dirt-digging dialogue in my back yard, I finally had mercy on Alan and so didn't say anything else for an extended time to give him time to digest or question where we were. After my silence …)

"So that's the plan for the Church? Sounds OK. But it's still a long way from that plan to where I am and what I see. So you might as well drop the next shoe."

We're closer than you think. That's the *plan* for building the Church. It's not institutions but *communities of disciples* that Jesus calls. Those communities, in turn, learn how to make disciples until the whole larger

---

[17] Matthew 28:18-20 (with my paraphrasing).

The Enchanted One: Jesus

human community is permeated with the reconciling and recreating message of Jesus Christ in the flesh and blood lives of Jesus' disciples.

It means, however, that *every* believer, *every* follower of Jesus, becomes an *activist*. Every follower becomes a vessel of Christ's authority and of his final command. Jesus, in all of his life and teachings, gave to those disciples the pattern that he will use (through them) for building his Church. That is the pattern for building New Creation communities. Those are the communities in which God will dwell by his Enchanting Spirit. Those are the communities through which the Seeking God will continue to bring his Light and Life into the midst of the death and darkness , *not only* of our human cultural scene, ... but also into his decadent church, ... into empires, and into the hidden back roads of this disenchanted human community. That is the mission of God in Christ until the *world* is reconciled to God and brought again within the *perichoretic embrace* of the Trinitarian community. It was for this that God created it!

How's that for a *plan*?

It was getting on late in the afternoon. I finally had to admit: "I'm pretty well pooped out! How about you?" Alan, being fifty years my junior probably had energy to spare so wouldn't admit to being tired. About that time, my wife Betty popped out the back door with the warning: "Don't you guys overdo yourselves! And, Alan, why don't you stay and have a bite of supper with us. I've got a crockpot full of hot beef stew, and I can whip up a salad. We'd love to have you."

He and I agreed to that, then we could continue the conversational journey after supper and see where it got us.

Alan protested that he was filthy dirty (we both were). He hadn't brought a change of clothes, so we solved that by my loaning him a pair of Bermuda shorts and a sweatshirt (they almost fit), and sending him off to the shower in the guest bathroom, and I made off to do the same in ours. Later, refreshed and clean, we devoured the good food, and also shared some of what we had been talking about with Betty. When we had finished Betty's wonderful meal, she asked: "Will you two rinse off the dishes and put them in the dishwasher and spiff-up the kitchen. I've got a seven o'clock meeting with some neighbors. It would be a big help."

"No problem."

Journey Five
Jesus Forms the Infant Church

Supper was over. Betty had gone to her neighborhood meeting. Alan and I had cleaned up the kitchen, made ourselves a cup of coffee and retired to the back patio to view the fruit of our afternoon's labors, and to look with some fascination at the evening colors in the western sky. So there we sat, barefooted, coffee in hand, reflecting in silence about where we were in our ongoing conversation. Alan finally broke the silence.

"I dunno, ... it sort of staggers my imagination to think of the consequences of what those guys were into. Most of those disciples were pretty young, weren't they? They must have had businesses and probably families and friends. It's hard to imagine them just pulling up roots, rearranging their priorities, putting all those connections into some lesser category, and making their relationship to Jesus the focus of their lives? Wow! That's pretty awesome.

"Can you imagine the dynamics of that bunch? You had what must have been a couple of hot-heads in James and John. You had at least one political fanatic in Simon the zealot. Add in at least one pretty profane fisherman. There was the 'company agnostic' in Thomas. And no telling what other colorful characters and eccentric personalities were mixed into the twelve. What a bunch! Add to all of that the earthy reality that at their mostly young age, if they were anything like me, they probably had testosterone surges along with other pressures, don't you think? And I can't even imagine what it was like to deal with the dynamics of Roman occupation and the tensions that brought with it. They had to figure out all of the economic realities that come with daily life. There were always those 'super-religious' types from Jerusalem making life miserable for them. Like I say, I have a tough time even imagining it. Quite a mix! So what happens now?"

I love your descriptions. And I love your identifying yourself with their realities. Did you ever stop to think how much we have probably "sanitized" this story of Jesus and the twelve in our *over-familiarity* with it? And no telling what other filters we have put on it to make it more congenial to self-interest.

I sometimes think of a colorful description from Kazantzakis' story of Zorba the Greek about just how sterilized life can become. The narrator is contrasting his own captivity to intellectual formulae and to rationality ... with the rambunctious, sensuous, joyous and unpredictable earthiness of his friend Zorba. As he thinks about it he laments to himself his own sterile existence:

> " ... it all seemed so bloodless, odorless, void of any human substance. Pale blue, hollow words in a vacuum. Perfectly clear distilled water without any bacteria, but also without any nutritive substances. Without life. ... no more seed, no more excrement, no more blood. Everything having turned into words, every set of words into musical jugglery, the last man goes even further: he sits in his utter solitude and decomposes the music into mute, mathematical equations."[1]

Maybe what we're talking about is not so much "mathematical equations" ... but just maybe, maybe, ... we've "decomposed" the Church into some proper theological equations. Maybe we've formed it into some kind of "bloodless, odorless" spiritual otherness, ... something safe and "without sperm, or excrement, or blood." Your wonderment about the earthy realities with which Jesus' twelve disciples lived is very much on-target for the journey that you and I are into.

---

[1] Nikos Kazantzakis. *Zorba the Greek* (New York, NY: Simon and Schuster, 1952) 133-4.

You can't spend two years (more or less) living together without getting beneath each other's surfaces and each other's hiding places. All of our sins and foibles and weaknesses and agendas and idiosyncrasies and short-tempers, ... all of the pettiness and insensitivities—all that stuff soon becomes obvious to one another when you're living in the close proximity and pressures of daily and unpredictable circumstances.

It's just such a *reality check* that you're raising here.

It's what makes it all the more interesting to figure, realisitically, how Jesus would *form* his New Creation community out of such unlikely (to us) persons. He knew full well all of their potential for better or for worse. And, if Jesus were *not* creating something indescribably beautiful and awesome, ... then it would seem to be contradictory to even talk about the Church being in any way an integral part of our joyous message of Jesus Christ – the *gospel!*

"Alright. So just how *is* the Church any kind of integral part of that gospel?"

Oh, I don't know. I suppose that it is altogether conceivable that some church institutions might have *nothing at all* to do with it! That's a harsh judgment to make, but it is not an unbiblical judgment.

I don't know about you, but I've known a lot of the church experiences in my life that have been totally unreal. I'm talking about basically good people who all looked at the same Bible that fascinates you and me, ... and yet somehow they and I were on totally different wave-lengths. There was a lot of looking at the message through what I choose to describe as a set of "devotional glasses." It was all pleasant and 'spiritual' but it didn't go anywhere. It all came out as something less than the flesh-and-blood-stuff of daily and very earthy life.[2]

For the most part there was a disconnectedness between Sunday church gatherings and the rest of the week. And what that meant was that whatever the *church* was, it seemed to have little discernable or self-conscious identity with anything like a joyous community of New Creation. It was hardly living out of any discernable dynamic relationship of love and obedience

---

[2] The Church, early on, had to struggle with an aberration known as Docetism. Docetism denied the true humanity of Jesus, and consequently turned the whole of the faith into something much less than incarnational, much less than flesh and blood. It all became 'spiritual' and otherworldly. We're still plagued with that false notion.

within the Trinitarian community. Such an idea seemed not even on the scope of those folk.

Jesus never succumbed to that kind of unreality. That kind of *disconnect* was basically a Greek notion. The Greek philosophers viewed anything material or earthy as a lesser sort of reality. To be *spiritual* was to find reality in the *other*, in the philosophical and the religious reflection. It demeaned bodily and earthy realities. Unfortunately that kind of thinking has tended to infiltrate the church all along the way. It was reinforced in the 17th and 18th centuries by it's cousin, an intellectual movement called "the Enlightenment" (which still influences us more than we know). The so-called Enlightenment tended to consign all religion (Christianity and the rest) to a category of inner and subjective experiences. Religion, or faith, might be personally meaningful to an individual but it had no viability in the real stuff and discourse of daily life and thought. Religion had no legitimate place in the *public square*. *Religion* was just your personal and inn*er experience* of well-being.

That kind of philosophical *worldview* is quite inimical to what Jesus did and taught (and it's inimical to the Church!). Jesus, after all, was a Jew. He was a Hebrew, and the Hebrew view of God and the world was *holistic*. It was all interconnected. It was all very earthy. God was the Creator and it was God's world. God made it *all* for his own glory. In the Person of Jesus, that same Creator-God (the God of Abraham, Isaac and Jacob) came right into the middle of his own creation. He came in flesh and blood. Jesus never allowed any such disconnection!

But, sad to say, much of my own church experience certainly did!

"Do you think Jesus ever discussed sex or politics with his guys?"

Count on it.

In the intimacy of those couple of years with them, Jesus certainly didn't serve up abstract life principles and then leave his disciples to haplessly figure out how to work it all out. I doubt if there was any subject "out of bounds" in the hours they spent together in private. What made the communal life of Jesus and the twelve so transformative was that Jesus was actually modeling it, … he was actually *incarnating* the very things that he was teaching them. He was doing what he taught right in front of them. They saw New Creation lived out in front of them in a whole spectrum of unlikely circumstances. They also saw the Son interacting with his

Father in prayer! They were tasting *enchantment*. They were experiencing the outskirts of the divine *perichoresis* as they walked with Jesus.

Have you ever noticed that it's near impossible to learn something that you've never experienced? So just register the fact that Jesus' church-building model gave those disciples a *hands-on* experience. It was not abstract. They *experienced* Jesus. Jesus *was*, in himself, the vivid New Creation model of what he was teaching.[3] Let me *underscore* that! No, let me *double underscore* that! Jesus was investing his own life in the existential context of their daily lives in order to form them into his own likeness and image.

He was together with them in the midst of all of their struggles and questions and doubts, their positive and negative experiences and responses. The disciples had the unhurried time to process all of this entirely radically new *alternative* way of living and thinking which Jesus opened to them and demonstrated before them. They had time to question, to argue, to be questioned, to be challenged. They began to learn the new language, the new symbols, and the new paradigm of the kingdom (revolution?) of God.[4] They experienced and touched and talked to the Love of God and the Word of God in the Person of Jesus Christ! It was *never* abstract. They had a model and a mentor.

"I feel cheated. That's what I really want. The closest I get to it is with my three friends on campus—and we're all just beginners. But to be with Jesus, to see him, to be able to process life … Wow! Awesome!"

"Awesome" is the word.

When we're talking about the Church, then, that kind of transformational process has also got to be essential to the *plan*. It *was* the *plan* which Jesus left with his disciples for the Church. It's at the heart of what the Church is all about. All of us still need not only to *hear* Jesus' teachings clearly, but we also need to *see* them being lived out in models and mentors. And especially do we need a context in which to process, to discuss, and to pray our way into Jesus' teachings together. That is especially true for new believers (such as yourself). We need models of

---

[3] Hebrews 1:1-4 describes Jesus as the "express image of God."
[4] I acknowledge my debt to Brian D. McLaren for this insight that "kingdom" might better be translated for our 2ist century ears as "revolution of God". Cf. *The Story We Find Ourselves In* (San Francisco, CA.: Jossey-Bass, 2003) 116 ff.

discipleship, real genuine flesh-and-blood persons with whom to *process* the life and love implications of Jesus' teachings until our lives are formed by them. Ultimately we need to learn how to be able to reproduce that same disciple-making process with others.

So now we're looking at a *major clue* to the agenda of Jesus building his Church!

The clue is called *disciple-making*! It is the commission of Jesus to the Church.[5]

Why? The Re-Creation of the True Human Community: The Church

"OK. Some of this is going over my head, but I think I'm computing it. Tell me again why Jesus is doing all of this? Give me some handles. If I have a clear idea of *why* the Church is being built, then it'll be easier for me to know how to sort out the stuff that clutters the scene. And by the way, you talked about Jesus teaching them some 'new language' and I need to know what that's all about, too."

I think we can handle that. Maybe a couple of questions are related here. We need to be clear as to *why* the Church is being built in the design of God. Then, secondly, it'll help if we have an idea of *what God thinks it ought to look like*. Right? So let's charge on.

You and I have been working on the thesis that God created the human community in his own image and likeness so that it could join with the Trinitarian community in expressing the wonder and glory of God's creation. The human community has no true meaning or authenticity apart from God, apart from the Trinitarian Community. We're still working with our thesis of the *perichoretic community*, of the nature of the relationships that exist among Father, Son, and Holy Spirit – that's our theological clue. We're working with the Biblical teaching that God actually *wants* to dwell with us and among us, and that he actually created us to dwell in joyous, creative intimacy with himself. That's true human community.

Got it?

"I'm with you. So … ?"

---

[5] Matthew 28:19.

So Jesus comes back to that divine intent with his assertion about building his Church. Such authentic human community is God's design. Jesus says that his recreation of it is irresistible. It is God who is working out his purpose in recreating that new community of those who love him in what Jesus designates as his Church. God calls out men and women (Paul reminds us) *according to his purpose.*[6] And the purpose of God's calling? That purpose is to conform them to the *image of his Son.* That means that we are to be conformed to the image of very Son who is before us in Jesus. God's intent is to conform those whom he *calls out* to the likeness of Jesus. (Remember: Jesus is the Truly Human One.) Jesus loves and glorifies his Father. He does his Father's work. He keeps his Father's word. He is totally one with his Father. He is the quintessence of authentic humanity. He is the firstborn of the new humanity.[7] Somehow that family likeness is to be enfleshed in those whom God calls, namely, in his Church.

So think of that! Think of a whole new community of people all being so transformed that they reflect the image of God just as Jesus does. What you get, then, when you ask: "Why the Church?" … is the answer is that God is now *calling out* a reconciled human community of real men and women who, through Christ, are to be partakers of the divine nature.[8] And behind that calling is the design of God to dwell in the midst of that community of his people. That, you will remember, was his ultimate intention in the first place. For us, then, it is God's purpose to demonstrate *through the Church* what is God's own eternal design for the *authentic* human community, … and do it *visibly* before the watching world!

Now we're talking about what the Church is really all about.

"So we're back to *perichoresis*, right?"

You got it. The only authentic human community is one that lives and loves and relates to God and to one another out of the very Life of God which dwells within it. It is a community of real flesh and blood persons living their human lives out of the divine nature within them by the Spirit of God, the Spirit of the Father and the Son! That is precisely what provokes me to conceive of the Church as the *Enchanted Community.*

---

[6] Romans 8:28-29 in loc.
[7] Ibid..
[8] II Peter 1:4.

Jesus Forms the Infant Church

Keep in mind, however, that such community is only possible through God's miraculous work of New Creation in Christ.

"OK, OK. Back to reality. Nice theory. Words are cheap. But how did Jesus go about that. After all, that was a pretty fractured scene he was dealing with – and still is! How do you recreate *perichoretic* community out of a bunch of somewhat clueless and autonomous individuals, if not downright incorrigible rebels (like the rest of us)? How do you even show them what it is?"

Ah! Now we're getting closer.

When you first asked me what was my "take on the church" those months back, I knew ultimately that we had to get to this very point. The first thing Jesus had to do was to give them a whole *new paradigm*. After all, he was proclaiming to them his New Creation (Kingdom) of God, but they were totally formed by the *old creation* culturally, ethically, and religiously. They were accustomed to (and formed by) the paradigm of Judaism. But Jesus came to inaugurate a radical alternative, a true counter-culture.

First of all, then, he had to free them from the rigid strictures of that existing paradigm of Judaism (preparatory though it was). He had to get them free from their captivity to the culture of Torah, temple, priesthood, and much more, … while at the same time showing them that he was the fulfillment of the design of God, and the promises given to Israel. He would have to set them free to see all of those structures as only preparatory, only a shadow of things to come.[9] Jesus had to reinterpret all of those 'shadows' in terms of himself. He had to redefine the temple. He had to redefine the sacrifices. He had to redefine the priesthood and the atonement. He even had to redefine Israel. He had to redefine all of those in the light of his own Messianic mission. His redefinition and his message were: that in himself God's *radically new dominion* had come. Then he had to unveil to them that the Church which he would irresistibly build was to be formed out of that same *mission of God* – to "make all things new" through his Son.

Everything Jesus taught spoke of a different and counter-cultural kind of human assembly – a truly alternative human community . His followers were to be a mobile, incarnational, transformational, and missional community. The Church he was (and is) building was to transform them

---

[9] Hebrews 8:1-8

into the living, breathing demonstration of his New Creation. The Church was, then, to be God's demonstration of authentic human community – community as God intends it to be. His purpose was to build his disciples (both individually and communally) into that transformational fellowship of men and women who would live-out the true "image and likeness of God," and would do it within the *perichoretic* embrace of the Triune God. That is not some merely human self-improvement society or any merely religious institution. It is to be God's *New Creation community in Christ.*

Jesus had to form them ever so intentionally and so obviously because the existing and dominant paradigms of their culture were deeply entrenched and formative. He opened them up to this new paradigm so that (when he would finally leave them) he could say to them (in essence): "OK, guys. You're on. It's your turn. For the very same purpose that the Father has sent me to you, so I am I now sending you to those still outside."[10]

His task in making them disciples was to form them into his own likeness and mission. He wanted them to know how to live, how to think, how to love and how to engage in the mission of God. And, do you know what? In the end, … they would know exactly what he was talking about.

He would be able to give them that *outrageous* commission: "Just like I have made disciples out of you, now it's your turn to go and *make disciples* of **every people group in the world.** And just like I have taught you to observe my commandments, so now it's your turn to teach all of your new disciples to hear and obey them."[11]

And that would have made perfect sense to them.

He could also tell them: "I'm giving you a new commandment, which is that you are to love one another just like I have loved you."[12] That wouldn't have sounded abstract to them at all. They would have been observing that forgiving love in action through Jesus, with all of its practicality, over their many months together – even when they denied him! They would have had a living, breathing human model of precisely what God's divine and costly love looked like.

---

[10] John 20: 21 (my own paraphrase, obviously)
[11] Matthew 28:19-20 (my own paraphrase)
[12] John 13:34

Jesus, you will remember, was the perfection of "the likeness and image of God."

Jesus' *plan* for the building of his Church would be, obviously then, that of reproducing himself in that community of his followers. His design was that they, in turn, would know how to form communities of disciples by following the example he had demonstrated with them. Every community was to be *reproductive* of that "image and likeness of God" that had been displayed before them in Jesus Christ. It's not all that complicated. It may be difficult—but it's not complicated. Make disciples! And Jesus didn't hide the costliness of the *disciplines* of his calling. He let them know that "the gate was small and the way was narrow" – that discipleship would engage their minds and wills at the most profound and demanding level.[13]

That continues to be Christ's mandate right down to this present day. The Church is not only to teach its members all that Jesus did and taught, ... but just as Jesus did, the Church must also *model* those teachings and that message. Jesus, after all, had perfectly modeled, in human terms, everything that he had taught them about God's inbreaking kingdom.

That is absolutely critical to *Church-building*.

So let me say it again (because this gets horribly eclipsed in all too much of the church's preoccupation with institutional clutter): Jesus would not only *proclaim* the message of the inbreaking kingdom of God, but he would also *demonstrate* exactly what he was proclaiming, and what that kingdom looked like in community form. That infant Church, composed as it was of those original twelve disciples, was being transformed into God's own image and likeness. They *saw* his teachings in flesh and blood reality right there in front of them every day. They were being built into his Church!

Have I said that often enough?

"No comment."

"Well, yes, on second thought, I do have a comment.

"I'm having to admit that my brain is getting 'fried' with all these fascinating concepts that are so absolutely foreign to any of the church stuff that I identify with."

I know. Still, that is what the Church is all about.

---

[13] Matthew 7:13

Jesus was building his model Church in that very community of those disciples. Or maybe to say it another way, he was building *God's new, and authentic, and truly human community* in the company of his disciples. His express purpose was quite obviously so that they, in turn, would reproduce themselves in others as he would give them the power to do so. That is exactly what happened. Jesus would build his Church through them so that as they obeyed him the Church would grow like "leaven in a loaf" (to use Jesus' metaphor).[14]

New Creation communities would produce other New Creation communities until, ultimately, the promise given to Abraham about "all the nations of the earth being blessed" would be fulfilled. That is the design of God's Kingdom, or of God's New Creation in Christ. That is God's design for the Church. That is God's design for the human community to be rescued and reconciled again into its intended communion with Father, Son and Holy Spirit.

That is the Church!

What Do You Think Jesus Wanted It to Look Like?

"Let's come back to planet earth. I think, maybe, I've got this 'perichoresis' bit down, and probably the 'New Creation community' stuff. But what in the world does it all that look like? Jesus must have had some kind of a vision of it like any good architect would. Gimme a few handles here. If you were one of those disciples, would you have had any clue what in the world you were being asked to live-out? Personally, I've still got too many filters on me to get the picture, particularly when I deal with the West Park Church question. Can you help me on that one? There must be some specifics in there somewhere that would give me a clue about what that new community was supposed to smell like, look like, live like, think like? Are there?"

---

[14] Jesus communities were not anything like company (ecclesiastical) franchises with buildings and staffs, but rather communities of natural, spontaneous and contagious growth. Again, this is so alien to our practice. We tend to want to skip the Square # 1 of disciplemaking and go directly to Square #3 which may be some kind of institutional form for the sake of the mission!

Unfortunately, Alan was too close to the truth. The Church has spent a lot more time on the *form* of the church institutions, on its rites and order, on its theology and orthodoxy of its message, than it has on the practice and essence of New Creation. That has probably turned-off a whole lot of people. Words are cheap. Forms can be vacuous. Ecclesiastical clutter can obscure the Church's God-given purpose. Jesus, on the other hand, was pretty pointed with his disciples about being *doers* of his word. Somebody in recent times has come up with the useful term *orthopraxis*, which is about the *practice of the truth*. Alan's question got to the heart of what that practice and demonstration would look like in the Church.

Since you ask, the new community should probably "smell like, look like, live like and think like," ... are you ready for this?

"Try me."

It should, provisionally, smell like, look like, live like, love like, and think *like God!*

"I'm beginning to expect such answers out of you. I want to see how you get to that one. But OK, press on."

Alan, just do the math!

The principle runs all through the New Testament. Paul at one point would say to the Church: "Be imitators of God as his dear children."[15] Or again: "Be imitators of me as I am of Christ."[16] Jesus would tell his followers to let their light so shine visibly that men would see the glory of God in them, or glorify God because of them.[17] Then there is Peter's astounding comment about our being "partakers of the divine nature."[18]

If we were all created to live *in, by, with,* and *for* God, ... in God's image and likeness in the first place, ... and *if* that 'true humanity' is one of the victims of the rebellious and tragic decision to attempt to leave God out of the human equation – to seek human autonomy, ... and *if* Jesus could say: "He who has seen me has seen the Father," ... and *if* Jesus so lived to

---

[15] Ephesians 5:1.
[16] I Corinthians 11:1.
[17] Matthew 5:16 (paraphrase).
[18] II Peter 1:4

do his Father's will and to seek his Father's glory, … then, … first of all , we're seeing the very Life of God in the flesh and blood 'true humanity' of Jesus. Right? We're seeing in Jesus true humanity, humanity as it was intended to be. So that would mean that when Jesus invites us: "Come unto me! Follow me! Believe on me!" … that somehow he wants us to be totally identified with who he is.

"Makes sense."

Which means you've got to seriously listen to what he says, and you've got to watch what he does in the light of that divine design. (Did you ever wonder why we have four different but complementary gospel records?)

Jesus spelled it all out it out with his promise that if we love him and keep his teachings, that same response will bring us again into the Father's love … and that he and the Father will come and make their home in us. Jesus talked in a most uncomplicated way about their response of faith and obedience, which would result in his people being once again embraced into the love and life of Father and Son, and would be animated with God's Life by the Spirit.[19]

Are you tracking with me?

"I'm tracking."

By the way, in Jesus' public ministry when some *bandwagon effect* started and large numbers were jumping on board of popular movement, seeking excitement and self-fulfillment … Jesus would stop them cold in their tracks with his sobering words which revealed how deeply they were captive to their autonomous rebellion. At the threshold of his calling into his New Creation was his call for *radical repentance.* He continually challenged them with that call for a total rejection of (or 'death' to) their autonomous self principle. That repentance was always the threshold of his call to authentic discipleship, of whole-hearted obedience to himself. He used the graphic metaphor of eating his flesh and drinking his blood to indicate what kind of absolute identity with his very Life would be the critical and formative discipline of their lives. The offense of such a radical calling immediately thinned out the *bandwagon* responders or 'fair weather followers' of Jesus.

Over and over again Jesus reminded his still somewhat obtuse and innocent disciples that what he was *forming* among them was anything

---

[19] John 14-16 in loc.

but a humanly possible religious society. What he was creating in them individually, and creating among them communally, was by any description a *miracle*.

His Church was to be God's New Creation in flesh and blood community.

But we've got to go even further back than that.

Jesus continually tried to impress upon those struggling-to-understand disciples how totally he identified with his Father. He was insistent in reminding them (as well as his adversaries) that he only spoke his *Father's words*, that the Father was in him and that he was in the Father. He publicly testified that the works which he did were his *Father's works* and that he was doing everything that he was doing because he was determined to *glorify his Father*. His will was also his *Father's will* ... and on and on. The corollary to that was that Jesus rested on his confidence of how very much his Father loved him. That is why he was so artless in saying that to see him was *see his Father*.

Keep all that in mind as we work on what the Church should look like.

"This is beginning to get scary."

It does get your attention. You will remember that we put down a 'marker' (back there somewhere in our conversation) that the Church is included in "the missionary dialogue of the Trinity."[20] So for our purposes here we have to assume that all we have just noted about Jesus himself ... is, then, also to be formed in the community which he is building. That would mean that to see Christ's Church is to see the Father who is living in it by the Spirit! That would mean that the Church is to be the community of the Father's will, of the Father's word, of the Father's works. Look at it! He tells them that others are to see their good works and so see the glory of God.[21] As astounding as that concept may sound to our unaccustomed ears, it is absolutely clear as Jesus was telling his bewildered disciples that he is about to go away, and that he was then telling them that just as the Father had sent him into the world so he was now sending them into the world.

Same mission.

---

[20] Jose Miguez Bonino (1995) p. 141.
[21] Matthew 5:16.

So we have the Church: God visibly dwelling in human community engaging in his 'search and rescue mission'. That's what Jesus was building. That was his vision.

"How does he do that?"

You have to think, first of all, of his call to *radical repentance*. Think of his call for a *radical trust* in himself and his consequent call for *radical obedience* to his teachings. They were being called into a new way of living and thinking – into an 'upside-down' kingdom.[22] Those all come to mind. Jesus had to keep reminding them that the building of his New Creation community was not some humanly explainable enterprise. If they were to be embraced within the fullness of the Trinitarian Community it was only by God's calling. It was only through their being reconciled with God, and that reconciliation would come through Christ and by his cross. But even more than that, it was only as they were baptized in the yet-to-be-sent-Spirit that they would then be inhabited and empowered (*enchanted*) for such New Creation living,

Such a calling and divine empowering of ordinary humans would be inexplicable and yet unmistakable before the watching world – too 'upside-down' to fit merely human categories.

"This is all getting scarier by the minute. Are you serious?"

Absolutely. Remember, you started me on this.

A major piece of Jesus' church-formation with them had to do with prayer. How would the Church demonstrate the "missionary dialogue with the Trinity?" How did Jesus demonstrate his own missionary dialogue with his Father? Jesus showed them by his own ongoing dialogue with the Father through prayer. Jesus showed them how critical it would be for them to also stay carefully tuned-in with the Father through prayer and by the Spirit.

So how would he form them as a community of Good News? He would form them by reminding them that without their dynamic relationship to himself that they really couldn't do anything at all. It was only with him and in him and through him that they had access to the Father in all the fullness of that relationship.[23] How did Jesus form them in the disciplines necessary for this?

---

[22] I am always indebted to Donald Kraybill for his *The Upside Down Kingdom* and his memorable explication of this whole alternative life that we are called into by Jesus.(Scottdale, PA: Herald Press, 1978).

[23] Colossians 2:9

Jesus did it by painting a word picture of a *mutual indwelling*. First, if his followers would make their dwelling *in him* and if his teachings found residence *in them*, then they would be animated to bear the fruit of the New Creation. He added a further bit of detail by reminding them that if they loved him, they would be loved by his Father, and that he and the Father would come and dwell in them by the Holy Spirit. They would be thus embraced again within the community of the Triune God. He added a caveat to that beautiful picture which was most critical to their calling. It was not going to be all roses! He forewarned them that this identification with him would bring with it the human antagonism that existed toward himself. It would surely be visited upon them. "Don't be surprised." To follow him came with a price to pay in suffering. He never, never hid that from them (or from us).

Jesus wanted the world to look at his followers (at the Church) and to see *the wonder of the Rescuing God*. It was always to be the community of the One who came in love to seek and to save lost – those bewildered, inauthentic and guilty creatures of his. The Trinitarian Community (that was Present in Jesus Christ) takes up residence in God's New Creation community which is the Church! The communication of God's love, of God's word, of God's will, of God's glory which took up residence in Jesus was now to take up residence by the Spirit in the people whom God calls through Jesus Christ.

With that much in mind, look at how Jesus created in his twelve friends (at least) his infant paradigm community. Look at the beginnings of the New Creation community in which he will reside by his Spirit. That infant community becomes for us our own paradigm community. It is the community in which God dwells, and by which he does his work in the midst of this very rebellious and self-destructive creation. The Church is the community of the "missionary dialogue of the Trinity." It is the community formed by his word. It is the community which does his will. It is the community which works his works and so seeks his glory. It is the community which is one with the Father and the Son by the Spirit. It is the community which lives God's Life and as such is the "dwelling place of God by the Spirit."[24]

---

[24] Ephesians 2:22

"I can't believe I'm hearing this? This is unreal! Am I really supposed to take you seriously?"

Well, yes! If you seriously want to get any kind of a Biblical answer to your question about what Jesus (the architect) wanted his Church to look like. Go back to your question: what does it look like? The community of Jesus' disciples (the Church) is to look like the teachings of Jesus lived-out in flesh-and-blood, lived out in a new and alternative humanity. Look at it: Jesus came right into the midst of all of this tragic human brokenness, autonomy and rebellion to exhibit God, ... "the Word was made flesh and dwelt among us, and we have *seen* his glory ...."[25] Then Jesus called his followers to join him in that same mission right in that very same tragic human scene. He didn't call them to some 'subjective spirituality'. He called them to visibly live-out the glory of God for the very reason humankind had been created in the first place.

"Maybe I'm a bit dense, but dare I ask (for the sake of my own confusion) just 'how' he set about to create something so wild and outrageous as you're describing to me?"

How Did He Set About to "Build" the Church?

I think that's a fantastic question. How would you do it? How would you form a bunch of ordinary men and women into something so totally beyond their grasp, ... into New Creation consciousness? How would you form them into that mission? How would you spell out the implications of following Jesus in the ordinariness of their daily stuff? Those are the questions that are too easily swept under the carpet in our zeal to build prospering 'church institutions' instead of the Church.

What grows on me, Alan, (and you can test this out) is *that it has to be done in a very personal, intimate, interactive, and intentional community.* It cannot be done where all is theoretical and impersonal. We are so captive to impressive ecclesiastical institutions and traditions and forms, replete with church professionals and the familiarity of the rites, ... that such basic formation is marginalized, if not forgotten altogether. (We'll come back to that.) I see Jesus doing precisely that with the intimate community of

---

[25] John 1:14

his twelve friends over those couple of years they were together. I don't see how you can miss it in the gospels.

I am personally quite persuaded that those six sermons that Matthew records are primarily Matthew's recollection of Jesus' dialogical times with them. Jesus taught them and then he *processed* those same teachings with them in their prolonged times together. He *took time* with them to spell out what the nuts and bolts of their discipleship were to look like. I believe that those recorded sermons (as we call them) could have been public preaching, but more likely were done in intimate times with them, forming their thinking.

At a deeper level, consider that Jesus was the very *Life of God* right there with them. And if you were to ask: How does God think and respond and act and love in the midst of the mess of human brokenness? I would answer: Just look at Jesus. In those sermons (or teachings) Jesus walks them into *how* the Life of God was to look in them and in the community of those who follow him. Those teachings spell out the *how* and *what* of New Creation visibility. They taught what it was that would make them to be the Salt of the earth and the Light of the world. They gave a pattern of that which men and women would actually *see* and *know* of God at work, like: " ... let your light so shine before others, so that they may see your good works and give glory to your Father who is in heaven."[26]

"So just what is it that these 'others' are to see?"

Hang on to that question. Look at the setting of the first of those recorded teachings. Look at what we call the "Sermon on the Mount." Jesus had been out there in Galilee publicly proclaiming the good news of the in-breaking kingdom of God. There had been large crowds listening to him. So what does Jesus do? He takes his twelve friends away from the crowd and off to a remote hillside. There in that very small and personal community of intimates he began to spell out with them the 'fine print'. He processed with them what was to be their *lifestyle* as participants in God's new kingdom. That would include their behavior and thinking and the character of their relationships with each other. He walked them into what their kingdom lives (or New Creation lives) were to look like in the earthy realities of every day life. Matthew (bless him) recorded the essence of those teachings (in that sermon).

---

[26] Matthew 5:16.

Right from the get-go this teaching has about it the very *aroma of the Life of God* which was to be lived out among the followers of Jesus. It spells out the lifestyle of the people of the New Creation. The pulse of God's identification with human helplessness (in all of its economic, social and religious contexts) is so obvious in those teachings.

Let me try to paraphrase the opening that Matthew records.

It's not abstract. Look at what life lived in harmony with the Life of God looks like and smells like. Look at what God intends to create in them. Their New Creation lives are to be lived in the context of a broken and disenchanted humanity. It is life lived in the midst of helpless poverty. It is lived in the midst of inhumanity and injustice. It is to be lived-out with all humility and disciplined strength (meekness). It is lived in the context of hostility and false accusations. It is lived with the willingness to suffer abuse, deprivation, slander and persecution for the sake of what is right and good. They (and we) are to be the divine instruments of good news with and to the poor. The Life of God in the lives of the people of God insists upon mercy, on justice, and on a zeal for what is right.

That is Life as God intends to display both in us and for us. That is the Life of Jesus which they saw in Jesus, the 'truly human one'. It is the Life they saw lived-out in their midst. It is the Life which Jesus, in turn, purposes to live out in his Church by the transforming work of his own Spirit.

That kind of Life cannot be hidden. That is the kind of life that is visible. It is Life-giving and wholesome. It is the Life exhibits who God is. It exhibits God at work in those of us who belong to him in his New Creation. What follows (in that and the other sermons in Matthew's record) are Jesus' teachings with his twelve friends.[27] In those recorded teachings he was forming them into all of the dimensions of that New Creation living and thinking and community that he wanted them to understand. He painted for them a picture of what it was to look like when the Life of

---

[27] Frederick Dale Bruner in his two volume commentary on Matthew (*The Christbook* (chapter 1-12) and *The Churchbook* (chapters 13-28) identifies 1) The Sermon on the Mount. Introduction to the doctrine of discipleship (chapters 5-7); 2) The Sermon on Mission. The doctrine of evangelism (chapter 10); 3) The Sermon of Parables. The doctrine of the kingdom of God (chapter 13); 4) The sermon on the congregation (chapter 18); 5) The Sermon of the Signs. The doctrine of last things (chapter 24); and 6) The Sermon of Judgment. The doctrine of the last judgment (chapter 25).

God and the character of God and the will of God were lived out among them personally, interpersonally, and missionally. Jesus' teachings deal with difficult and complex subjects, such as God's judgment and of the final things of human history. Their purpose was to form the Mind of Christ in his followers.[28]

"Uh, like, I feel short-changed, or something. Somewhere I missed something. That's the kind of mentoring me and my guys would love to have. Where do you look? All I get in West Park is the offer of more programs that don't seem to go anywhere, or don't seem to have much to do with forming the Mind of Christ in me. So where am I supposed to look?"

I could only counter with a question back at him: If our pattern here is a valid one, and if you've been shortchanged, then … who's going to reclaim the pattern and begin to practice it within the community? I could only propose to him that such was what we were engaged in here, namely, that he and others like him with similar integrity might be the very ones to perform that reclamation. If we are just to hang-out passively and wait for somebody else to be the practitioners of what Jesus modeled … we might just wait a long time. He looked at me quizzically but encouraged me to proceed.

Look at Jesus and the twelve as the paradigm of the *primary church*. Within the dynamics of that small and intimate group it was possible for Jesus to process with them those same teachings. Those teachings are a portrait of New Creation life. They contain a density and profundity that has challenged the Church for over two millennia. Their content is of such radical magnitude that it is difficult to imagine it being grasped by a popular crowd, however enthusiastic they may have been in their attraction to Jesus. Such crowds all had built-in emotional, traditional and cultural filters. They were on a different wave-length.

But in that smaller group of twelve Jesus could process those teachings with them. He could deal with their misunderstandings and with their captivity to the *mind-set of the dominant culture* with all of its filters. He

---

[28] Cf. I Corinthians 2:16.

could deal with their limitations (cluelessness), and do it in the warmth and gentleness of his friendship with each of them. In such a company he could literally pour his Life into theirs. He could begin to recreate their thinking and behavior into the radical new thing that he was inaugurating.

I don't think that such a process would be practicable or even possible in a larger assembly. So *the size and dynamics of the community* are the first part of your answer.

The second piece of the answer to your question is that Jesus spent *significant time* with those twelve friends. Disciple-making requires lots of intentional and significant time spent together. Jesus goal was to reproduce himself in their lives so that he could later tell them to go into all the world and reproduce themselves ("make disciples") of others just has he had done with them. If I can revisit *perichoresis* here, Jesus is engaged in the interactive, interanimating, interpenetrating, self-giving life of the Trinitarian God, and he is doing it with these twelve friends. In so doing he was introducing them into what life of the ultimate New Creation community was to be.

So think small!

"Whoa! I always thought the Church was to think 'big', like the bigger the Church the better. Did I miss something?"

No. Think small.

Think about it. It was only in his sustained and private time with the twelve that they could have asked him the very questions that you are now asking me. The radical implications of those New Creation concepts demands that they be digested and prayed over and discussed. That quite simply cannot be done in a large assembly. You can't love in the abstract. You can't love someone you don't know and you certainly cannot love with the same love with which Jesus loves us. No! It takes real persons with *names* and *faces* and *stories* and with whom we are in *real communication*. That means pouring yourself into others. It is only in such small gatherings that you can process together such experiences as those of hostility and suffering, as the tragic and the daily complexities which constitute the context of our lives. It is also in such small gatherings that we are able to share the joys of the adoration, the freedom, the joy and the song of the New Creation.

It is only in such a *primary church* context that we can be responsible to each other as well as accountable to each other. Jesus was modeling such transformational community with his twelve friends. When you live together, when you walk miles and miles together, when you eat meals together, when you see each other in your off-guard moments, when you are engaged in public evangelism together … it is difficult to remain strangers! Something happens. There comes a bonding. There is a sense of mutuality and responsibility to and for each other. Jesus was showing us how to do that in his life with the twelve.

When you process the rest of the Sermon on the Mount, that all makes sense. It makes sense only as you see real life with God's eyes, hear with God's ears, and understand out of God's heart. It is such capacity to see and hear and understand that the Spirit gives to Jesus' followers. The Sermon on the Mount is not at all some idealistic or utopian fantasy. Rather, the Sermon on the Mount unfolds to us how the Life of God is to be lived-out in the community of his people by the Spirit. It deals with such subjects as confused sexuality. It deals with legal agreements. It deals with our enduring being wronged personally, and with dealing with real enemies. It deals pointedly with the stewardship of life and possessions.

All of those are very practical pieces of life to be lived out as God's *Enchanted Community* in the midst of the *disenchantment* of "this present age." When Jesus told his followers to pray: "Your Kingdom come! Your will be done on earth ….," he was, in effect, calling them to receive from the Father the power to be God's visible Kingdom (or New Creation) people right in the middle of "the stink and stuff" of real (and often tragic) life.

If I am even close to being on-target here, when Jesus commanded his disciples (on that last evening) to love one another as he had loved them and as the Father had loved him, then there was no way that they would have heard that as some ethereal and invisible love. No way. They would have known that such God-love was pragmatic to the core. They had seen it demonstrated. They had been living with it for many months.

In another of Matthew's six recorded teachings (the one frequently called the Sermon on the Congregation) Jesus wonderfully described how God-in-them was to deal with all of the very non-ideal vicissitudes of human community.[29] It was Jesus' description of how the Life of God

---

[29] Matthew 18.

(the Spirit) living in his followers was to express itself toward all of the *one anothers* within his new community. Look at it! Look at how very practical it all is. The teaching deals with *ambition* in the congregation. It deals with *interpersonal offenses* and with conflict resolution. It deals with *sticky interpersonal relations* that every community has had to face (if it were honest).

One of the most often overlooked nuances of that sermon, by the way, is that it provides for those "little ones" who tend to be invisible and are so easily overlooked in a community. Jesus spelled out the community's responsibility for the immature and the fragile persons among them. God doesn't overlook them and so it follows that his Spirit-people must not overlook them either. That demonstrates love in flesh and blood. Such communal relationships are to be so visible that "all men will know that you are my disciples."[30] (Again, I don't believe that such love can take place in large and impersonal assemblies. It requires a smaller, knowable group of real persons with names and faces and stories!)

That Sermon on the Congregation spelled out for them how Jesus is to live-out his Life and love in the lives of his New Creation people. It taught how they were to relate to each other, with all of the imperfections and human emotions involved.

Is that easy?

Of course not.

But as the Spirit of the Father and the Son animates the community's life those are the natural and unmistakable expressions of the design of God and the Life of God within it. Those teachings instructed *how* the Great Commandment: "Love one another as I have loved you" was to take on flesh and blood and be visible to the watching world.[31]

Am I beginning to answer your question? Does it begin to look, smell, think, love, and respond like God?

"It sure doesn't sounds like Zorba's 'pale blue, hollow words in a vacuum' does it? I'm getting the picture you're drawing, ... but with a *big* BUT – this still doesn't look very much like the church stuff I've

---

[30] John 13:35
[31] John 13:34.

been exposed to. And I can't even imagine how it could be applicable in the scenes I know about. So, are we lost in some ecclesiastical fantasy-land here?"

Maybe we are, but I don't think so. Think of where we've been. Jesus was not only introducing a whole new paradigm for his followers (who had been formed by the paradigm of Judaism). He was actually introducing a new paradigm for the faith community. Such radical shifts are always traumatic and not easily accepted. That means that what Jesus was doing in his ministry was not unlike the setting where we find ourselves. The Church always seems to have a proclivity for diluting (or forgetting) the *radicalness* of the New Creation community that incarnates that gospel. God's people have a history of forgetfulness. They easily revert back to the paradigm of the temple and the priesthood, and to the familiar and comfortable rites.

What we need to learn from those Biblical records is that Jesus did not call his Jewish disciples to forsake the temple. What he did, rather, was to go about founding a community of his disciples within that existing paradigm which would ultimately transcend it and grow beyond in unimaginable ways. He did not advocate a 'break-away movement' even though the new wine of the Kingdom of God would ultimately require the new paradigm (wineskin) which he was in process of inaugurating. That may sound like a contradiction. But if you will look at the record of those Jewish followers of Jesus, they kept their links to the Jewish community even when they moved out into the missionary enterprise of the next generation.

Part of the contribution that you and I will have to make in a scene like West Park Church will be to be the gentle reminders of *what* the Church is, and *why* we are there.[32] I think that there is always a ministry of

---

[32] I was reminded while writing this of the second volume in *The Chronicles of Narnia* in which the 'old Narnia' has been forgotten and buried from memory by most of the Telarmines who have occupied it for generations. But there was an old dwarf, Dr. Cornelius, who became the tutor to the fledgling Prince Caspian who confirmed quietly the reality and existence of Narnia where there were Naiads and Dryads and centaurs and unicorns and dwarves and talking animals. Narnia where there was beauty and joy and where there was dancing and music and celebration. These had been the basic norm. Dr. Cornelius was the link within a hostile and alien monarchy with the memory of the True which was so obscure. I like his role. I want to be a rememberer and a tutor in the Church even in the most unlikely and forgetful realities of that scene which I know and in which I live.

reconstituting, or *refounding* the integrity of the New Creation community. There's a sense in which all of us who are part of God's New Creation become continual *evangelists* to the community, remembering, reminding, rejoicing each other with what God has done and what God has called us to in Christ.

That is the role and ministry that I see for myself. The people of God have a long history of forgetfulness. It's not a matter of junking *what is* but of pealing back the layers of subversion and forgetfulness—and such a critical ministry begins with just a few. That brings me to the point of *small transformational (evangelizing?) communities* inhabiting church institutions (just for the sake of practicality). That is happening quietly and out-of-sight in West Park Church, and it is also probably in a great host of somewhat forgetful and subverted church institutions of all traditions. Those *small transformational communities* are like "leaven in a loaf."[33]

I want to come back to the *community dynamics* here. I don't think that Jesus could have processed anything so 'radically other' with the large public multitudes to whom he preached. I am persuaded that those teachings were his very intimate and transformational discussions with the twelve. In such a limited group context there was inevitably a personal and dialogical process which ingrained these teachings in those intimates. I am always grateful for those six sermons Matthew recorded. But then remember that the apostle John indicated (at the end of his record) that "if all the things Jesus had taught them were written down that it would fill many books."[34]

My imagination can only assume that it was in those extended times with them Jesus could have begun to open to them that the only true blessedness, the only true *Shalom*, was to be found in living out of that very *perichoretic* relationship within the Trinitarian community, which you and I have looked into. He could help them to see that *true humanity* and

---

[33] Historically, the founding of many of the monastic orders within Roman Catholicism were just such transformational communities. This is not to mention dissenting communities and clandestine communities of faith and obedience that crop up periodically in unexpected places in the history of the church. One thinks of the Waldensians or the Lollards in pre-Reformation times.

[34] John 21:25.

true human community would find their true and ultimate expression only in living out of that Life and Light of God.

"I guess it doesn't surprise me that your imagination would go in that direction. You're sort of hung up on that, aren't you. Yeah, but I really like it, so, OK."

There is more. But you get the idea, Alan.

In initiating the building his infant Church with that community of twelve, Jesus got to the heart of true and reconciled and compassionate community. We can observe there true community as God designed it to be. We catch the sweet aroma of the divine *perichoresis*. The law is love, divine love, forgiving love, seeking love, sensitive love. But it is always strong love. Jesus would acknowledge that there was always a *fine-line* between carelessness in living out such love on the one hand, and excessiveness in pressing principles to the point of divisiveness and hurt on the other. But God's purpose for us is to demonstrate God-love and God-caring in our relationships with each other.

Those things simply cannot take place in a society of strangers (or of impersonal 'others')! So we're back to (what I consider) the basic premise, namely, that the working units (or the primary forms) of the Church necessitate some kind of more intimate communities, some kind of households of mutuality. There have got to be intimate contexts in which God's "little ones" are taught to observe all that Jesus has commanded us. I think that such is the paradigm which we see in Matthew. It can only lead to this conclusion: the building of the Church is done *like this*!

The *plan* for the Church emerges. The form and pattern, the thinking and lifestyle, the model-mentor are all there in the story of Jesus and his disciples. There is just one critical piece yet to be revealed and that has to do with the *power*. It has to do with the new eyes, the new ears, the new conception of the heart that would enable those followers to engage in actually living out of the Life of God. The New Creation is not to be a matter of *talk* but of *power*, not just of words but of *demonstration* of that power.[35] It will help to remember Paul's ascription of praise: "Now to him

---

[35] I Corinthians 2:4, 4:20.

who is able to do far more abundantly than all we ask or think according to the *power* at work within us, to him be glory *in the church* and in Christ Jesus …" (Italics mine).[36] It is that *power* to live *into* the glory of God that has to be critical to our quest. So we move on to …

The Last Tumbler Drops

The last violet and green colors of the vanishing day were fading, so I dropped the question: Are we building the Church yet?

"Not quite. You still haven't quite come through clearly enough for me on the enchanted bit. Are we going to get there?"

Alright. I suppose we can go there before we hang it up for the day.

You can imagine that it didn't take too long before those twelve disciples were feeling totally overwhelmed ….

"Sure, I can imagine it, because I'm feeling pretty much the same myself!"

I get the message, but let me tie this up.

They would be the even more overwhelmed when they all forsook Jesus and scampered away to save their own skins after his arrest and execution. They would begin to realize just how totally weak and vulnerable they were. It was only slowly dawning on them how *radically other* his life and teachings were. The whole thing was all so totally awesome and unlike anything they could imagine themselves being and doing. They undoubtedly communicated their incredulity and unbelief to him. In our present day context, they would probably say: "Come on, Jesus, get real! This is too much."

What is so wonderful about Jesus is that he knew all of those things about them anyhow (just as he does about us). He knew very well that he was not beginning some new and popular *human religion*. He knew he was not offering them just a wonderful set of commendable and altruistic principles. He knew, rather, that he was (and is) proclaiming *God's radical and subversive New Creation*. If you will let me – Jesus was openng up to them an *enchanted* new reality. Jesus knew that all authority had been given to him both in heaven and on earth. He also acknowledged that

---

[36] Ephesians 3:20-21.

those friends of his were, of themselves, totally helpless to live-out and obey what he was putting before them. His response to them would go something like this:

> "Of course you can't live this kingdom life on your own. Without me you can do nothing. Without me none of this works. But if you will make your residence in me, and allow my teachings to take up residence in you, then my Father and I will come and actually live you. Don't ever think that I am going to leave you here helpless like a bunch of orphans. My Father and I are literally going to come and indwell you by our own Holy Spirit. Then you all will be fully empowered with Our Divine Life. Then your community of disciples will be my *Enchanted dwelling place* in the midst of the disenchanted human scene. ... but only when our Spirit comes upon you."

Of course, you know I'm paraphrasing and doing a 'cut-and-paste' job on a lot of Jesus' teachings (with a dash of Paul's). But in those closing days of Jesus ministry he would make reference on several occasions to the final piece of his redemptive work. That final piece was about the imminent coming of the Spirit. In his prayer to the Father (in John 17) he would say to his Father-God that he had given his followers "the glory" that the Father had given to him. I (with many others) take that to be a reference to the Holy Spirit, who is the third Person of the Trinitarian Community. In another place he "breathed on them, and said: Receive the Spirit."[37]

But then at the close of Luke's record, Jesus told the disciples: "I am going to send you what my Father has promised; but stay in the city until you have been clothed with power from on high." [38] Or in the opening of Luke's account of the early church: "You shall receive power when the Holy Spirit comes on you, ..."[39]

Now we're talking about true *Enchantment*.

We're talking Divine empowerment. We're talking divine Presence within this non-descript, floating community of Jesus' bewildered and imperfect followers. That reality will come out later in many descriptions

---

[37] John 20:22
[38] Luke 24:49
[39] Acts 1:8.

such as: "Christ in you, the hope of glory." And especially: "Now to him who is able to do immeasurably more than all we ask or imagine, according to his *power* at work within us, to him be *glory in the Church* and in Christ Jesus throughout all generations ..."[40]

Does that describe an *Enchanted Community*, or what?

"I'm beginning to get the point?"

The absolute necessity of the working of the Spirit in the design of God for this new community is like the 'last tumbler' in a lock. The last tumbler must fall before it all unlocks. It is what unlocks the authentic *Enchanted Community*. The apostolic Church would know this *in spades*. They subsequently gave themselves to obedience to the commands of Christ because they knew that only by obeying that they could know the *Enchanting Presence*. Humanly conceived *christian institutions* can exist. They can even realize some rather impressive religious activity, ... but do it all without the Spirit. They can conceivably exist rather 'successfully' but have nothing at all to do with God's design for New Creation.

That's the dilemma that you and I are struggling with now. Right?

"Right. And maybe next time we're together you'll help me track what happened next. OK?"

No problem. But at least we both need to remember that when Jesus told his bewildered disciples that he was sending them on the same mission for which the Father had sent him, ... that he was *not* offering them some abstract mission design. He was actually in the process of equipping them to be precisely such a *missional community*. He was equipping them to be a community that was *Enchanted* because of the Presence of his Spirit.

Let's call it quits. I promise you that next time we can get together I'll work on some real "handles" for us to use as we look at what *is* in the present church scene. And, by the way, thanks for all your help this afternoon. I hope I haven't done you in.

With that we collected his muddy clothes, and a few things he was borrowing to read, and I saw him off at the driveway.

---

[40] Ephesians 3:19-20

Journey Six
The Emergence of the Enchanted Community

The next day, Alan sent me an e-mail:

> To: bob.henderson@belbury.com
> From: alan2@gitech.org
> Date: May 30, 2003
> Subject: Magic, Joy, Song—Where?

Bob: As I remember it in one of our earlier conversations,[1] you and I poetically described what happened when the *disenchantment* entered God's good creation as something like a computer virus. I recall you saying that the *magic* and the *song* and the *joy* and the *hope* and the *trust* … all faded, or maybe vanished when Adam and Eve made that tragic choice. After our time yesterday (by the way, thanks for the gift of your time with me—I needed it!) I can see where we're going with some of this, … but when you're talking about *enchantment*, then … I need to know where do the smells and sounds of enchantment come in? Like, artistry, creativity, the song, the joy, celebration of life and creation and the environment—where do they fit into this? Are these going to be

---
[1] Journey Three

pieces of the Church? How does the Spirit give us eyes and heart for all that exists beyond the boundaries of the community of Jesus' followers? Can we go there? What happens to all of that?
Alan

I responded:

To: Alan2@gitech.org
From: bob.henderson@belbury.com
Date: May 21, 2003
Subject: Let's explore it!

Alan: We can definitely go there. Maybe that's a whole dimension of the community life in the New Creation that's worth our exploring. I think it doesn't take a rocket scientist to figure out that if the Spirit moved upon the face of the waters in creation in order to bring it all into being out of the primordial chaos, … and if it's that same Spirit who has been given to Christ's followers in the Church, … then somehow creativity in all of its fullness including song and art and nature and dance and mirth and the sense of *magic* at God's Presence should not be surprising, should it now? Somehow, all of God's creation should be impacted. Let's hold the question, but let's not forget to explore it as we go along.
Bob.

The phone rang just after breakfast several days later. Alan had just found out that he had an unexpected break that afternoon and wondered if I could possibly be free to meet him on campus to pick up the conversation. I was and we did. We met at the coffee bar in the campus student center, got our mocha and settled in at a table on the terrace just outside. He didn't wait for me to begin.

"Bob, I was serious in my e-mail. The whole idea of New Creation beginning to re-enchant the disenchantment fascinates me. I hope you weren't just playing word-games with me. And I don't know whether you have even thought through the implications of what you've been teasing me with. But I sure have. In one way I could get really frustrated with you and all of your flights off into the theoretical. But in another way, it sure makes sense. I really do want to know what the church is all about, especially how my participation in it would look.

"So it occurs to me that if we were even close in our picture of the enchantment present in that human community as it was originally created, and if that could have included magic and hope and song and laughter and creativity and selfless love all flowing out of the community's Life within the Trinitarian embrace—if that's even close (and I think it is), then it stands to reason that when Jesus began to build his New Creation community that we should be able to anticipate some green sprouts of that same sort of enchantment reappearing as the Spirit recreates community and dwells within it.

"That whole scene may have been blighted with the disenchantment that descended when those first guys introduced the virus of autonomy into the scene. But *if* the Church *is* the community reconciled into communion with God by Jesus Christ, ... then can I expect some of that delicious enchantment to begin to reappear?

"What do you think?"

I frankly sat there stunned at what he was asking.

I had never seen such a picture painted in any of the theologies of the church that I had ever read. I was blown away at how he had grasped the whole content of our journey thus far and had, frankly, taken it a quantum step beyond where I had taken him. In all of my life I had never heard those evidences of the Spirit's habitation in the Church verbalized (which may say more about my limited experience than about what might have been out there). I could only respond: "Yes! I think you're on target." I, at least, can't conceive of the Spirit of Christ producing sterile and repressive religion which is devoid of any of those characteristics of the Trinitarian community, or devoid of the image and likeness of God in his Church. That couldn't be the plan. I continued ...

I'll tell you what I think. Right away I think I see in those accounts of the apostolic church the evidences of high joy, of gladness of heart, of shared lives, of shared meals and hope and anticipation and singing. Why don't we 'plunge back in' and pick up where we left off and see what emerges in the early Church?

"I'm listening. I've gotta see where this crazy trip is going to take us."

The Deep Longing For …

Something deep in the *disenchanted* psyche of those who are still outside (of God's New Creation) responds to and longs for the Utopian dream of Eden. It knows that something is missing.[2] It longs for that community of existence where it all comes together. Think of how many of our classic myths and fairy tales and legends have been written out of such longings.

The blank spot in those quests, however, is that 'merely human' (translate: incomplete or disenchanted) men and women still cannot conceive of a reality that can only come together out of intimate communion with the Triune God who is their Creator. Such a notion simply does not register with them. As a matter of fact, most probably could not even conceive or portray what their own Utopian Edenic dream of fulfillment would look like. The *virus of autonomy* has so distorted and darkened their understanding of any such Peaceable Kingdom that they have no category for it. Having deleted God from their systems, they cannot conceive of any community dwelling in reconciled harmony with God and with all of God's creation. That being so, their quest always falls short and is frustrated from the start.

All of that makes it the more interesting for you and me that as Jesus began to spell out the disciplines and the behavior of those who would constitute his New Creation (the Kingdom of God), … he reminded them right away that it would be their visible, and radically-alternative, and beautiful way of life which would (among other things) catch the attention and spark the curiosity of those who were still 'outside'. Our New Creation lives are intended to awaken the somnolent longings in others for their heart's true home. Such *enchanted* lives are intended to

---

[2] Reflecting back to our C. S. Lewis and Narnia metaphor, we are talking about those who have never been through the back of the wardrobe into Narnia and so consider it all fantasy and foolishness.

have an effect on those others that will cause them to conclude that some supernatural source is behind such beauty.[3]

The idea of such alternative lives which demonstrate God's New Creation should not seem so strange or surprising to us. After all, it had been splendidly demonstrated in Jesus himself as the firstborn of this awesome new reality. In him that beautiful and joyous Word of God had already moved into the human community *visibly* and *publicly* (albeit in humility and hiddenness). Jesus (along with his infant community of disciples) had roamed the back roads and seashores of Palestine in conversation with the most unlikely and irreligious persons, ... and he had gotten their attention not only by what he taught, but perhaps maybe even more by how he lived and responded. He healed, he fed, the cared, he set people free to live robustly and even abundantly in the midst of their mundane and fragile and perilous daily existence. Jesus hardly even seemed *religious* – just different and profoundly authentic in his humanity.

That first generation Church (or New Creation community) was a visible phenomenon. It grew robustly and contagiously and uncontrollably in its very unlikely and hostile context with all of its political, religious, social and economic dimensions. It becomes the more interesting to us that Peter would speak of the Church's *good works* as the visible and effective means of getting the attention of its hostile and often Christ-hating neighbors.[4]

Alan, that is really, really important. We need to look into the pieces, the elements, the realities that make the Church to be what it is intended to be, namely, *the aroma of Christ* unto God.[5] God's people are to *smell like God*, not only to those inside the Church ... but to those outside. What is it that makes the Church smell like and look like Jesus? What is it that makes the Church to be the ongoing *Presence of the Enchanting Word* in our human neighborhoods? It certainly is not some ineffable religious aura, or some vague spirituality. It is rather the joy, the song, the creativity, the hope, and the love of the alternative human community. It is humans who think like and behave like Jesus did. It is the authentic Church. It has very identifiable characteristics which are different and life-producing. Its characteristics, according to Jesus, are *Salt* and *Light* and *Life*.

---

[3] Matthew 5:13-16
[4] I Peter 2:12; 3:13-17.
[5] II Cor. 2:15

"I think you're a dreamer, Bob. You're totally lost in an illusion."

Maybe so.

But maybe even more, I'm a realist. I've had to work through my own *disillusionment* with the Church's ever present human proclivity of reverting to a *disenchanted* form, to a *merely human religious society* with little or nothing to do with God's New Creation.

We really, really do need to chase that one.

"I'm listening."

We need to identify whatever are those continual and ongoing disciplines that give substance to the kind of *radical repentance*[6] that Jesus called for. We need to reclaim that *conversion* which transforms the Church, and creates it a genuinely alternative community—which makes it into an authentic expression of God's own life. We need to identity what makes it a *counter-cultural movement* that is visible in the midst of the darkness and death of this disenchanted scene in which we live. What was it that could make a bunch of frightened, very fickle, and ordinary human beings into something so *remarkably, radically, and observably other*? After all, their previous lives had been formed by a deeply ingrained affinity to life *without* the Spirit. Why was it that the apostle would be writing to them again and again about *putting off* their affinity to that autonomous life, and *putting on* their new life in the Spirit?

If the Church (that's us) is to live in the real presence of both "this age" (or this world, disenchanted as it is), … and also in the real presence of "the Age to Come" (or the New Creation in Christ), … then there would have to be some kind of an *alternative consciousness*, some kind of power and conviction that would produce in that Church a *New Creation consciousness*. I don't think it is possible to grasp the New Testament letters unless we also understand and identify what such a dynamic is all about. It may also help us understand why the *humanly unexplainable* (translate: *enchanted*) Church has shown such a proclivity to revert to a church that is *humanly explainable* (*disenchanted*). I think that would also describe the church with which you and I have experienced and are struggling.

---

[6] I can't think of any other way to verbalize Jesus' insistence that to come after him required that his cross be operative in their lives. Such a call to reject the brute autonomy that exists in the human scene, such a decision to enter a very small gate and walk a narrow and disciplined path , cannot be designated anything less that radical repentance.

The Emergence of the Enchanted Community

The Church as the "dwelling place of God by the Spirit" must certainly have some *discernable building blocks*.[7] The presence of those building blocks will potentially call forth again the magic, the song, the joy, the hope, … all of that which was lost in the primordial rebellion. That speaks to your e-mail question about the laughter, the song, the hope, and the magic that was lost with that human declaration of autonomy.

That is what I mean when I speak of a *kingdom consciousness*, or a *New Creation consciousness*. OK?

"Got it."

Enchantment Comes Crashing In?

"When you and I were talking the other night, you were telling me something about 'when the last tumbler dropped' and about the mystery of the Spirit's coming. So, like, when those guys, (you know—the disciples) got left on their own, what happened next? Is that when the *enchantment* crashed in on them?"

No. Actually, that *enchantment* had already come crashing in when Jesus invaded the human scene. It happened when the Seeking God became flesh and blood in Jesus the truly *Enchanted One*. He was the Word of God sent to us to be the firstborn of the New Creation.[8]

But, … the last tumbler dropped when the full meaning of that invasion broke in upon his followers at Pentecost. It broke in with such force, and in such an unmistakable and irresistible way, that they were totally transformed by it. That whole new Spirit-Presence powerfully recreated them into a community that was nothing less than a radically *other* and *alternative* humanity. Christ was being formed in them individually and communally by the dynamic of that Spirit.

Your question about "what happened next?" is an essential one, however. It is absolutely critical in our quest for Church. Whatever happened next will give us our clues about whatever it was that formed them into the essence of God's New Creation. If we can identify what it was that was most important to them in their whole new experience as

---

[7] Ephesians 2:22
[8] Romans 8:29

community, ... then we just may be able to find out what made them into such a transforming force (Salt and Light) in their neighborhoods—and the world. What we need to know are the unmistakable dynamics of that first generation church. What did *enchantment* look like in that bunch of ordinary folk living in unlikely places?

What's really so awesome is that we actually do have the written records of their own story, and we have it from eyewitnesses. We have some preserved correspondence from the first several decades (or more) of their life together. Those records provide us with a fairly accurate account of the Church's movement from Jerusalem out through the Roman Empire. That also gives you and me plenty to chew on.

"Duh!"

Alright, so that's an understatement.

But what becomes immediately obvious is that at the moment of Jesus' ascension to heaven (or out of sight), the disciples were still *stuck* back there with their anticipation of a *merely human* next step. They were still thinking in terms of some dramatic messianic display and divine intervention with regal authority. Stuff like that. They were totally unable to conceive of how radically different was Jesus' way of thinking and living into which that the Spirit would call them—even though Jesus had been pointing them to it all along. They could still only conceive of his *kingdom of God* teaching as something having to do with a splendid earthly dominion.

We need to remember that the Jewish people had always been possessed by a very dominant preconception about the role of their long-awaited messiah. Their anticipated messiah would re-establish the glories of the monarchy of David. It is not strange then that the disciples seemed unable to see beyond that pattern from their past. Their messianic concept would mean, somehow, that Jesus would be dispatching the Roman imperial occupation forces along with every other alien influence from their Jewish lives and nation. Something like that.

"Hold it, Bob. Now that you mention it, I'm don't think I anticipate anything 'radically other' myself when I do church. Hey! I mean: What I expect (because of what I've experienced) is some (hopefully) well-done religious theater with music and oratory and well-appointed surroundings, and the American flag displayed comfortably in the corner. Do I expect anything *enchanted* or transformational? Not really, … but excuse me for interrupting."

No problem. You've got lots of company. But let's follow the story.

Jesus had to demolish that mistaken notion in his final moments with them.

In his final meeting with his disciples and just before he ascended they were still standing around asking him when he was going to establish the kingdom. Any connection between that concept and his promise to build his Church seems to have totally eluded them. What he did in those final moments was to give them a *non-answer*: "It's not for you to know!" He would only tell them to wait in Jerusalem *until they received power by the Holy Spirit.*

Then he's gone.

And they're standing there gazing up into the sky totally bewildered. What in the world was he talking about? Do you know what? If I had been there I would have been right there with them bewildered too, wouldn't you? So what do you do next? The only thing they *could* do was to do what Jesus had told them to do. They got together, they cloistered themselves, … and they prayed. They prayed on the basis of what they only barely understood. And they waited for whatever *the next* was.

They had no categories to even begin to imagine what was about to happen.

What happened next was so absolutely critical and mind-boggling that nothing else in the rest of the New Testament makes any sense at all unless we *get it*. First off, the timing in Jerusalem was strategic. It was fifty days after Jesus had been executed. The events surrounding that public execution and the rumors of a resurrection were still fresh in the talk of the city. The occasion was the Jewish feast of Pentecost. A huge cosmopolitan crowd of pilgrims had come to Jerusalem from all over the Roman world. Then … what happened (to use your description) was that the Holy Spirit came "crashing in" upon that small, bewildered, praying, room-full of Jesus' followers.

The very same *enchantment* which Jesus' followers had witnessed in Jesus now became dynamically present in them. The Spirit of God came upon their meeting with such overwhelming and consuming power that the same *enchantment* was now upon them and animating them with the very Life of God. Take note: that would be the same Holy Spirit who was the *enchanting* dynamic which we originally saw active in the Garden of Eden. Remember how we saw that original human community so created in God's image and likeness that they were be able to dwell somehow within the intimate embrace of the Trinitarian Community. Now that same Spirit came even more dramatically and irresistibly into that community of Jesus' praying disciples.

Jesus was building his Church!

The Light finally broke on them! They were given eyes to see *God's big picture*. It turned out precisely as Jesus had told them it would. Jesus had told them that it was expedient for them that he go away so that the Spirit could come. Then he told them that when the Spirit did come that he would both glorify the Son and would also bring Jesus' teachings to their remembrance. That's exactly what happened.[9] In the context of a decidely unfriendly Jerusalem those disciples were transformed and emboldened to exalt Jesus Christ as the Messiah of God. They now saw everything in the light of another Presence, that of the Spirit of the Father and the Son who dynamically inhabited their midst.

They began to realize and experience with great joy what the apostles would later call *the powers of the Age to Come*.[10] The Story of God's Great Salvation became *their own* story. They saw themselves in the light of Jesus' teachings and his commandments and his commission. They were participants in the God's Ultimate Story.[11] They were irresistibly called into God's mission and that mission was to demonstrate and herald God's New Creation in Jesus Christ to everybody—to people in Jerusalem, in Judea, and in the uttermost parts of the earth. That all became the flavor of their new community.

Thy kingdom come!

Not only did they *see* it, but for the first time they actually had ears to *hear* what it was that Jesus had been teaching them all along. They had new eyes and new ears. Their hearts now responded to the sheer ecstasy of that

---

[9] Cf. John 16:14 in loc.)
[10] Cf. Hebrews 6:5.
[11] For insights into God's Ultimate Story, cf. comments on *Eschaton*, and *Eschatological* below.

unveiling. Luke stretched to paint a word picture of that moment, only it defied words. That Pentecost event could only remind him of something *like* the sound of a strong rushing wind. And the visible manifestations looked something *like* tongues of fire. Whatever it was all about, it was all so absolutely unmistakable and consuming in their midst. Their obtuse hearts and minds finally began to be able to get the message.

Jesus had told them that it was absolutely necessary that he should go away so that the Spirit would come. Now it comes through. What the Spirit Presence produced among them was a thrilling urgency to get on with being the obedient practitioners of Jesus' teachings. The Spirit inflamed them with a consuming love for Jesus. What they now understood was that the very Presence of Jesus was awesomely, powerfully, and personally in and among them by his own Spirit. That is what he had promised. The *Enchanting Spirit*, whom they had seen and known in Jesus, was now in and among them giving them the same wisdom and power, the same sweetness and strength that he had given to Jesus.

"My signal is getting weak here. My lights went on slowly when I was first pondering Jesus, and what would happen if I put my trust in him. But now I'm struggling to comprehend such an event as that in a whole community of people. It's absolutely foreign to my church experience. Are we even to expect such Spirit Presence in the church today? What is the bridge between that event and us?"

All I'm relating here is that for that first generation Church the Spirit of Jesus was not some abstract doctrine. The Spirit was dynamically present as a Living Person recreating them to be God's new and truly human community. Paul would speak of *the Holy Spirit and power*.[12] The *enchantment* of God had dramatically come into their midst. Their focus was moved from themselves to the glory of God in Christ. Their small community became unmistakably *enchanted*, divinely inhabited. Jesus was among them then and there by his Spirit. What we looking at is that infant community being transformed by the Spirit. It was that in that transformed community that Jesus was *building his Church.*

The Spirit was building Christ's church in such an unimaginable way. He was building it in homes, in public, around dinner tables, in clusters and colonies of disciples—like leaven! It's easy for us to miss that point.

---

[12] I Corinthians 2:4.

Furthermore, Jesus was building his Church in what was a totally non-congenial setting, a missionary context.

Remember *perichoresis?* Then, notice how those disciples were now learning to live consciously and corporately in the embrace of the *perichoretic* community of Father, Son, and Holy Spirit.

The Eschatological Community

Can I drop another fascinating word-description on you?

"You have already assaulted me with the two weird concept-words: enchantment and perichoresis, so why not another?"

Brace yourself. I hope you can handle one more because I want to drop a third one on you. Try *eschatological.*

"Say what?"

That is another one of those loaded words that the Church occasionally uses to carry a lot of freight about the *end times*. It really has to do with God's *ultimate purpose*, or the *final act*, or even the *grand consummation* of God's design for creation. The word has probably been mostly used by the church to talk about the coming return of Jesus Christ. But it's really much bigger than that. It really has to do with the very *mission of God* to and for his world. From the first coming of Jesus (and his inauguration of the kingdom of God at that coming), the New Testament writers would then consistently declare that we are now living in the *last days*. We are, in other words, living in the determinative consummation of God's grand redemptive purpose for his (rebellious) human community.

That's something else you've got to understand about that infant church. From the beginning those followers were formed by the inescapable awareness that they were, in fact, God's *missional* community. In other words they were God's *eschatological* community. That was the purpose for which they had been *called out* by Jesus Christ and they were very self-conscious and intentional about that. It was through the Church that the promise of God given to Abraham and realized in Christ would now find its ultimate consummation.[13] God had promised Abraham nearly two

---

[13] Cf. Ephesians 3:9-11. " ... and to bring to light for everyone what is the plan of the mystery hidden for ages in God who created all things, so that through the church the

millennia before that through his genetic offspring ("seed") all the nations of the earth were to be blessed. The followers of Jesus began to understand that promise to have been fulfilled in Jesus the Messiah.

"So Jesus Christ was the key to the blessing of the nations. Hey!"

Are you OK with all of that?

"'Blown away' may be a better way of saying it."

And well you should be. But let's just say that without that understanding we will never really comprehend the Church as it is intended in the heart and mind of God. You will never comprehend it apart from the necessity and dynamic empowering of the Holy Spirit. You will never comprehend it apart from the Church's being consumed with its own *eschatological* and *missional* essence! There's simply no way to grasp the Church as the good news apart from those realities.

So, What Do You Do With Three Thousand New Believers?

"Talk about 'blown away'. I can't even imagine the emotional, conceptual-intellectual, even physical impact of that Pentecostal moment, can you? And talk about the 'back of the wardrobe!' I mean, ... just think: their whole conceptual framework had just been radically redefined. And there they were right the middle of an alien context of those threatened out of their socks by this new thing in their midst. My first thought would have been: How did we get into this? Where do we go from here? Who's ever going to believe us?"

You got it! They were the followers of an executed felon. They were living in the midst of a jealous religious community and a paranoid occupying Roman army. But now they were totally consumed and recreated into a joyous, even ecstatic and reckless, people persuaded that God has visited them in Jesus the Messiah. Nothing else, but *nothing else,* mattered in the slightest.

---

manifold wisdom of God might now be made known to the rulers and authorities in the heavenly places. This was according to the eternal purpose that he has realized in Christ Jesus our Lord."

"I guess that made them sort of subversive and suspect to the whole dominant scene, right?"

You've got the picture. But Jesus had been raised and exalted and the Spirit had come. It was dangerous. It was true!

So what do you do with that? How do you keep it quiet?

"You don't!"

Still, we still have to ask ourselves: what was it *specifically* that made them a threat? After all they were basically a disenfranchised and controversial bunch of *nobodies*. How could they be a threat to anybody? They could only be identified (or defined) as a community which was formed by a whole new and all-encompassing awareness of life. Their community had another, and a humanly inconceivable, *worldview*. They had a totally different sense of the meaning of it all. Now they had a *contagious hope* and a *missional purpose* for their lives. Even more, they had a profound new awareness of their communion with the Triune God who now had taken possession of their lives through the Spirit.

They were set free to participate in that which the apostles would define as the "glorious liberty of the children of God."[14] The Spirit energized them with such boldness (with what they now understood about Jesus) that they compulsively rushed out into the mixed mass of bewildered and amazed Pentecost pilgrims. They were unafraid. They 'went public' to explain what had happened to anybody and everybody who would listen. It didn't take long for the whole populace to become aware of the commotion and excitement.

There is one wonderful piece of that whole episode which has fascinated the Church over all these centuries. Those people who were now *enchanted* by the Holy Spirit began to *speak in other tongues*. Were those angelic tongues of praise? Maybe. Were they the tongues of other languages? Maybe. But whatever those *tongues* were, at least for that entire multi-ethnic and multi-lingual crowd, it meant that they miraculously *heard* the message of Jesus and the resurrection in their own languages. So right from the start you saw emerging a bit of the *magic* which you and I have discussed pertaining to my use of the word *enchanted*.

What happened after that was that the same *Enchanting Spirit* now accompanied their responses of obedience. That anointing became so

---

[14] Romans 8:21

The Emergence of the Enchanted Community

very obvious in their public witness to Jesus. They were inexplicably bold as they explained what was happening. They had a kind of power and authenticity that they had never experienced before, or even imagined was possible. The result? The minds and hearts of about three thousand of those listening folk were seized by God. Don't ask me to explain. Multitudes believed. Those who received the message of Jesus, and the New Creation, were then publicly identified with the community of Jesus' disciples by being publicly baptized.

Alan, I need to confess that having been a pastor for fifty years, I really have a tough time even beginning to imagine such a scene. There's nothing in our church's **Book of Order** to deal with that kind of a massive conversion!

"Did you ever have to baptize three thousand people, Bob? No, don't answer that. Like, a super-big 'Wow!' But go on. I've read that story before, but it's taking on some new implications for me. Where did they go from there?

"And, Bob, ... just for the sake of my periodic *reality check*, where do *we* go from here?"

I'm as impatient as you are, Alan. After all, we're probing into the *essence* of the Church which Jesus *was* then and *is* now building.

It's too easy for us to get carried away by some fantasy about an *ideal* Church. We dream about a church that would transcend all the grubby stuff that you and I both know is part of our human scene. Face it: in one sense those disciples were still a bit disoriented. OK? After all, their newly *enchanted life in the Spirit* was so totally *other*, and had just taken such a radical new turn, that it was nothing less than awesome. They could not possibly escape being happily bewildered. At the same time, they were still a very new community made up of very imperfect persons.

We need to remember that.

I am quite sure that the Spirit of God among them made them realize their human weaknesses more than ever, not to mention their ever-present proclivity to miss the point of it all. They would have been painfully aware of their potential get distracted from their mission and to disobey God by pursuing some merely human religions agenda. Peter, most of all, knew of that potential. He knew that most excruciatingly. Though he was their spokesperson at Pentecost, it was he who had denied Jesus at the critical moment of his arrest and trial. He was the one who fervently protested his self-sacrificing loyalty to Jesus only hours before, and then out of fear publicly denied that he even knew him.

It's equally critical for us to be continually reminding ourselves that the Church is made up of redeemed rebels. We all still have that capacity to revert to type. Remember, too, that those newly converted people were still living in the same neighborhoods with all of their same familiar associates and friends, many of whom were still part of the darkness. It was actually (and frequently) family members or neighbors who were most hostile to that new thing that was happening.

Add-in the fact (never even slightly veiled in all of the apostolic writings) that there was another ever-present malignant and supernatural *personality* engaged in opposition to all that they were. That personality is called the "god of this age." That "prince of darkness" hated Jesus, hated those new believers, and now hates all that is going on in God's children of the Light. Our present human scene cannot be construed in any way as *neutral* territory. *Satan* works continually against the Church to distort, to bring again the dissonance, to lie, to call forth again the *autonomous* spirit, and to destroy. He was, and is, in every way the enemy of the Church.

"Deliver us from the *evil one*?"

Absolutely! That is the stuff we're working with in the Church. Let's just keep that in mind as we proceed.

Narnia and Harry Potter Revisited

"I'm really, really trying to keep up with what you are proposing here, Bob. And I really am still trying to connect the dots back to my original questions to you. Let me go back to my off-the-wall beginning references to the entrance into Narnia through the back of the wardrobe, … or the entrance into the world of wizardry and to Hogwarts School through Platform 9 ¾ (in the Harry Potter stories). … I sort of hear you saying that an authentic Church makes it, somehow, like those who have experienced the reality of Narnia and who know the reality of Aslan and the Great King beyond the Sea, while at the same time still living their ordinary lives as ordinary school children in England. Only occasionally they will find others who have seen and know the same *other realm* as they do. They are, like, living in two worlds at once.

"Or maybe the Church is like those with the power of wizardry, and who participate in that strange realm, but then live ordinarily on this side of Platform 9 ¾ in a community of 'muggles'.[15] And muggles can't see anything other than their muggle world.

"But in both of those stories there was an opposing and dark personality. The Narnians knew the destructive forces that were always seeking to subvert or destroy Narnia. They remembered the White Witch, and all of that. In the Harry Potter stories there is always that destructive power of Voldemort, the wizard who used his wizard power for destructive purposes. At the same time there were those who understood that they were to use their wizard powers for good purposes. Something like that.

"Maybe it is too much of a stretch to try to relate those stories as illustrations of the Church. Still, I am listening to you talk about Jesus building his Church, and then about empowering it with the Power that comes from the very Presence of the Eternal God, and maybe I'm beginning to glimpse your description of the Enchanted Community.

"I'm not sure I should even dare make such a connection with those favorite stories of mine, … but at least it helps me. It helps me to think beyond the pale odor of the *disenchanted* and the 'merely human' in the religious institutions that I have experienced as church. Am I missing your point?"

I had to chuckle.

I guess I could have given Alan a good *postmodern* answer and said: "If it works for you." But, yes, I was intrigued by his connection. C. S. Lewis was a Christian with an enormous imagination. He obviously had all kinds of things in mind when he wrote those children's stories. I'm not at all sure what lies in the psyche of J. C. Rowling, but at least the lady has opened the imaginations of a generation to something other than the

---

[15] In mercy to the uninitiated reader, *muggles* are the ordinary non-wizards of Rowling's stories. They are the people who haven't a clue about the world of wizardry and so write it off as fantasy.

world of *modernity*. *Modernity* is confined to the humanly observable and explainable. Wizards don't fit in that world.

I think that the Church, if it is to be the Church, must think into the awesome world of the Spirit. The Church has to enter into that world where what "eye has not seen, nor ear heard, nor the heart of man conceived" is the *worldview* out of which, and by which, it understands its life and power and mission.[16]

So I pondered his point for a few minutes, and then could only say: "Maybe you're on to something. Let's move on to what happened next."

A Parenthetical Digression

One difficulty in thinking our way into such an image of the church is probably going to lie with the unfortunate proclivity (which the church has continually displayed) of redefining itself in terms of: 1) the *disenchantment*; 2) *this present age;*[17] 3) the *merely human* and its institutions; 4) the *demonic*; 5) the *natural*; or 6) *religion*. That proclivity, unfortunately, has caused it to do such redefinition *rather than* defining itself according what seems apparent in scriptures and to what seems its divinely originated essence as: 1) the community of the Age to Come; 2) the community of the supernaturally inhabited; 3) the community of Spirit-habitation (or *Enchantment*); 4) the community of "what no eye has seen, … no ear heard, … nor the heart of man as conceived;"[18] 5) the community of God's New Creation (or kingdom of God); 6) the community of the "pattern given on the mount"[19] or 7) the community of the (*eschatological*) mission of God.

The Church easily forgets its *alternative* essence.

When the apostle wrote to the Christian community in Rome: "Be not shaped by this age but always (literally) 'be being transformed' by the renewing of your minds so that you may be demonstrating the true design

---

[16] I Corinthians 2:9-10.
[17] Cf. Hebrews 9:9 which is a reference to the dominion of darkness, and stands in contrast to "the age to come" which refers to the eschatological Kingdom of God.
[18] I Corinthians 2:9
[19] Hebrews 8:05

of God for the human community" (loose paraphrase)[20] his reasoning behind this was so that God's very own love, holiness, creativity, hope, justice, joy, word, goodness (not to mention the Trinitarian mind and will) should all have a visible and demonstrable dwelling in the Church. The Church was to be such a demonstration right in the midst of that disenchanted human scene. Such Enchanted Community could be realized in small groups of twos or threes, in families, in households, or in other committed communities of intimate and authentic divine Presence.

After all, we are those who (to use the Narnia metaphor) have been through the back of the wardrobe. We know Aslan. We live in two worlds. Or to use the Harry Potter metaphor, we are wizards who have been oriented to the powers by going through Platform 9 ¾ to Hogwarts School, ... and though our normal existence might be in the community of *muggles* ... we live in two worlds. Our danger (to continue the metaphors) is that we are prone to *sacralize* (make sacred) and refocus on the wardrobe, or on Platform 9 ¾, and in so doing to progressively diminish what it is that lies beyond them. It is easy to forget or to dilute the otherness, the eschatological essence, the Trinitarian Presence, until all that makes the Church authentic it is only a memory, ... or displaced altogether by what is the *merely human and provisional church institution*.

Illustration: the first century church at Laodacea was in this process of forgetting who they were.[21] The people in that church would never have considered denying Jesus as Lord. That wasn't even their intention. Rather, they had just become so preoccupied with their own inner life together as a community, along with their comfort and well-being, that Jesus Christ was essentially left on the outside looking in. John pictured Jesus knocking on the door asking to be invited in again. He wanted to be included in their life together, to dwell among them.

Never forget, Alan: it is Jesus who is building his Church.

All of the eroding, counterfeiting, contemptuous, or controlling efforts of this demonically inhabited age will not prevail against what Jesus is building. God keeps interrupting. God keeps breaking in. God keeps creating his own communities of Light and Life and doing it in surprising ways and in unexpected places. God keeps on creating new forms of

---

[20] Romans 12:1-2.
[21] Revelation 3:14-22

community in order that he may sovereignly accomplish his own will and design. God is fulfilling his mission and his promise to bless every people group in the world by Jesus Christ (as difficult as that is for us to grasp).

The same Spirit (the Spirit of the Father and the Son) who moved creatively upon the face of the waters at the creation, ... that same Spirit still moves irresistibly and *out of control* creating authentic Spirit Communities through Jesus Christ. The Spirit creates the Church. The Spirit does it in *uncontrollable* ways which are beyond our imagining. *Church institutions* (or institutions of christianity) often contain such *authentic Spirit-communities*—I want to make the distinction between those two expressions. However, those institutions in and of themselves are only human constructs. They may be (and often are) reminders or signifiers of God's design in Christ.

But what we're looking for are not the *controlling institutions of christianity*, but rather those *enchanting* community disciplines, those flexible forms, which are designed to be continually transforming us into people of the Age to Come, into God's New Creation communities of the mission of God. What we're looking for are what Jesus uses to create us into those people in whom, and through whom the Trinitarian Community lives redemptively (real but not always discerned) in this present scene of darkness and disenchantment.

By the Way ...

"Wait a minute. Do me a favor. One confusing aspect of that story is: whatever happened to all of the Jewish religious system that this new community grew out of? After all, it *was* God who instituted those priests and sacrifices and tabernacle and all that stuff. There were all of those (to me) ambiguous promises about the temple and the land that somewhere in the future would have some special place. What happened to all of that?
"Is that an OK question?"

Do you want the encyclopedic answer or the abridged answer?
"Make it short."

That's a great and most appropriate question. It is also a question which a lot of people never think to ask. Or if they do ask it, they pursue answers in weird ways. Basically, one of the reasons that Jesus was so controversial, and so resented by the Jewish leadership, was that he radically redefined all of those significant parts of their tradition. Jesus essentially said that those cherished parts of Jewish tradition all were fulfilled and given new definition by his own mission as God's Messiah. He was their fulfillment.

What he taught, sometimes by inference and sometimes quite explicitly, was that he, as God's Anointed One, became the temple. He was the *dwelling-place of God*. The Church soon understood that Jesus was both the high priest who offered the sacrifices, and the Lamb of God who offered himself as the one perfect and forever sacrifice for sins. He claimed to give messianic interpretation to the Torah by himself being the living Word of God, and by interpreting their Torah in terms of his New Creation. The true Israel, henceforth, would be those who followed him as his disciples. And the whole earth with all of its ethnic groups became the arena of God's mission, his own *holy land*.

All of which gives some substance to what I referred to earlier in our conversation as *eschatological*, or the ultimate unfolding of God's design.

What you discover as you get on over into the apostolic period is that the early followers of Jesus understood themselves as Church in the light of those very redefinitions. The Church becomes the true temple, the dwelling-place of God. The Church becomes a *nation of priests* under Jesus our Great High Priest. The sacrifice of Jesus Christ on the Cross becomes the great *atonement*, and the focus of our adoration. Jesus is now our means of our being set free from the guilt and power of sin, free to live and walk in the "glorious liberty of the children of God."[22] Wherever we may live as God's Spirit-people (people who live by the Spirit) that selfsame place becomes *holy ground*. That is meaning of Christ's incarnation and it becomes the meaning of our incarnational lives as, in Christ, we are the Salt and Light of this world. That is my understanding of the *Enchanted Community*.

That's the brief version.

What are you thinking now?

"Awesome! Enchantment right in the middle of all the stinky stuff we live in. It'll take a while for me to digest that one."

---

[22] Romans 8:21

Journey Seven
Signs of Authenticity - I

"All this makes some sense thus far. But I think maybe I'm still not clear about what the Church is all about in personal terms. I need to know what my participation would even mean. What am I looking for? I still need to know what are the evidences of authenticity that I'm *looking for* in trying to figure out my involvement, … or maybe, what I would be *working for* if and when I decided to get involved?

"Alright, don't say it. I remember that there is all of that residual DNA of darkness, and all of those seductive influences of the culture of disenchantment that factor into the picture. But what I really need is something like the *status dialog bar* on my computer screen. You know, that thing at the bottom of the screen that indicates how much of a document is downloaded? I need to know what indicators there are in something like West Park Church of its authenticity as the Church. Maybe something like an *authenticity status dialog bar*. It sure would help! If such evidences were hardly present, it might be a 'Caution: Go Slow' signal to me.

"Can we go there now?"

It was a Sunday morning. It was the first time in several weeks that Alan had been free from the demands of his research runs. They had totally consumed his time. I confess that we were also skipping church. Alan had caught up on his sleep, and had only a brief break before he had to be at it again. We mutually agreed that we were really walking on holy ground in our conversations, so the two of us together could joyfully claim Jesus' promise to be with us as we were together.

We had decided on brunch and so were sitting at table in a sidewalk café on Shadowlawn Avenue along with a whole lot of other, often animated and voluble, urban dwellers on that pleasant morning. I picked up on his question: "Yes. We can go there and will."

Connecting the Dots

You and I have been moving between two poles: The first pole is what we saw in the creation account when the Creator God created man in *his own image and likeness* with all of the consequent blessedness of living within the complete embrace of the Trinitarian community. That's where my use of the concept of *perichoresis* came into our conversation. That was our signal. But you also need remember that God created us to flourish within a community of others – "it is not good for man that he should be alone." Both individually and communally God created us so that we are only complete (truly human) as we dwell in intimate relationship with the divine community and as the divine community animates the human community. We are incomplete apart from that. Such completeness is actually what God has designed us for out of his love for us.

The second pole is at the other end of the Biblical story. It comes in the Revelation to John, where we hear a voice saying: "Behold the dwelling place of God is with man. He will dwell with them, and they shall be his people, and God himself will be with them as their God."[1]

It is there, between those two poles, that I threw you those three delicious words: *enchanted, perichoresis,* and *eschatological.*

Remember?

"How could I forget?"

Then back to your original question. That reality is precisely *why* the Church is such an integral part of our gospel. The Church is the human community rescued, reconciled, and created new by Jesus Christ. Then

---

[1] Revelation 21:3

by the Spirit of the Father and the Son inhabiting it, it is restored in its intimacy with, and its embrace within, the *perichoretic* community of Father, Son, and Holy Spirit. The human community is enabled again to engage in conversation and communication with the Father and the Son by the Spirit. The mind of God, the heart of God, the mission of God, the kingdom and will of God ... all become dynamic in the New Creation person and in the New Creation community—the Church. It is only as that communion takes place that the human community becomes the true human community that God designs. Our *good news/gospel* is incomplete without that corporate dimension of God's great Salvation.

Why the Church? It is to demonstrate and incarnate authentic human community as God created it to be and to flourish in communion with the divine community. God's design was that he should dwell right in its midst of the human community. Likewise, those whom he created were also to dwell in communion with each other and in total harmony within the community of the Trinity. It is only within such divine and human relationships that they find their true humanity. True human community is being recreated as Christ's followers relate to one another (how to say it?) out of that same *perichoretic* mutuality which exists within the community in which the Father, the Son, and the Holy Spirit are always giving themselves to each other in utter mutuality and love.

Such mutuality and love becomes our paradigm for relationships within the Church. The vision in Revelation 21 displays that ultimate (*eschatological*) design as being finally accomplished. It points us to that *consummation* when God has created all things new. It is when God's creation dwells adoringly in him, and when God dwells personally among his people in unsullied harmony. That is the *eschatological* design. Such is the Kingdom of God. It was *inaugurated* at Christ's first coming. It is now in dynamic process within the Church that Jesus is building. But it always looks forward to that *consummation*.

Between those two poles we saw the horrendous tragedy of those first human parents misusing their God-given moral capacity to choose, and so violating the divine command and intent, as well as their own true humanity and true human community. They hid from God and became strangers to each other.

Signs of Authenticity - I

It all went down hill from there. That is where 'life without God' entered the human scene. That is where *disenchantment* became the norm.² But it left behind that human heart longing for it's true home, and for the true community of others in which to share life. The divine design for human community surfaces again when Abraham's heirs (the children of Israel) are delivered out of their captivity in Egypt. When God met dramatically with those exiles on their pilgrim journey he declared to them: "I will dwell among the people of Israel and will be their God."³

That theme (or design) of *community dwelling in God and God dwelling in the community* literally flavors all of the Biblical writings that follow. It comes to an unexpected and extravagant fulfillment in Jesus in whom "… the Word (God) became flesh and *dwelt among us* and we have seen his glory, glory as of the only Son from the Father, full of grace and truth."⁴ The story of Jesus is the story of the Seeking God invading his human community (or as Eugene Peterson has so deliciously paraphrased it: "… moved into the neighborhood").⁵ God entered the human community as *the truly human one* in order to demonstrate that sovereign design. God came in Jesus, the Anointed One, to reconcile all things to himself—at great cost.⁶

In Jesus, God took the initiative. Notice how Jesus came and called together a community of disciples. He didn't call them and form them as solitary New Creation persons, but rather as New Creation persons within his New Creation community. Let me say it plainly: Jesus began to form those whom he called to be the *eschatological* community, the community in which God dwells by the Spirit. That community, in turn, reciprocates in joyful adoration and obedience. Jesus opened the door into the New and Living Way. He reconciled us to God by the blood of his cross⁷ and called us into a reconciling community of others.

---

² Several years ago a poignant personal account appeared in a book by Gen Xer Douglas Coupland entitled: *Life After God*. It records his sojourn through the landscape of his cultural darkness and in closing he simply says something like: "What I really need is God." It is such an eloquent statement of the longing for the 'heart's true home'. (1995, Washington Square Press)
³ Exodus 29:45.
⁴ John 1:14
⁵ Cf. *The Message* on John 1:14
⁶ II Corinthians 5:19ff.
⁷ Colossians 1:20

The apostle picked up that same theme when he described the Church as the "dwelling place for God by the Spirit."[8] That theme becomes the more awesome when Peter told us that: " ... (God) has granted to us his precious and very great promises, so that you may become *partakers of the divine nature*, ..." (italics mine).[9]

With all of that to swirl around in our heads, we come then to that fascinating eschatological consummation in Revelation 21 where the angel heralds: "Behold the dwelling place of God is with man. He will dwell with them and they shall be his people, and God himself will be with them and be their God."

Now then, Alan, ...

... anything else we say about the Church, and any attempt we make to lift up any signs of authenticity must somehow flow out of that theme that resonates between those two poles. Does that resonate with you?

"It really resonates. Charge on!"

The church has traditionally answered your question about the Church by defining itself in (what is to me at least is) a weird way. If I can put it this way, the church has defined itself most often by those *roles* it has assigned to some special leadership persons, whom it designates as *clergy*. The origins of that category are to my mind both dubious and hardly Biblical. It is to those *sacralized persons* that the church has assigned the functions of: 1) preaching the Word of God; and 2) administering special symbolic rites, which it designates as *sacraments*. First off, such a definition makes the majority of the church—the non-*clergy*—by implication and practice to become passive recipients of those *clergy* functions. 'Ministry' has thereby been defined as a clergy role. Everyone else, who is not *clergy*, (which is most of the church) is relegated to a status which it designates as *laity*. Such a designation is also dubious.

"Boy, are you ever going to get in trouble with the system."

I know. I already am. But if I were honest with myself, I would have to say that those definitions, though venerable, sometimes helpful, and widely adopted, ... are also frightfully inadequate if any of that which we are processing here is valid. I really *do* think that such definitions of the church are several steps away from the patterns that are more obvious

---

[8] Ephesians 2:22
[9] II Peter 1:4

Signs of Authenticity - I

in scripture. They may even be a not-too-subtle form of *subversion*. The most obvious problem with such definitions is the absence of any such *priestly-clergy class* of persons in the New Testament accounts.[10]

The New Testament portrays the active participation and giftedness of the whole community, and this not to mention that it designates all of its participants as *saints*. The whole community (and every believer within it) is alive and dynamic by the Spirit, and it is growing out of any human control. All who are involved in the Church are to be part of the mission Christ mandated. *All are called to the ministry* of living out their New Creation lives day by day in their own immediate *disenchanted* world. I have to say all of that simply so that you will not make *authenticity* in the Church dependent upon clergy.

I think, in answer to your question, that we can come up with six or seven *signs of authenticity* that (at least to me) demonstrate both the *enchantment* and the *authenticity* of the New Creation community—which is the Church.

Let me insert a word of caution at this point.

It is quite too simple to conceptualize the Church and its authenticity *in theory*. It is quite something else to be involved in a local church expression that vacillates between authenticity and institutional idolatry, between Spirit-animated faith and what I have called *merely human religion*. What I want to designate for us as the *signs of authenticity* for the Church should first of all become the *personal disciplines* of authenticity for you and me as we engage the Church.

Here is my own list (I'm sure that there are others, but these are mine):

1. The Sign of Dynamic Spirit-Presence in the Community.
2. The Sign of Jesus Christ as the Center and Focus.
3. The Sign of Prayer as the Church's Primary Activity.
4. The Sign of the Word of Christ Dwelling Richly In, and Forming, the Church.

---

[10] As I write this, the Roman Church has just inaugurated Pope Benedict XVI in a splendid bit of pageantry what with rows of red-robed "princes of the church" and all of the mystique that is so fascinating. My only question is: what does it have to do with the Biblical patterns and with the Mission of God? Am I missing something?

5. The Sign of Christ-love for One Another.
6. The Sign of Alternative and Subversive New Creation Thinking and Behaving.
7. The Sign of the Church as Incarnating the Mission of God.

None of these *signs* stands alone. They are all *symbiotic, interdependent,* and *interactive*. Each points to all of the others. When any one of them is muted or absent, our caution lights should go on. Because that is true, then, it isn't even possible to rank them in any order of importance. But *signs*, if they are not visible, should at the very least be easily discernable and unmistakable. An 'outsider' or an 'inquirer' should be able to see (or sense) such signs being present. Such signs would point them to the true Light and true Life. They would point to Jesus Christ and to his New Creation for which such inquirers probably have no categories. He or she might not immediately understand them, but they would still be signs to them that *something* was going on in the community that would demand their attention – something *enchanted*.

So let's jump in and walk through them.

"You and I can 'jump in' but I'm sitting here looking at all of these happy pagans sitting around us who don't even have a clue that the church even exists ... or care. It's going to take more than your *signs*, I think, to make the church demand their attention. Or am I just being my cynical self again? But go ahead and jump. I'm listening."

We assured our server that we would leave her 'rent money' to compensate for occupying her table for so long. She laughed and replied: "No problem!" and darted off.

Sign: Spirit Presence

Alan, there is a very real sense in which the Spirit Presence may be the most elusive of these signs. In another way, however, it is the most critical since all the others are animated and receive their *authenticity* from this one. They are not possible apart from it.

Signs of Authenticity - I

In any observable church institution which you may encounter, everything may *appear* to be all properly 'church-like' ... and yet be without Life by the Spirit. What that means is that some church institutions can be essentially lifeless and consequently still a part of the *disenchantment*!

The Spirit of God within you will sense that, and your own spirit will respond to the Holy Spirit discerning the presence either of Life, or of semi-Life, or of spiritual death. I can tell you stories about having come into some venerable church settings and then sensing that something alien, something dark (even demonic) was present. Initially, it was not anything observable. I hardly trusted my own spiritual sense in coming to such an awareness. It was only later that it became more apparent why and how the Spirit had been quenched in that setting by decisions made in disobedience to the Word of Christ and the Spirit of Christ.

Conversely, I can bear witness to having come unexpectedly into other church settings and immediately having sensed the evidences of Spirit Presence. Something was alive and expectant and formed by the love of Christ and the Word of Christ. Again, it was not anything immediately observable.

It only fits!

Jesus had given to his non-comprehending disciples a couple of complementary realities. First off he said: "Without me you can do nothing" (or maybe "without me none of this will work!"). Then he gave them a promise and hope: "Nevertheless I tell you the truth: it is to your advantage that I go away, for if I do not go away, the Helper (Spirit) will not come to you. But if I go I will send him to you."[11] The coming of the Spirit of God and of Christ into that fragile group of Christ's waiting disciples at Pentecost was Christ himself coming to abide in and with his own. He came as he had promised to walk with them and in them as they lived-out the adventure of obedience.

Think what that meant:
- Jesus, the firstborn of God's New Creation was now dwelling in their midst communally and in them individually.
- The true Life of God was dwelling in them by the Spirit of the Father and of the Son.

---

[11] John 15:5; John 16:7

- They were literally having the *mind of Christ* and the *life of Christ* formed in them, and being energized among them, by the Spirit of God. That meant that they could *think* Christianly and *live* Christianly, ... and *love* and *serve* one another Christianly. New Creation was becoming a reality among them.
- The human community (in the Church) was thereby coming again into the intimate and *perichoretic* embrace of, and relation to, Father, Son, and Holy Spirit.
- God by his Spirit was recreating his own true design for human community in which he dwells, and in which he demonstrates his love in the love of his people for each other—as they minister to one another just as he ministers to us.
- It was the Spirit who called them (through "repentance toward God and faith in our Lord Jesus Christ"[12]) into his own community of New Creation, and into their new life by the Spirit.
- It was the Spirit of Holiness (or the Holy Spirit) who fashioned them as a holy people (or nation). The Spirit creates a people whose whole being is being brought into *synch* with the very heart and mind of God (cf. "You shall love the Lord your God with all your heart and with all your soul and with all your strength and with all your mind, and your neighbor as yourself."[13]).
- That means that wherever we are, in that very place we are those in whom Christ dwells by his Spirit (*enchanted*). That very place is *holy* because we are there!
- That means that the Spirit is present in us twenty-four hours a day and seven days a week. The God of the Incarnation becomes incarnate in his people by the Spirit when they are *gathered* for adoration, as well as when they are *scattered* into the most unlikely and improbable places of their daily sojourn. It is in those places that we each become Salt and Light as we are becoming conformed to Jesus Christ by this same Spirit of Holiness.
- That is the *Eschatological Spirit* whose work it is to create the Church. The Spirit's work is to energize every follower of Christ into the mission of God (*missio dei*). The Spirit enables them to

---

[12] Acts 20:21
[13] Luke 10:27

look with hope to the future, to obedience, to transformation, and to the consummation of God's New Creation, ... to that fulfillment of God's promise to Abraham that all the nations of the earth will be blessed in Jesus, the seed of Abraham.

- That is the Spirit whose Presence produces observable fruit, all of which, are evidences of the Life of Christ in us: love, joy, peace, patience, kindness, goodness, faithfulness, gentleness, and self-control (Galatians 5:22-23).
- That is the Spirit who energizes the Church for its mission by equipping it with *gifts* and *ministries* in the form of persons who respond to the Spirit, and who prove those gifts in the community as the community has need of them and confirms their gifts.[14]
- That is the Spirit who gives form and order and flexibility and versatility to the Church as it lives and obeys in the huge spectrum of different social and cultural contexts and as it moves out to make disciples in the world beyond its own familiar setting.
- That is the Spirit, who is full of surprises as the Church through its prayer and obedience honors the Spirit's dynamic Presence among them.

Such dynamic Spirit Presence cannot be hidden. It is very visible. It is a Sign of Authenticity. The Church is a Spirit Community.

The tragedy comes when a Church, which may have begun well, then settles down comfortably into institutional routine within its sanctuaries, and into a comfort-zone of more-of-the-same conservative mentality, and with no expectation or imagination. That tragedy comes when 'worship services' reinforce an ethos of *inspiration* rather than the Spirit-ethos of *transformation* and *holiness*. As that takes place, then the church becomes

---

[14] We will probably return to this later, but the only observable clue to the ordering of the communities resides here. Within the community there emerge those who by the Spirit are gifted in (effective and proven) teaching, helping, providing hospitality, administering affairs, reaching out to those outside with the gospel, providing oversight and making disciples, and such needed ministries. This also demolishes the clergy-laity *subversion*, which devolves into something more like an "office" to which one is elected, but which may not (and often does not) have anything to do with Spirit-giftedness. Gifts emerge in communities by the Spirit, not be the acquisition of a certificate or a degree from a Bible College or theological school!

more and more what the New Testament writers refer to as being "without Spirit" (ψυχικοσ) or humanly explainable.

The Spirit of God accompanies the Word of God. The apostle can say: " … my speech and my message were not in plausible words of wisdom but in demonstration of the Spirit and power." After all, Jesus had said: "The words that I speak to you are spirit and life." All of which explains the statement of the apostle that the kingdom of God does not come simply with *talk* but in *power*.[15]

That also clarifies the zeal of the apostle who persisted in telling the infant church to be continually putting off their old life and putting on the new life by the Spirit. It clarifies his warnings to them not to *quench* the Spirit and not to *grieve* the Spirit. It gives weight to his teaching that those who live by the Spirit should also walk in the Spirit. The authentic Church is no ordinary religious phenomenon. There is something (or *Someone*) dynamically Present in its midst. There is the Spirit of God. It only stands to reason after all since the Church is to be the dwelling place of God by the Spirit.

Alan, are you, maybe, beginning to get the reason behind my use of the description of the Church as *enchanted*?

"I'm just sitting here stuffing this Danish into my mouth, taking it all in!"

Well, while you're stuffing your mouth and taking it all in, we're at the place where we're going to have to slow down and be very discerning.

Take your *authenticity status dialog bar* idea, for instance. It may, in fact, indicate Spirit-Life where you least expect it. That sometimes becomes obvious in larger assemblies or gatherings. It is frequently true within smaller groupings or communities that exist inside church institutions. But there is no way to even remotely describe or define the Church out of the New Testament evidence apart from the Spirit Presence. It is never taken for granted. It is always invoked.

Any church institution that can carry on its life and its programs and its ecclesiastical rites without a conscious dependence upon the Holy Spirit, … *probably does*!

---

[15] I Corinthians 2:4, John 6:63, I Corinthians 4:20

"That makes sense. Which may explain that ancient Latin prayer: *Veni Creator Spiritus*. Or back to our metaphor: it also explains that whole other dimension of reality 'through the back of the wardrobe' doesn't it? What no eye has seen, no ear heard, no heart conceived, and all of that. Right?"

You get an A+!

"Question: The way you portray this Spirit-Presence, though—doesn't that raise the possibility, maybe the danger, of every Church becoming a law unto itself? Of claiming the 'Spirit authority' for its own life and practice, and simply ignoring what the Spirit may be doing elsewhere? Isn't that going to be a problem?"

Absolutely.

That risk and danger has always existed in the Church. When that happens the Spirit is grieved. Let's just put a Bookmark there and acknowledge how important it is to recognize that the Spirit is (and has always been) at work in ways beyond our comprehension. The Spirit works uncontrollably in many contexts and in many quite diverse ways over the centuries. That makes it critical for us, in the here and now, to seek to know and to be abreast of world Christianity, and of church history, and of the development of the church's mission.

It makes it critical for us to learn the lessons that the Spirit has taught to the church: the pitfalls, the surprises, the obedience-disobedience, the truth-error, the faith-unbelief, the life-death episodes from which we ourselves can be taught by the Spirit. Your point is very well taken. Such an exclusively self-focused perspective that is blind to what God has done and is doing elsewhere has always diminished the church. God has never been 'asleep at the switch'. The Spirit is always at work in ways that we can hardly conceive right now, and in places that we hardly know exist.

So let's move on. All of the other signs and evidences of authenticity that we come up with flow out of, and are energized by, that same Spirit Presence.

Sign: Jesus Christ, Center and Focus

Jesus is the Door into God's New Creation. He only is the Way into God's great salvation. Jesus must always be the focal point of the life of any authentic Church.

Enchanted Community

When we were looking at the definition of *perichoresis* early on, one of the descriptive words about that relationship within the Trinitarian community was *interanimation*. That comes very much to the fore on this Sign. Not only does the Father glorify the Son, but the Spirit also glorifies the Son.[16]

It follows then that the Church, which exists by and for Jesus Christ, should always have as its *raison d'etre* the glory and honor and praise of the Jesus, the Son of God. It is Jesus who gives us Life through his own life, death, and resurrection. Jesus must always, then, of necessity be the focus of any authentic Church. Luke began his history of the apostolic church (Acts of the Apostles) with the telling statement that he had written his first work (Gospel of Luke) to deal "with all that Jesus began to do and teach."[17] The inference is quite clear, namely, that in this second work he will deal with what Jesus then continued to do and still does by his Spirit. There is an identification implicit in that introduction between the working of the Spirit and the working of Jesus Christ.

It should be obvious to us that when we are looking for the signs of authenticity, we will tune-in very quickly to the church's focus on the centrality of Christ, … or the absence thereof.

"Obvious? Right! Tell me how is it obvious to a guy like me coming in from the outside? What do I look for? How do I look for it?"

Well, Alan, let's see. Simon and Garfunkle did a song about "the prophets of the day [being] written on the subway wall." So, maybe you look in places you don't expect. If I were looking for this sign of authenticity in a church I think I would look and listen-in to the informal and unguarded conversations and discussions. Because if Jesus is really at the heart of that church's life, then, in the unexpected places it will be obvious that Jesus is taken seriously. It will not be so much what comes out of its public face (the pulpit), or in someone quoting some orthodox creed.

When lives, families, daily life and occupations are oriented around Jesus and his Word, then Jesus will quite naturally be the subject of

---

[16] John 12:27-28; 16:14.
[17] Acts 1:1

significant conversations. The followers of Jesus will be able to articulate their faith in him in some kind of meaningful dialog with others. Daily life will be processed in the context of their mutual faith in Jesus Christ. That's what I would look and listen for.

But having said that, I would look and listen for the language of adoration of Jesus, of the Christ-focus in a church's occasions of worship and its public teaching. The apostles knew that the Church would grow into its participation with the divine nature through the knowledge of Jesus.[18] That's an essential component of authenticity.

Paul was Christ-focused that way. He made it quite plain that the compelling theme of all his public teaching was "Jesus Christ and him crucified."[19] In another context he would say that the very purpose that God has for all who are called into God's *eschatological* salvation is so that they be "conformed to the image of his Son."[20] Paul described his labors among them as being like a mother giving birth. His labors were for the explicit purpose of seeing Christ formed in them.[21] What should be obvious to us, then, is that it is the Father who *calls*, the Spirit who *recreates*, and both *glorify* the Son in the Church. That is how the Church itself inevitably becomes an instrument of the Glory of Father, Son and Holy Spirit.[22]

The Church, as it abides in the Spirit, is incurably, ineluctably, and unmistakably focused on the glory of Jesus Christ.

"Ineluctably?"

OK, so I got carried away. It's a good word. Look it up.

But back to my point. It is both thrilling and instructive and transformational for us to read again and again the encomiums of adoration in such passages as:

> He (Jesus) is the image of the invisible God, the first-born of all creation; for in him all things were created, in heaven and on earth, visible and

---

[18] II Peter 1:2-4.
[19] I Corinthians 2:2
[20] Romans 8:28-29
[21] Galatians 4:19
[22] Ephesians 3:21

invisible, whether thrones or dominions or principalities or authorities – all things were created by him and for him. He is before all things, and in him all things hold together. He is the head of the body, the church; he is the beginning, the first-born from the dead, that in everything he might be pre-eminent. For in him all the fullness of God was pleased to dwell, and through him to reconcile to himself to himself, whether on earth or in haven, making peace by the blood of his cross. (Colossians 1:15-20)

The Church in its gatherings through the ages has celebrated that focus in its life together. First of all, it has made baptism into Christ to be its public point of entrance into the community. Then, it continually celebrates its identification with Christ as it breaks the bread and drinks the cup together in its eucharistic fellowship. There it remembers Christ in his Body and Blood.[23] And think of all the hymns and songs the Church has written in praise of Jesus.

In another vein (which as the people of God in Christ we must never, never forget) are the *incarnational implications* of Christ living in and through us. God's purpose for our lives together in the Church is that Christ be formed in us. We are to be conformed to the image of God's Son in knowledge, in true righteousness and holiness.[24] Like our Lord Jesus (who lives in us), we become incarnate (Christ's presence) in the realities of our daily routines, and of this human scene. We are not exempt from all of the realities of culture, poverty, suffering, politics, materialism, grubby stuff, disappointment, joys, beauty, and death.

What is so awesome is that in the midst of those realities, God faithfully provides for us all of the unsearchable resources we need to actually *be* his

---

[23] I state this ever so basically, since the various traditions see this with different eyes. But I see Jesus as giving these reminders to the Church so that we never lose our fellowship with him: "Remember me when you are together." My own view is not so much on the liturgical propriety of the observance as it is in the authenticity of our solidarity with Christ, whether in families, in clandestine house churches or larger ecclesiastical settings. Records give moving accounts of prisoners improvising elements so that they could "eat the bread and drink the cup" together in unlikely settings. Baptisms, likewise, are wonderfully accomplished in all kinds of unlikely, formal and informal settings without all of the liturgical paraphernalia! Just "Don't forget me!"

[24] Romans 8:29; Ephesians 4:24; Colossians 3:10

Enchanted people, just as he did in Jesus the firstborn of the New Creation. The implications are obvious. Our lives are to demonstrate Christ in the ways in which we live and think and behave (Sign Six). We are to "walk in the same way in which he walked."[25] It is that Life in Christ demonstrated in God's people which makes them to be Salt and Light in this darkened and disenchanted world—whatever their daily contexts may be. No one who belongs to Christ can escape into that pitiful: "Oh, I'm only a layman" by which some lamely attempt to escape the incarnational calling which is ours in Christ. (But that's our sixth sign so we'll come back to it.)

Take note: the Jesus who is focal and central in the authentic Church is not some contemporary 'Designer Jesus', fashioned by some clip-and-paste fabrication of our human whims and likes and dislikes. Such crazy schemes have been tried by many in the Modern and Postmodern era. As we will see shortly, that is precisely why it is so very critical that the Word of Christ (the apostolic teachings about Christ) be the everywhere present and formative reality among God's people.

"I have a question: How does all that happen? How am I to know what Spirit presence looks like in persons? How does a group keep its focus on Jesus? Who enables the Word of Christ to be understood and practiced in a community? All your stuff sounds good, but it's too simple. There's got to be some provision to make all of this happen. So what do you think?"[26]

---

[25] I John 2:6

[26] Germane to this question would be a whole thesis on redefining the pastoral gift. The pastor-teacher gift in the New Testament is that of equipping God's people for their own works of ministry so that they become mature in Christ. Christendom made this gift into an office for "ordained clergy" when actually this becomes a tragic subversion of its intended purpose. The Ascended Lord gives gifts to his Church to enable it to fulfill the Mission of God. Essential to that purpose would be Paul's word to Timothy: "Commit the message to faithful men who shall be able to teach others also" (II Timothy 2:2). The Elders were to function as "examples of God to the flock" (I Peter 5). Somehow it all expresses the need for the gift of such reproductive leadership. That would mean that we probably need to confront the subversion embodied in all too much of the "ordained clergy" crowd who claim the title of pastor. That Spirit giftedness cannot be contained within that clergy designation. Practitioners of true disciple-making emerge in the community and their fruit is obvious in the fruit of mature, self-reproducing followers of Jesus.

It is all so subtle. A community of believers which may have begun well can subsequently become so focused on the blessings of each other's company, or on their mutual activities, ... or maybe on institutional success, ... that they ever so inadvertently shift the focus from Jesus Christ, and from obedience to him, ... to those other foci. It happens quickly. There are many ostensible 'churches' in which one wants to stand up and shout: "Does anyone here know Jesus?"

The Spirit of God glorifies the Son of God. Where there is the Spirit Presence, there the Son is exalted, and vice-versa. Interanimation! Our *authenticity status dialog bar* needs to register the presence of such interanimation. That sign of authenticity, then, segues us into our next evidence. The Spirit who was in Christ (as Christ was in intimate and dynamic communion with the Father in prayer) ... also creates the community of believers to be a people who are in continual and dynamic communication with the Father, Son, and Spirit ... through *prayer*.

Sign: The Primary Activity Is Prayer

There is something quite surprising in the New Testament accounts of the emerging young Church: *the priority activity was prayer*! The Church, which the Spirit was forming, was always praying! That priority has also been most obvious in authentic and transformational and *enchanted* Churches ever since. Given our present proclivity to proliferate 'church programs' in order to become 'successful'—this is a *big* surprise.

"OK, but first I have a practical question: if that Spirit Presence is so critical to the Church's authenticity, what should I look for by way of real people in real time doing something that indicated that they were onto those first two signs? How were those signs nurtured?"

It's all connected. Stick with me here.

Think about your question. It is the Spirit (first sign) who comes into us in Christ (second sign). It is also the Spirit who also initiates, provokes, and enables our prayers of communion with the Father and the Son (third sign). You could say that prayer is the Triune God embracing us once again into his own heart and mind and purpose.

"Are we back into *perichoresis*, or what?"

All of this is not in any way disconnected from our being formed into the image of the Son of God, and into the Spirit Presence. What became obvious from the *get-go* in the New Testament was that the Church's primary activity was *prayer*.

One wonders why that was so? Answer: *communication* with the Father and the Son by the Spirit was the only way by which those believers could possibly maintain the Pentecostal *enchantment* in the face of the humanly impossible commission given them by Jesus.

It was also by the Spirit that they knew how to pray, since it was the Spirit who was praying in them.[27] They knew that their only dynamic contact with the heart and mind and *power* of God was to be realized in prayer. They knew that their own lives were awesomely set free and transformed by Jesus. They knew that such liberation was not as the result of their own *merely human* efforts or their good intentions. If your were to ask how they could be empowered to be faithful in communicating the liberating message to those still outside in the dark, their answer would be that when they were together, whether in their house churches or in their larger gatherings—the prayed! Prayer was their dynamic lifeline to the wisdom and power of God.

They prayed out of adoring hearts to their Risen Lord Jesus Christ. Their prayers were adoration at the beginning and at the end. Their psalms and hymns were prayers set to music. They prayed about their decisions. They prayed out of repentant and believing hearts because they knew their own human frailty. They prayed about the hostility and opposition to their missional obedience. They brought their daily lives and necessities before God in prayer. They prayed about the impossible circumstances in which they found themselves. They prayed about problems and about relationships in the community. They prayed for a continual anointing of power and boldness in the Spirit. They prayed for God's vision concerning those elsewhere who still needed to hear the good news. They prayed for the glory of Christ in all they touched.

Like I say, the primary activity of the Church in its gatherings was prayer. *It was and is a sign of authenticity.* Look for it.

You don't even begin to understand that first generation community without understanding that *when they were with one another they prayed—*

---

[27] Romans 8:26

they prayed until they were all in one accord before God. That's *primarily* what they did! That was *the* focal activity! They all prayed. Paul will later say it with such stark simplicity and brevity: "Pray without ceasing!" Living as they did in a hostile and humanly impossible context, with an impossible mandate to "make disciples of all the people groups" meant that prayer was their only means of plugging-in to the mind of God, to the heart of God, and to the power of God. And so they prayed!

"Does that mean that I'm not looking for a church's big impressive, 'bells and whistles' worship services, but that I should ask: Where and when do the folks get together to pray? And depending on the answer I get, I should see that as another *status dialog bar* indicator of authenticity?"

You figure it out.

Jesus prayed. Jesus gave them a model for their prayers. Jesus promised them that they would do greater works than he had done. Then he promised them: "Whatever you *ask in my name*, I will do it, that the Father may be glorified in the Son."[28] If a church does not make prayer a priority in its corporate life, then, you can count on it: Its authenticity diminishes. When you find life-giving authenticity of Church, you will also find that somewhere behind that authenticity is the primary activity of prayer that produces that authenticity.

Sign: The Word of Christ Dwells Richly in Its Midst

One of the tragic evidences of the *church's decline into inauthenticity* in our own North American culture is that of Biblical illiteracy—people inside the church simply do not know the data of the gospel of Jesus Christ. Too many have never thought and studied and prayed their way into a maturity of understanding. That leaves them all too inept and vulnerable before the post-christian and secular *whitewater* in which they (and we) are presently living. They are not equipped to think Christianly in the midst of the complex cultural and ethical issues that confront them each day. They haven't been equipped to function as Salt and Light because the Word of Christ is not what forms their minds and lives.

---

[28] John 14:14. (italics mine)

Signs of Authenticity - I

Our God is a God who speaks! Jesus was unabashed in saying: "I am the way, the *truth,* and the life." Jesus was also the one who said that those who have his word and keep (obey) it are like the wise man who builds his house on the rock. The implication of that is quite inescapable. It is not just the knowledge of his word, but the practice (praxis) that is involved in our *knowing* his word. One of Christ's final commissions to his Church was that it is to go to every people group in the world and to teach them to *obey* all that he had commanded. The knowledge of Jesus' teachings and the understanding that they are to be obeyed is critical to the mission of God.

Our God speaks, and he speaks in order that we may hear and obey.

The writer of the letter to the Hebrew Christians begins with the statement:

> Long ago, at many times and in many ways, God spoke to our fathers by the prophets, but in these last days he has spoken to us by his Son, whom he appointed the heir of all things, through whom also he created the world. He is the radiance of the glory of God and the exact imprint of his nature, and he upholds the universe by the word of his power. (Hebrews 1:1-3)

Jesus promised that he had so much more to tell them than they could ever absorb, but ... that when the Spirit would come, then that same Spirit would bring all those things to their remembrance. That has been the Church's experience all through its missionary history. Those apostolic teachings, which we have in the *canon of scripture*,[29] have been the *lodestar* to which the Church has looked for its understanding of God and of God's New Creation in Christ.

Those scriptures, in themselves, are an *enchanted* set of documents. They are Spirit-breathed. When our eyes are opened by the Spirit, when our ears are opened by the Spirit, when our hearts conceive by the Spirit, then the eschatological design of God to dwell in the midst of his people is made quite clear in the Word of Christ. The Spirit provokes a hungering and a thirsting after the Word of Christ to be both known and obeyed.

---

[29] The Church has appropriated the Greek word κανον 'measuring rod' to designate the sixty-six Biblical documents which it considers officially received to contain the Christian rule of faith.

Enchanted Community

Paul told the Church to:

"Let the word of Christ dwell in (among) you richly, teaching and admonishing one another in all wisdom, singing psalms and hymns and spiritual songs, with thankfulness unto God." (Colossians 3:16)

If your *authenticity status dialog bar* picks up a community with a healthy engagement with scripture, then rejoice. God's people need to be conversant with the God of scripture. When they are allowing it to refine and animate their lives, then you can rest assured that the Spirit Presence is also at work. Conversely, when groups, or classes, or pulpits, or community gatherings *trivialize* (or are content to remain ignorant of) scripture, then you can know that the *disenchantment* has taken its toll!

The word of Christ dwelling among us, then, leads us on to ....

... Well, actually, maybe we've been at it long enough for one day. Let's hang it up for now, and get back to the rest of the signs whenever your schedule permits.

We had been sitting at the table on the sidewalk patio for nearly two hours, and the mid-day Sunday brunch crowd were beginning to arrive in numbers, so we began to check out.

"Bob, my schedule is impossible for the next couple of weeks. Why don't you just put them in an e-mail to me? At least that way I can try to digest them in the breaks from my work. Maybe we can get together and process them somewhere out there when I am freed up. I'm not certain whether you are helping me answer my question or not, but I'm really 'hooked' on your line of thought. I have only one request: When we've finished your 'Signs of Authenticity' piece, could we talk about something like: 'You are here! Where do you go from *here* to get to *there*?' You know, let's put ourselves in the place of most guys who are in my dilemma, and look at the realities and the options. I know we're never going to come up with the ideal Church. It may not even exist. But the Lord who is building this whole thing has made us, somehow, stewards of our influence and gifts. I'd like to pursue that. OK?"

You're on.

We paid our check and left a bonus tip because we had occupied the table for so long, and called it a day.

Journey Eight
Signs of Authenticity – II

To: Alan2@gitech.org
From: bob.henderson@belbury.com
Date: June 25, 2003
Subject: The Rest (?) of the Signs

Alan: I don't know about you, but I really enjoyed our time Sunday morning. I know I'm the one doing most of the talking, but you keep provoking me to some overdue honesty and fresh thinking as we pursue this together. Thanks.

The first four of the Signs of Authenticity I came up with, are in a very real sense foundational Signs for the inner life of the New Creation community. The next three that I want to try to unpack here pertain more to those outward and visible and healthy evidences of the practice that should flow out of the first four. These three signs are not only teachings and commandments given by our Lord Jesus for his people – but they are also the signs in which the Church engages those *outside* of itself in its *missionary confrontation with the world*. Even more, it is through these three that the Church catches the attention of those still outside. They are not only demonstrations of the Church's obedient response to Christ's word, but they are also where the Church's New Creation reality becomes visible as it redemptively confronts and engages those men and women who are still in the dark. Hopefully my use of those several weird words: *enchanted, perichoresis,* and *eschatological* will begin to take on some clearer focus here.

Early on you and I were looking at the human community as it is intended by God – created in God's own *image and likeness*. I dredged up that wonderful word *perichoresis* which the Church has historically adopted to describe the relationships that exists between the persons of the Trinity. I quoted a theologian who painted a beautiful picture of those three divine persons *being in* each other, *making room for* each other, *interpenetrating* each other, *interanimating* each other, *drawing life from* each other, *pouring life into* each other, *rejoicing in* each other, *seeking the glory of* each other, *existing in and through* each other, *coinhering* in one another by virtue of the dynamic communion which they constitute in their belonging to one another.[1] Remember?

Then I drew the conclusion that when God created the human community in his own family likeness, that the very same life which those persons lived together was by the life of God in them. What that meant for them was that their relationships with each other reflected and demonstrated the same interpersonal dynamics as that of the Trinitarian community. It was out of their embrace within the Trinitarian Life that they lived their lives with each other. They would be given to each other *and* to their Creator God in that kind of reciprocal intimacy and shared life.

I want to point us to the fact that all of the *"one another"* passages in the New Testament documents are only understandable by such an awareness of the Trinitarian Life and relationships (*perichoresis*) being once again created in us, and its consequent demonstration in the community of the New Creation by the Spirit of Christ. Those dots connect to the Church. That is how the community is to live and relate to each other and also to their Redeemer God as those called are participants in process of being transformed from darkness to light, as they are being conformed to the image of the Son of God.

---

[1] Colin Gunton, *The One and the Three and the Many* (Cambridge Univ. Press, NY. 1993) p. 163. Cf. also T. Torrance, *The Christian Doctrine of God: One Being, Three Persons* (T. & T. Clark, Edinburgh. 1996). P. 132.

Signs of Authenticity - II

All of which makes the tragedy of the human community's attempt to live apart from such human and divine community (in people's attempt to become their own gods) all the more tragic. Such attempts at autonomy, to be a law unto themselves, to find life in itself apart from the Creator God, can only lead ultimately into some kind of despair and death. Remember the list of dismal descriptions we came up with to portray the *disenchanted* community that resulted – *orphaned, suddenly alone, lost to their heart's True Home, intimates became strangers silence replaced song sadness eclipsed joy, darkness descended, hope faded, the magic, the enchantment,… but a memory, fear replaced trust, "You will be as God" they were told … but … it didn't happen, not the way it's supposed to be, death, dissonance, disenchantment, "All creation groans, … waiting …"*

The Church (as God's *eschatological* or *missional* community) is obviously to be an integral part of that joyous news of the Seeking God whose love is demonstrated in *making all things new*. The Church is the human community made new and dwelling again in its intended intimacy and communication with each other and with the Triune God for whom it was created. What that means is that the *Church as true human community* is an essential dimension and demonstration of our joyous news. That is what makes the *Church* such essential *gospel*. That is what makes it to be an integral part of God's good news in Christ. Such intimacy with others and with God is somewhere always an unmet desire lying somewhere deep in the human heart, no matter how far it has wandered. When that provision of divine love emerges in Jesus Christ (the truly human one) it is unimaginably good news. When it is displayed in the Church today it continues to be incredibly good news.

I observed above that our initial four Signs were foundational: the Presence of the Spirit of God who makes it all possible (otherwise we are left with the *merely human*); the adoration of Jesus who reconciled us to God and made peace by the blood of his Cross; the communication (prayer) between the community and the God whom they love and adore; and finally, the community formed by the Word of Christ.

Those bring us to these next three *signs* in which the New Creation community engages the very world that Jesus Christ came to seek and save. It is through these engaging signs that the Spirit of God makes the good news of God visible as New Creation. The fifth sign is that of the *love* that those in the Church have for one another which is the demonstration of the love of Christ among them. The sixth sign is (and I choose these adjectives advisedly and deliberately) is the alternative and subversive way of living and thinking that comes from the image and likeness of God expresses itself in them as God's New Creation people. And the seventh sign is their engagement in the *mission of God* – in the *compassion of Christ* for the all the peoples of the world whom God seeks (through the Church) to reconcile to himself. Such alternative behaving and thinking reflect the scope of God's redemptive love for his whole creation. This final sign is the Church's intentional *movement* as it becomes God's agent to seek and to save those still lost from their "heart's True Home." It displays their God-given passion to make disciples. It is the Church's identification with the Mission of God – the Father's mission to bless all the nations as promised to Abraham. It is the Church's response to the mandate given by Christ to "Go!"[2]

Sign: Christ-love for 'One Another'

Jesus couldn't have made it more plain: *A new commandment I give you, that you love one another just as I have loved you, you also are to love one another. By this all people will know that you are my disciples, if you have love for one another.*[3] It is both a commandment to be obeyed, and a sign (signifier) to those outside of divine love and authentic discipleship.

Love is a word easily spoken, but it is a discipline which challenges every autonomous fiber in our being as we are in the process of our being transformed into God's New Creation. It is only possible by our living and walking in utter dependence upon the Spirit of God and by renouncing our proclivity to autonomy. This involves a radical repentance. Our paradigm for such love is seen in the *perichoretic* relationships between the Father,

---

[2] Part of the mystery of God's extravagant good purpose for his whole creation is that of 'Common Grace' whereby men and women who are alienated from God, and have no vision of his glory and goodness, still are given the ability to do many wonderful deeds of love and generosity and humanitarian care. Some have called this *God's preserving grace* which causes the sun to rise on the just and the unjust, that keeps his creation from deteriorating into total destructiveness: *Every good gift and every perfect gift is from above, coming down from the Father of lights ... "* (James 1:17 ESV)

[3] John 13: 34-35

Son, and Holy Spirit. Those relationships define the kind of love with which the Father loves the Son, and so the love with which he loves us. Only ... there's a difference. God's love for us is undeserved on our part – but such love *is* the very nature of God. That renewed image and likeness, which is ours in Christ, is empowered by the Spirit to love as God loves. That kind of love is now to be demonstrated in our human lives.[4]

Alan, I am totally persuaded that the full content of Christ's command to love is only going to be found by looking again at all the *one another* passages in the New Testament. Jesus commanded us: Love *one another*. What does that look like? It means, first of all, that there are to be *real and significant other persons* with whom we are in living relationship. It can never be impersonal or abstract. Then we are faced with the fact that both we and those significant *one another* followers of Jesus are in all stages of imperfection. We are all 'in process' of moving out of our former lives as children of darkness and into our new calling to be children of the Light.

Just a sampling of the *one another* passages gives us something of that flavor. We are variously instructed in apostolic teachings that: *we belong to one another; we are to speak the truth to one another since we are all members of one another; we are to carry one another's burdens; we are not to slander one another; we are to forgive our grievances against one another; we are not to grumble against one another; we are to have the same care for one another in our diversity of gifts; we are to be at peace with one another; we are to live in harmony with one another; we are not to murmur among one another; we are to submit to one another; we are to be kind to one another, tenderhearted, forgiving one another as God in Christ forgave us; we are to do nothing from rivalry or conceit but rather in humility to count others more significant than yourselves;* ... for starts.[5]

---

[4] It is probably worthwhile for us to look at Jesus' prayer in John 17 asking the Father that his followers should be one just as he and the Father are one. That is not nearly so enigmatic a petition if we see the divine intent for the Church to be embraced again within the *perichoretic* community of the Triune God, and that the life of God should demonstrate itself within the relationships of the Church both in the relationships to one another, but also that corporately in their life of adoration and worship of that very One in whom they dwelt.

[5] Romans 12:5; Ephesians 4:25; Galatians 6:2; James 4:11; Colossians 3:13; James 5:9; I Corinthians 12:25; Mark 9:50; Romans 15:5; John 6:43; Ephesians 5:21; Ephesians 4:32; Philippians 2:3.

That cannot be any natural "love-those-who-love-me" kind of love. Rather it is the redemptive and patient and gracious and undeserved love of Christ being lived out among his New Creation community. It is the demonstration of Christ's image in us. Only so can it be a sign to those watching us from outside! It can be quite 'tough'. It is not sentimental. It is always kind and gracious. It is not a 'feeling'. Quite the contrary: it is a selfless and determined act of our wills. When we can listen to others; when we can love and accept those of other religions, other ethnic cultures, other lifestyles (yes, and sexual expressions), even when we may not at all approve of them; … when we can forsake our comfort-zone church life and become God's bridges into those lives through thoughtful dialogue and caring, …then it is a powerful sign of New Creation authenticity to those very persons whom Jesus came to seek and to save.

Church institutions (or societies) are a step away from this dimension of love. Church institutions can affirm that all of our Signs of Authenticity are valid and even necessary, … but so long as they are impersonal and theoretical they remain detached and abstract. Love is never abstract. It is never detached. Love takes place in a *community* and is near-impracticable in some larger *society*, or *institution*. Love is real and specific other persons to whom and with whom I am bound in the Spirit. I am to be bound to them in mutual caring, service, accountability, submission, and missionary obedience. All of the *one another* passages simply help us understand how profound is this commandment of our Lord Jesus Christ.

Christ's love in us and through us to the real and specific 'one anothers' is a sign of our authentic discipleship. Check that one out on your *authenticity dialog bar*.

Alternative and Subversive New Creation Thinking and Behaving As a Sign of Authenticity.

If you want to know why a good portion of the society does not take the church seriously, you might want to begin by looking a this sign. This is a lifestyle sign. I wrote above that I chose these adjectives advisedly and deliberately, and so I did. The Light of God dwelling in his people confronts the darkness. The Life of God inhabiting his people by the Spirit confronts the cultural ambiguities and death. This sign has to do with our responses to Jesus' teachings and commands. It is the "by their fruits shall you know them" sign. It is the evidence of New Creation authenticity, and it is perhaps the most difficult and demanding. It is not simple nor easy to make thoughtful ethical responses to the cultural darkness. It takes intelligence, imagination, energy and love. It is where God's New Creation people are different and become self-consciously counter-cultural, even subversive.

It was G. K. Chesterton who observed that the Christian idea had not been tried and found wanting but rather found difficult and not tried. The public polls highlight how incredibly absent this sign has become in the church notwithstanding all of the 'Christian talk' that proliferates and the presence of so-called 'churches' abounding in every community. Those polls indicate that the behavior patterns of those who profess to be serious Christians are not all that different from the irreligious and secular populace. As if that were not serious enough, we have come to the pass where 'Christian thinking' almost sounds like an oxymoron in many circles.

This sign is Public Square stuff. It is where the Church engages this present age as Light and Salt. Such engagements involve us in areas of serious debate and in conversation with the plausibility structures of our particular communities, and with our culture at large. It can be very difficult and often intimidating. It is one reason that we need the community of faith in which to discuss, process, and pray about our responses. Such sensitive engagement and thoughtful conversation and debate are all too rare. This sign requires the moral and intellectual disciplines with which our new nature as Spirit-persons should be energizing us. It is where we come into "missionary confrontation" with cultural decay, social injustice, the not-black-or-white issues of ethics, education, politics, economics, sexuality, power, cultural idols, and a myriad of other daily experiences in the workplace. It is lived in the neighborhood and in our national life. It can also be very costly.

When we see God's New Creation people as a people *called-out* in order to be those who are not captive to the economic, political, and social-cultural "principalities and powers," ... then we begin to read scripture with a whole new set of eyes. We begin to see how we are called to live our New Creation lives in the midst of this often confusing culture which so fearfully falls short of God's glory – and to do so as the wonderfully and redemptively subversive children of Light. We are called to live in the midst of the gritty realities with joy and hope.

One historian observed that those early Christians prevailed over their hostile pagan culture because they *out-thought, outlived,* and *out died* their pagan counterparts – and that culture was really hostile. It could cost you your life! We in North America, ostensibly, have freedom of religious expression, all kinds of time-consuming activities that are carried on under the rubric of 'Christian education' – and yet we have produced a Church that is abysmally ignorant of scripture, or its own orthodox heritage and its history, and is totally frightened of controversy.

A wonderful old spiritual laments that "everybody talkin' bout heaven ain't a-gonna go there." In our public scene there is almost an overkill of "Jesus talk" co-habiting with a frightful conformity to the world around it in both thought and behavior. Somewhere the church forgot its calling to be a radical alternative, a New Creation, aliens and exiles who exhibit the wonderful deeds of him who has called it out of darkness into his marvelous Light.[6]

Jesus made it quite clear that those who are 'outside' are to see and take notice when his New Creation people *think and behave Christianly* – when the Life of God in the people of God is demonstrated in their thinking and lifestyle. We are called upon to resist "conformity to the world" and conversely we are called to be "transformed by the renewing of our minds." That is the glory of God in the Church. That is where God dwells by his Spirit. That is where the New Creation community engages the world profoundly and *creatively*. That is where we engage the world *transformationally*.[7]

When the Church sinks into mindlessness and depthlessness and cultural sterility – when it avoids complex and controversial issues – there is created a huge void. Jesus always calls his people to live robustly *incarnational* lives. What that means is that we will often find ourselves

---

[6] Cf. I Peter 2:9-12

[7] The late Francis Shaeffer used to speak of being "co-belligerents" with those who did not identify with our Christian faith and yet held to behavior patterns in justice and peacemaking and righteous living which are our heritage as Christians. In our engagement with the world, we find strange and unexpected bedfellows by the common grace of God.

in confrontation with the culture of the darkness around us. At the same time we will confront it with gentleness, sensitivity, knowledge, and redemptive purpose. The Church is called by its Creator to *get inside* the thinking and lifestyle of its pagan context so that it understands it, and in so understanding to be able to expose its emptiness, and then sensitively point it to the Light.

For the church to seek escape from being controversial (in order to avoid conflict) may very well be an act of direct disobedience to the clear teachings of Jesus. Jesus makes some pointed statements about obedience to his teachings: "Not everyone who calls me Lord, Lord is going to enter the kingdom, but only those who *do* the will of my Father." Then there is that metaphor of the person building his house upon a rock being like the person who has Jesus' words and doing them.[8] Even the familiar missionary mandate at the end of Matthew speaks of "... teaching them to *observe* all that I have taught ..."[9] Take note, however, that to obey such radical and subversive teachings as we find, for instance, in the Sermon on the Mount can be very costly. That may be the reason that we find such obedience so tragically rare. It also provides a clue about the church's frequent tendency to truncate that part of the gospel!

For our purposes here, we are looking at the Signs of Authenticity which are *visible* to those outside. Look at the telling word following right on the heels of the Beatitudes in Jesus' Sermon on the Mount. It goes like this: "*... let your light shine before others, so that they may **see** your good works and give glory to your Father who is in heaven.*" [10] Or Peter writing to a Church 'under the gun' of persecution as he lifts up the lifestyle of the believing community as a sign: "*Keep your conduct among the Gentiles* [unbelievers outside the Church] *honorable, so that when they speak evil against you as evildoers, they may **see** your good deeds and glorify God on the day of visitation.*"[11] He goes on to say that the community of believers is to look to such confrontations as purposeful occasions in which to enter into redemptive conversation with those curious outsiders and point them to the *hope* that motivates their *enchanted* lives and behavior. That is just to

---

[8] Matthew 7: 21ff.
[9] Matthew 28:20
[10] Matthew 5:16 in loc.;
[11] I Peter 2:12

say, Alan, that the *enchanted* lives of New Creation folk, and of the New Creation communities, are to be clearly visible as an alternative way of living, behaving, and thinking to the watching world.

It only follows: God's DNA is dwelling in us by the Holy Spirit. The lives of those who are part of God's New Creation will naturally *think* and *live* out of that image of the Son of God being created within them. After all, it is into God's family likeness that we are being recreated. Right? Such an image involves a radically new and alternative kind of living and thinking. It is what makes faithful followers of Jesus to be Salt and Light. As the old saying goes: "to talk Christian talk means that we are to walk Christian walk." It is one thing to demand orthodox beliefs of the Church and to insist that it engage in 'spiritual activities'. But if there is not that *orthopraxis*, that practical living-out of the teachings of the New Creation in obedience to Christ – then some distressing kind of contradiction, some rank smell of *inauthenticity* becomes that Church's witness rather than the "sweet aroma of Christ."

It is fascinating to watch how our cynical society responds to and appreciates New Creation behavior when it sees it present in Christ's servants. It sees it in those who engage in the great humanitarian efforts, and who become colonies of light in the cultural darkness. Such examples speak to them that something they don't understand is going on, and just might be worth further investigation. The report goes that both Mahatma Gandhi of India, and Fidel Castro of Cuba, at some point in their lives indicated that they would probably have become Christian *if only* Christians had demonstrated the teachings of Christ! And it was most revealing in the positive example of Mother Teresa who received a state funeral in a Hindu nation because of her New Creation work in the slums of Calcutta. Why? Because of the authenticity of her Christian living, thinking, and behaving. The values and lifestyle of those who own Christ's Name are to express God's compassion for the helpless, the crushed, the victims of injustice, and the plight of the world's victims of poverty. According to the New Testament we can only expect the society around us to take the Church seriously when and if this Sign of Authenticity is present and visible.[12]

---

[12] Missiologist Charles Taber has written: "The life of believers, individually and collectively, is intended to incarnate the biblical reality of human dignity. The church is called to be an alternative society, living in a contrasting style in the midst of the

One of the enigmas that always disturbs me is how easily the church skirts around this sign. It is easy (even expected) for the church to talk about the wonderful story of Jesus, to celebrate Christmas and Easter and Pentecost. It is comforting to revel in the promises of the gospel. But when it comes to the *demands of the gospel* – which are also essential if we are faithful to the gospel – the continual temptation is to by-pass them in order to get on to something other than those lives of active obedience to which Christ calls us. Such a truncated gospel may promote 'spiritual folk' who easily mouth devotional platitudes, ... but it tragically dilutes the integrity of our gospel of *New Creation*, which is to be visible in the midst of the realities and hard questions of everyday life. When the New Creation community is scarcely different from the unbelieving community around it, then something is tragically amiss.[13]

Such is the highly visible sign in which our character as God's true humanity, as God's Salt and Light in this decaying and darkened society, is to be truly transformational. Such is where our own daily character is to demonstrate and exhibit God's character. Such is where we become God's *instruments of righteousness*. Such is where the *beauty* and the *music* and the *dance* of New Creation become a reality. Such is where we become stewards of our Father's creation and where we glory both in the natural

---

world. Its members are, in God's design, not self-promoting , as the world is; they are not competitive, s the world is, they do not advance at the expense of others, as the world does; they do not take advantage of the weakness of others, as the world does. They love one another and do good to and for one another. Failing that, there is no compelling reason for the world to pay attention. Which is to say that the only means by which Christians can commend a truly godly vision of human rights is to incarnate them in their individual and collective lives, to announce God's actions and intentions that constitute the Gospel, and to act justly in the name of God." (From an article: "In the Image of God: The Gospel and Human Rights" in The International Bulletin of Missionary Research, Vol. 26, No. 3).

[13] In this vein, Andrew Kirk, significant missiologist from the UK writes of his early career in Buenos Aires: "My time in Latin America was immensely significant in my understanding of mission. I became more certain that a gospel message that could not address directly and fittingly the major social and political questions of the times was, at best, defective and, at worst, a false Gospel." (International Bulletin, Vol. 28, No. 2. April 2004. P. 71.) Or, as I write this, Ron Sider has just written a telling volume *The Scandal of the Evangelical Conscience* (Baker, 2005) which footnotes how widespread is this contradiction between profession and behavior.

environment and in the human *polis* what with its neighborhoods, cities, corporations, nations and beyond. Such is where our minds and hearts and loyalties and behavior and energies are an expression of the glory of God.

Such is where we become *aliens and exiles* as we are faithful to the subversive and redemptive otherness of God's New Creation. Such is never easy. It is a struggle in which the Spirit of God is continually at work to energize us for the enormous struggle required.[14] Such is where the *Enchanted Community's* New Creation authenticity will stand in beauteous and redemptive contrast to any conformity with the values and agendas of this present *disenchanted* world. We are to be known by our fruits! All of which brings us then to the next of these *interanimating* signs.

Sign: Community Focus on The Mission of God

This last of our Signs of Authenticity (or the signs that I, at least, have come up with) could be and maybe should be the first. It is the *Missionary* or *Eschatological* sign. All of the other signs flow into this one, and all flow out of it. It is the one sign that "connects the dots" from the promise given to Abraham (that his seed would bless the nations) ... to Christ the Seed, ... to that day when "this gospel of the kingdom shall have been preached in all the earth"[15] and when Christ shall return to consummate his New Creation work.

> "Then comes the end, when he (Christ) delivers the kingdom to God the Father after destroying every rule and every authority and power. For he must reign until he has put all his enemies under his feet. The last enemy to be destroyed is death. For God has put all things in subjection under his feet. ... When all things are subjected to him, then the Son

---

[14] Cf. Romans 6 in which Christian people are instructed in the disciplines of "dying to the flesh" and putting off our former servitude to sin in order to live unto righteousness. It speaks eloquently of the resurrection life of Christ in us which enables us to live such alternative lives.
[15] Matthew 24:14

himself will also be subjected to him who put all things under him, that God may be all and in all."[16]

So what is that it is all about? It is about the Church being *the vessel and the agent of the Mission of God*. As such the Church's purpose is to bring God's blessing to the nations through the *good news* of Jesus Christ. It is about the blessings of *peace* with God through the blood of Christ's Cross. It is about *reconciliation*, about the good news of *forgiveness*, about *hope* and *new life*. The Seeking God has come in the person of his dear Son to seek and to save those who are lost (that's all of us!). He has come to bring good news to the oppressed and marginalized and hopeless and guilty and those without meaning. And now, those whom Christ calls become his Body: the Church. They become the authentic agents and communal demonstrations of God's New Creation in Christ. They engage in their daily ministries as Light and as Reconcilers to those still in darkness. They sing God's new song!

Check that one out on your *authenticity dialog bar.*

Jesus told his disciples (that's us): "As the Father has sent me, even so am I sending you."[17] The *Sending God*, who is in us through Christ, is made known as we become agents of his compassion for those who have never seen or known or heard the Word of Life. The good news of Jesus comes through us to those "… having no hope and without God in the world."[18] Jesus gave us his commandment that we should go to every nation, to every people-group everywhere, and make disciples. That is one of his final words before his ascension. In another account he told them that they (we) were to be his witnesses beginning where they were, but then outward to the uttermost parts of the world.

It becomes quite obvious that as Jesus was sending out his infant Church into the hostile world he never intended for his people to dig-in, settle down, and establish a secure institutional life for themselves. His people were always to be a pilgrim people engaged in that very mission which was his until it was completed. "As the Father has sent me, even so am I sending you."

---

[16] I Corinthians 15:24-28
[17] John 20:21
[18] Ephesians 2:12

Alan, this sign is easy to see on our *authenticity status dialog bar*. Whenever a New Creation community is praying for and engaging those around it, those who are still outside of it, those who are its neighbors in the city, or those living in darkness half-way across the world—then that is a brilliant sign that something *enchanted* is burbling healthily in that community's inner life. By the way, when you told me that you and those you pray with on campus were praying for your other contacts who were living out such empty lives, I took heart. A church institution that is only concerned with its own institutional success and survival and programs and maintenance, and that at the same time seems practically indifferent to Christ's passion for those outside … that community reveals a deadly pathology, and a lamentable evidence of inauthenticity!

Strong words? Absolutely. The Church is, if anything, a *missional community*. Its dependence upon the Spirit of God, its focus on Christ the Savior, its formation in and by the Word of Christ, its life of prayer—all those signs are for the purpose of producing that community of love and good works that reaches out to those who are still outside with the extravagant invitation to be reconciled into the Father's embrace through Jesus Christ. The Church is called to be transformational. It is called to permeate the human community like leaven, and to use its influence to bring light to this present age with the Light of God's design. The Church exists for those outside of itself (not an original statement but borrowed from Archbishop William Temple—just so you'll know). Otherwise the church is not only inconsequential, but is actually a contradiction of its own calling. Or as one friend put it: If you cannot relate your life (or the life of your Christian community) to the Great Commission (the Mission of God) then your life is irrelevant to history![19]

Alan, this is really much more critical as a sign than many realize. If the Church's adversary, Satan, can deceive the Church into diluting or marginalizing this missionary mandate of Christ, then the whole of the ecclesiastical enterprise can become quite incestuous and demonic. It requires the missional discipline of the New Creation community to keep its resources and vision focused on accomplishing that mandate.

And that can involve us in some difficult choices.

---

[19] This quote comes to me second-hand from Robert Coleman, friend and missiologist who has blessed many of us.

Let me leave you with an interesting 'for-instance'. Jim Petersen tells of himself and his wife coming back from a very fruitful missionary career in Campinas, Brazil, in order to become staff to their missionary organization at its headquarters in Colorado. On the plane they were discussing and praying about how they could continue their missionary faithfulness living in American suburbia. The dilemma which awaited them, living among typical secular middle-class North Americans, was that about the only day available for good neighborly contact and conversations was on Sundays!

Their neighbors, like most irreligious folk, scheduled their weekends so that Saturday was their day to mow the grass, run errands, take the kids to activities, etc. But then, on Sundays they slept late, kicked back, read the paper, and chilled-out in leisure time. So the Petersens found themselves in the dilemma of discerning between going to church and in so doing feeling guilty about not reaching out in hospitality to their non-Christian neighbors, ... or staying home on Sundays and inviting their neighbors in for coffee or grilled hamburgers hospitality ... and in so doing feeling guilty about not going to church![20] Such dilemmas are not uncommon, but the missional priority is there.

If this missional Sign doesn't register significantly on your church's *authenticity dialog bar* it is quite distressing. It evidences that such a church has quenched the Spirit, denied Christ, and disobeyed the word of Christ. After all, the Church as New Creation community is created by Christ to demonstrate true human community in God, and as such to bring the promised blessings of New Creation to all the nations. It is in its integrity and faithfulness to this calling that it reflects the "missionary dialogue of the Trinity."[21]

But that is not at all a simple task. The church that takes seriously Christ's missional call must of necessity be continually and seriously *exegeting* its own cultural setting. It must be attuned to its culture's language, its nuances, its contributions and deterioration, its worldview, its social complexion, its plausibility structures, its music, its politics, its

---

[20] Jim Peterson, *Church Without Walls.* (NavPress, Colorado Springs, CO. 1992).
[21] Cf. Miguez Bonino

economics, its poetry, its prejudices, its other gospels—all of that which makes up its complexity. It *must* do this if for no other reason than that this is where our gospel of the Reign of God, of God's New Creation, is being incarnated. In so doing, the church affirms its solidarity with real humanity. We are always in a missionary confrontation with the real world in which we live. That being so, we must understand the cultural and philosophical insides of our context better than those who are in captivity to it do.

So those are my own *Seven Signs of Authenticity* which have helped me, at least, in seeking to evaluate expressions of the church. All of which may lead us to the wherever and whenever of our next time together. Maybe then we can pick up your original question. I promise, I really promise, to remember that question: What do you make of the Church? We're getting close. We'll begin with a "You Are Here" reality check between ourselves. Hope your research is going well. Let me know when we can connect. Bob

Journey Nine
You Are Here: What Next?

To: bob.henderson@belbury.com
From: alan2@gitech.org
Date: June 29, 2003
Subj: Where Now?

Bob:
I'm processing your seven Signs of Authenticity. It all sounds good. But where in the world do I go with it? I'm back to the question about *if* and *how* I decide to get involved (or not get involved) in West Park Church. If not there, where? What would become my role or obligation to whatever it is that Jesus has in mind with the whole church thing? I'm repeating myself.

I'm probably going to hang out back at our bookstore coffee shop a couple of mornings August 13 and 14. That's where we began. Can we, maybe, bring it all together there and then maybe I can make a decision or come to some conclusion that is (relatively) satisfactory? Does that sound like an OK plan? Name the date.

Alan

So on a rainy Thursday morning in the middle of August, Alan and I landed where we had started, in the corner of the coffee shop at our favorite bookstore. I was probably as hesitant to try to make something out of our entire sojourn as he was eager to satisfy his own integrity with regard to the Church. Frankly, I was not only hesitant, I was actually intimidated. After all, mine was just one person's 'take' or experience of the huge mystery of the Church with all of its twenty centuries of history.

For whatever 'presence' the Church has had over these past two millennia, it is still somehow the creation of the Holy Spirit. Consequently, it refuses to be taken captive by human structures. It is unpredictably *enchanted* as it appears and then dissipates with all the mystery of such a Spirit-dwelling. Try to define it too carefully … and it will break out into some new and unexpected expression. Yet its roots are deep in apostolic teachings and practice. Its authenticity is manifested in a diverse array of communities around the world and in many cultures all of whom share a common calling by Christ into New Creation.

What I also knew was that Alan was not alone. There are myriads of God's faithful people who are his fellow (and often bewildered) sojourners—just as Alan and I are. Most of those sojourners don't have the luxury of "church shopping" or of endlessly pursuing some ideal church of their dreams that "has it all together" (which church is an *illusion* anyhow!).[1] They can only faithfully take their places in whatever community is at hand, be it ever so puzzling, often messy, sometimes indistinctly authentic or inauthentic. There … in that far-from-perfect setting and out of their adoration, out of their devotion to Christ, and out of their loving obedience to him, … they pray, and encourage, and equip, and persevere. It is there that they may find one or a few others such as themselves. There they break bread, make disciples, and form *households of faith*, which then become pockets of authentic Spirit-life within those larger assemblies, … and there those faithful people patiently and faithfully walk as "children of the Light."

---

[1] Sadly, there are those who spend their whole lifetimes going from church to church looking for a more authentic one. It is sad to watch. Authenticity begins with each of us where we are, not with someone else somewhere else! Jesus was *the* authentic One and he summoned others one by one and formed each into authenticity (with one failure: take note!).

What we also know from the two thousand year history of the church is that no matter how well-intentioned a church may *begin* its life, and no matter how authentic it may be at one period of its existence, ... such communities (no matter how impressive their visible presence) always face the proclivity of reverting into *disenchantment*. In time, after a generation or two, they grow forgetful or dilute or displace or distort their reason for being and their calling by Christ, ... and in so doing become *merely human religious societies*.[2]

Coffee in hand, we settled in and I asked: Are you ready for this?

"What have I got to lose? You've been teasing me along for months, and I want to know where you are going to land. Then maybe I can decide where I'm going to land, what I'm going to do with it. Jump in! I'm listening."

Let's Review

You've noticed that I have veered away from your original question. I haven't really answered it.

"I noticed." (He was giving me that indulgent grin.)

You asked me *what* was my *take* was on the church, and I have spent most of our months together answering the question of the *why* of the church. Let me simply register with you that I am more and more persuaded that you can't really discern *what* the church *is* until you understand *why* it is in the design and purpose of God.

That is the reason why I have taken you on this 'merry chase' back to the beginnings, back to that original primordial human community created in the image and likeness of the Triune God. That community (Adam and Eve) lived initially in a relationship of perfect harmony with the holy God as well as with each other in God. (That's what *shalom* is

---

[2] Let me acknowledge my debt to Gerald Arbuckle, a Roman Catholic brother who has very helpfully studied how an 'order' devolves into *chaos* as that order dilutes, displaces or forgets its "founding myth" i.e., that founding set of beliefs and principles upon which it was founded. He has written of this in *Refounding the Church* (Marynoll, NY: Orbis Press, 1993).

all about.) I took you into the church's ancient concept of *perichoresis* in which the church has attempted to conceptualize the beautiful, loving, interanimating, self-giving relationships that exist between the three Persons of the Triune God.[3] I have lifted up those relationships as being our paradigm for the kind of relationships that are to exist now between persons within the Church among those reconciled persons residing together within the embrace of the Trinitarian community.

But more to your original question is that it goes to the heart of the divine intention, which intention is unfolded in God's promise to Abraham that God would bless all the nations through Abraham's seed. That blessing has to do with the divine intention to recreate true human community as a necessary dimension of God's great Salvation through Jesus Christ. It is through that New Creation community, in which the fullness of the Godhead is exhibited by the Spirit, that all of the people groups of the earth are to be blessed.

"Whoa. Isn't that a bit of an extravagant statement?"

It is only if God's stated *eschatological* blessing of the nations is extravagant. There are extravagant descriptions of God's design for the Church, such as Paul's "*For in Christ all the fullness of the Deity lives in bodily form, and you have been given fullness in Christ...*"[4] I can only conclude that such fullness is that for which the true human community is created. Apart from such true and reconciled community, humanity is always frustrated, hopeless, empty and failing—not to mention 'guilty' in that it falls sadly short of the design of God. Do you think that makes sense?

"Did anybody ever tell you that you have a weird mind?"

Frequently. But then God's promises are always beyond our asking or imagining. So "weird" may be more normal than abnormal. My understanding of the Church as *Enchanted Community* always presses the boundaries of credulity. Remember that I pointed out to you Paul's description of the Church as "the dwelling place of God by the Spirit" being one of my reasons for proposing such an outrageous description. The New Testament documents seem quite unequivocal that the Church is to dwell in God, and that God is to dwell within the Church by the Spirit. That means that it is no ordinary, or *merely human* society.

---

[3] Cf. references from Colin Gunton and Thomas Torrance in Journey Two.
[4] Colossians 2:9

"That would mean that the members of a Church community inhabited by the Spirit are really to know and communicate and share an intimacy with each other, and with God, because of that very divine Life that inhabits them—out of the power and dynamics of their mutual Spirit-Life. Awesome! Is that why you have been suggesting that the Church community is to exhibit and live-into God's design for true human community?"

Go ahead and say it: "*eschatological* community." What else? It may be provisional at this moment in history, but it stands out magnificently at the very end of the Bible: "*The dwelling place of God is with man. He will dwell with them, and they will be his people, and God himself will be with them as their God.*"[5]

I have connected Jesus' statement "I will build my church" with all of that. I have intentionally identified the dominant New Testament usage of "the kingdom of God" with Paul's usage of "new creation" simply because I think it is more easily grasped by the non-Hebrew mind, but it all refers to the same *eschatological reality*.

You will also remember that you raised your eyebrows at me when I hung the description of *enchanted* on the Church. I'll stick with that description for the obvious reason that *if* the Church is the dwelling place of God by the Spirit, and *if* by the power of God at work the Church is the glory of God, ... and *if* I am correct in interpreting Jesus' prayer: "the glory that you have given me I have given them"[6] as referring to the gift of the Holy Spirit to the community, ... then, ... then *something* awesome is at work, something more than any merely human effort, something that is *other*, something of *magic* and *mystery*, ... something that *no eye has seen, nor ear heard, nor the heart of man imagined*[7] is Present. All of that says to me that the Church is more than a little *enchanted*, don't you think?

"So what do I do with all that?"

To begin with—just to get your attention—let me propose that the New Creation *authenticity* you are looking for in the Church ... begins with *you*.

"That's scary!"

---

[5] Revelation 21:3
[6] John 17: 22
[7] I Cor. 2:9

It really begins with your own *disciplines of New Creation authenticity*. You yourself are (somehow in the mystery of God's working) actually the fruit of the Church whether you realize it or not. The Church in some form has faithfully (and authentically) somehow brought the God's good news down to you over many generations and through the centuries. Your own *calling* into it is now to be part of the present link with what God is unfolding. Your authentic New Creation life is so that those inside the Church and outside of it will have a visible witness of what the true gospel is all about.

"So I can't wait for somebody else to be authentic, huh? I can't wait for some yet-to-be-experienced community out there somewhere to be the responsible agent of New Creation? For me it begins with me, right? It begins as I bite the bullet and connect up with another, or several others, and begin to work out the reality of New Creation community in and among ourselves. Like maybe you're backing me into the answer to my specific question about West Park Church?"

A Backward Walk Through Scripture

Let me shift gears and try something on you that I've been thinking about. Let me walk you *backward* through Paul's letter to the Ephesian church. There is a fascinating statement near the end: "*This mystery is profound, and I am saying that it refers to Christ and the church.*"[8]

Paul introduces that word *mystery* to describe the journey that has just preceded this statement. If you will walk backward from that statement, you will see that the word *mystery* comes at the end of a brief passage about the relationship between husband and wife, about their *mutual ministry* to one another as members of Christ's body. It speaks about the intimacy required between two such persons "in Christ" relating as husband and wife (vss.22-29). They are told that they are to care for one another just as Christ feeds and cares for his Church. The paradigm is Christ himself. Christ gave himself for the Church, and in that same self-giving way husbands are to *give themselves* to their wives. Wives are told to be subject

---

[8] Ephesians 5:32

(or responsive) to their husbands in the same way that the Church submits itself obediently to Christ out of love and devotion.

Interesting!

But that example doesn't stand apart from the larger context. The text preceding that one speaks about the beautiful relationships within the Church community in which all of Christ's followers are called upon to *submit to one another* out of reverence for Christ (vs. 21).

Remember now, I'm walking backward from 5:32.

That redemptive and reconciling and loving and caring submission to one another is carefully described. In all of our relationships (let me put all of this in the first person) *we* are to *speak to one another with psalms, hymns and spiritual songs, making music in our hearts* (Vss. 19-20). That means that there is to be a conversational ministry between the believers that nurtures each other. We are mutually called upon to be *filled with the Spirit*. That can only mean that the community and its members are to be continually and consciously giving to the Spirit of God his transformational and dynamic place in their midst. It means that we are to be quite consciously *Spirit-dependent* (vs. 18).

That description, in turn, is preceded by our calling to be continually turning away from what constitutes "the darkness" and always turning to what constitutes "the Light." There is a dynamic transformational process going on. It means is that we *together* (the Church) are to live lives of what can only be called lives of *continual repentance*. It means that we are always in process of being transformed (vss. 3-15). That *transformational dynamic* is to be expected normally within the Christ's New Creation community. Lives are to be in the process of continual and dynamic change. We are a community being transformed from one that is formed by the *darkness* into one that is being formed by the *Light* (vs. 8). The individual and corporate lives of those of us who are the Church are to be a brilliant alternative exhibits of living and thinking right in the midst of the "stink and stuff" of our daily realities. That involves us in lives of goodness, righteousness, and truth (vs. 9).

Now get this: *together* with *one another* we are to be *imitators of God as dear children* (vs. 1). That can only mean that our paradigm for our relationships and for our behavior within the Church is to be the very character of God himself—the family likeness. We have our model in Jesus. He is the Word made flesh. Christ's life was one of total self-giving to the Father and for us. He was devoted to doing his Father's will. It is to be so with his children. Jesus is our flesh and blood paradigm: *Christ in you* ... What that means for us is that all the 'bad stuff' that has afflicted us and has so distorted the image of God in us, all of the behavior and thought patterns of the *disenchantment*, are to be continually discerned and renounced by the Spirit's help. That makes us different, even *weird?*

Got it?

"Got it."

So we've walked backward from verse 32 of Ephesians 5 to verse 1. The obvious thing in that passage is that the Church needs to have a clear and self-conscious sense of being exactly what it is, namely, it is to be a community of those who are *called out*. That's what the Greek word for church means: 'called out'. It is *called out of* all that defines the darkness of disenchantment. It is *called into* the Life and the Light of New Creation.

Put your imagination into play here. If you keep walking backward in the letter you will ultimately come to the description we have landed on so frequently: *the Church is to be the dwelling in which God lives by his Spirit* (2:22).

"So I guess you're not too far off base in describing the Church as enchanted. OK, but hold it right there.

"Let me see if I can help you, Bob. I'm struggling to absorb, and to process, all this stuff you're unloading on me. Maybe what I'm hearing is that the authentic Church is more like a *movement*. Then only, and maybe secondarily, is it an *institution*. You've been indicating a movement in which the Triune God moves out to us in love through Jesus, the Son. Then through Jesus, and by the Spirit, God calls us back into reconciled and intimate relationships—first with himself, then within a community whose model is the Trinitarian community. Something like that.

"So, as the Spirit of God moves within us individually to relate us to each other, in so doing the Spirit creates a new and reconciled community. That means a community in Christ and a community with specific others. That community is, at the same time, also a community within the Trinitarian community, or human community as God intends it to be and as it is supposed to be.

"Then the Spirit of the Missionary-God moves through us to reach those who are still outside. It goes on and on ... until all the nations of the earth are blessed in God's wonderful message of reconciliation through Jesus Christ. Ultimately that would bring us to the consummation in that Revelation 21:3 vision you quoted about God dwelling with us, and being our God.

"How'm I doing?"

Fantastic! You've given me the key I wasn't quite able to put into words. The Church really is essentially a *movement*. It is a movement of God's Spirit that (when it is authentic) produces *missional communities*—communities in which its message becomes visible. That *movement* creates communities of New Creation along the way.[9] Such church communities not only demonstrate New Creation but also are support bases for the mission. They become communities to give *thought* and *substance* and *equipping* and *prayer* to the movement's missional obedience. That is no minor point. Those communities demonstrate the authenticity of the message of Christ *visibly*.[10]

Alan chewed on that data for a while in silence. You could see the wheels turning in his head. Then …

"That's interesting. You know the guys I interact with at the university don't really buy into the idea of truth being anything other than what you want it to be. Any truth is your own construct. And for them there certainly is no overarching interpretive story or meta-narrative that gives meaning to their lives. I'm not at all sure that means that they don't have all the same questions about meaning and the transcendent that all the rest of humanity shares.

---

[9] A fascinating study is that of all of the missionally minded communities who have moved out into the scene as self-supporting models of New Creation life and witness and hospitality. One thinks of the monastic movements, especially of the Irish monastics who moved across to Scotland and England and then to Europe. But what is unrecorded are those who unheralded have done the same across the world over these two millennia. In recent years Charles Mellis wrote a study of some of this in *Committed Communities: Fresh Streams in World Missions*, (Pasadena, CA.: William Carey Library, 1976).

[10] The communities may even, for a time, take on institutional form for the purpose of facilitating such supporting and equipping.

"But as you were talking just now I was wondering if the visibility of Christ's message in New Creation communities might not be inescapable to them—you know: 'that men may see your good works and glorify the Father ....' What if they really saw love, and meaning, and caring, and thoughtful discussion, and all the fruits of the Spirit at work in such a community? It would be difficult for them to deny, wouldn't it? So maybe the authentic Church could be a critical agent of our evangelistic obedience in such a culture. What do you think?"

What I think is that you and I are not the first to come up with that conclusion. Postmodern culture is indifferent to mere words. People are assaulted by truth claims constantly. But when the Church's faith assumptions are fleshed out in an authentic community, then real substance is given to those assumptions, and to the Church's faith. (Tragically, the opposite is also true and the church can become a contradiction to its own message.)

Back to our discussion about a scene like West Park. Such New Creation communities may, for a time, even take on institutional form for the purpose of facilitating such supporting and equipping. But, ... whenever that *church institution* displaces the community's focus on the Spirit-movement and puts its near-total focus on its own inner-life and institutional maintenance, ... then something about that institution becomes inimical to the mission. Such institutional preoccupation easily distracts the Spirit-community from the *eschatological-mission* of God. I have watched it happen too often. It has happened, tragically, over and over and over again in the Church's history ... too often.

The Church as *Spirit-community* is to be the local incarnation of God's New Creation. It is to be a living demonstration of the transformational power of the new Life in Christ. Churches are to be the exhibits where our *Seven Signs of Authenticity* are at least *provisionally* lived-out. We saw that pattern in our 'backward walk' through Ephesians. Spirit-communities like that are always focused outwardly. They are part of a dynamic process. They are where the *Vision* of all the peoples of the earth being blessed in and through Jesus Christ keeps the Church authentic.[11]

"Let's come down to planet Earth. What does that do to all those churches that are proud of their clergy, their impressive buildings, their

---

[11] Genesis 12:2-3; Matthew 24:14.

denominational ties, their prestige in the community, and all that kind of stuff?"

It means that it's all pretty disturbing. It means, of course, that any church institution that focuses primarily on itself, on its own institutional (physical) form, on its own inner organization, on its authorized 'clergy' ... is probably a *subversion* of the movement—not to mention a grief to the Holy Spirit.[12] The movement is from God, through Christ, and by the Spirit *calling* men and women to live *in Christ*. That same Spirit is to be at work in every one of them to conform them into the image of Christ. In that image they enabled by the Spirit to will, to live, to think, and to relate to each other as God intends that they should. The whole purpose of that transformation is so that the same Spirit can, in turn, *send them out* as part of God's own eschatological-missional design for his Church.

"Like, 'As the Father has sent me, even so do I send you,' right?"[13]

The consummation of God's design is the building of a dwelling for himself in and among his own New Creation community. That is his glory. The Church is a *movement* from God in Christ and back to God.

"So we've come full circle back around to that Latin American guy you quoted to me way back there—that we find the Church's source in the missionary dialogue of the Trinity.[14] Makes sense."

Perspective and Context

I knew I needed to be cautious here. I knew I was challenging some venerable understandings of the Church. I really didn't intend what I was saying to become a stumbling block to Alan, or anybody else.

I really do take the two millennia of church history very seriously. I also take very seriously *all* of the church institutions which are a part of that history. I consider any dealing with the Church (like with what Alan

---

[12] I am persuaded of this by Ellul in his *The Subversion of Christianity* (Grand Rapids, MI.: Wm. B. Eerdmans Pub. Co, 1986.). Ellul makes the case that when the church 'sacralized' special places (church buildings) and special persons (clergy) that it thereby denied the incarnational nature of the Christian church and the Christian message, and thereby 'subverts' Christianity. Amen.

[13] John 20:21.

[14] Ibid. Miguez Bonino, quoted in Journey Two.

and I were doing) something to be approached with "reverence and awe."[15] Somehow it's all *holy ground* to me. The footprints of God are all over it. Those church institutions can be, and have been, an enormous resource for the movement of God's Spirit in the world. Yet, on the other hand, they can be very distressing distractions when they lose their focus on the design of God for their being. They are, at best, symbols and signifiers of what God has done and is doing in Christ. That remains somewhat true even when those symbols and signifiers have long since been forgotten by the institution's present inhabitants.

Maybe it is only a personal confession, but my best thinking is that the authentic Church should not be identified with its institutional forms. It should, rather, be identified in the *authentic communities inhabited by the Spirit* which *are* part of God's missional movement—and which often inhabit those selfsame and forgetful church institutions.

Mystery!

It is also true that the authentic Church is continually faced with new challenges. It is always being refined and refounded into its God-given purpose by the Spirit. Let me say it: all of our heritage in the Biblical and apostolic teachings, as well as in the theology of the church, contains the record of the struggles of the church to be faithful in its missional calling. All of that is to be cherished. Those records contain the contributions made by previous generations which give depth and substance to the present Church's missional incarnation. That is evidenced in the writings of a huge number of wonderful teachers over the generations. You can make your own list. I think of many such as Augustine, Aquinas, Calvin, Luther, Menno Simmons, along with Ignatius Loyola, Dietrich Bonhoeffer, David Bosch, right down to Dallas Willard and John Paul II in the present ... and innumerable others along the way.[16]

---

[15] Cf. Hebrews 12:28 about our attitude in approaching worship and the things of God.

[16] Curtis Chang has made a formidable case that Augustine's *City of God* was his effort to assist the church in it mission of reaching the jaded, upper-class, educated pagan elites of late fourth century Rome. Likewise, Aquinas' *Summa Contra Gentiles* was his response to the missional challenge of the Muslim community in Spain, and his getting inside the Islamic worldview with the purpose of evangelizing these who posed a new and remarkable cultural challenge to the Christian faith. Cf. Chang, *Engaging Unbelief* (Downers Grove, IL.: Inter Varsity Press, 2000).

You Are Here: What Next?

Alan, just looking at you and your generation, I cannot think of a more exciting, unpredictable, completely new array of contextual and cultural factors than the ones in which you now live. There isn't any sense in pretending that we're operating in the predictable and congenial more-of-the-same setting of *Christendom*. No longer! We are in a fascinating new 'post-everything' (postmodern, anti-modern, hypermodern, ultramodern), neo-pagan, and altogether liminal *cultural whitewater*.

Add to that the fact that we are also living, for the first time, in such a global and bewildering merging and mixing of ethnic, religious, cultural, and social forces that it leaves one totally *limp*. The accessibility of information internationally has removed all of the walls of isolation between nationalities, religions, as well as ethnic and denominational cultural patterns. Who can deny that the vast culture of Islam is now on our own doorstep,[17] or that China looms larger and larger on the world scope with its estimated eighty million followers of Jesus? Like it or not, we are here. We are in the middle of this strange new world.

"Do you want to throw into that mix the growing awareness that the dominance of the 'Christian West' is now in its twilight?"

Absolutely. Plus, the hegemony of traditional denominations has essentially dissipated into insignificance.[18] In the formerly Christian West (the Northern hemisphere primarily in Europe and North America) we are now witnessing once powerful church institutions in disarray. We see them often in messy and murky confusion in the face of an omnipresent secular consumer-culture, and media-culture. The church's influence wanes as it loses its missional raison d'etre. Someone termed this present scene as the *whitewater of post-christian North America*. It's that and more. It's a "strange new land."

I (along with many others) have the premonition that in the coming century we will see the Church move beyond the ancient rivalries between Orthodox, Roman Catholic, Protestant, Pentecostal, and other

---

[17] My home city of Atlanta is replete with Islamic mosques, Hindu temples, and meeting houses of a host of other world religions in its many neighborhoods.
[18] I must confess that I resonate with H. Richard Niebuhr's dictum: "Denominationalism represents the moral failure of Christianity." Quoted by Lesslie Newbigin in *Foolishness to the Greeks*. (Grand Rapids, MI.: Wm. B. Eerdmans, 1986) P. 144.

independent traditions. The very missional context will demand that once again we *all* recognize that we (the Church) are *all* the "one holy catholic and apostolic Church" (as confessed in the Nicene Creed). We will both learn from each other and be enriched by the traditions of each other. Then we will see the Sovereign Lord *morph* the Church into some surprising form of missional newness such as we (formed as we are by centuries of division) can hardly imagine. Unimaginable, but thrilling. "The gates of hell will not prevail …"

"You really are a dreamer, aren't you?"

Standing In the Rubble

Parenthetically, as I record these journeys some several months later (November), the cogency of our conversation in that coffee shop takes on new importance. Recent events involving several conspicuous court cases and some profound and very public controversies over previously unquestioned community ethical and moral principles are a telling reminder that the hegemony of *Christendom* is collapsing around us. Why should we be surprised? For years perceptive observers have been telling us that we were back into the pagan culture similar to the first several centuries of the church's history (before *Christendom*).

For these past two hundred years the United States held (even if unconsciously) a Hebrew-Christian worldview, so that its symbols and ethical practices were essentially unquestioned. But the political foundations which named the ultimacy of "life, liberty, and the pursuit of happiness" (rather than the glory of God and obedience to his word) still assumed a common Hebrew-Christian worldview. As the culture has drifted away from that worldview those same cherished constitutional words do more to give license for autonomous, secular, neo-pagan, and self-aggrandizing pursuits. Rather than espousing the values of a Hebrew-Christian worldview our culture now finds these very symbols and practices to be archaic or offensive to itself, and so sues to have them removed.

We're learning the hard way that we are presently immersed, totally, in a truly non-congenial and missionary context. Our New Creation worldview with its resultant though patterns and behavior patterns serve to make us "aliens and strangers" in our own country. Thus it is that these court cases can (or ought to be) be for us a redemptive "wake-up call" to remind us of our missionary incarnation.

Future observers might well mark these recent days in 2003 as a seismic shift, or a cultural diastrophism (look that one up!) in the missionary role of the Church. But probably most churches will sleep through it. They are more likely to only whine about how "all those wicked people out there are attacking our way of life!"

Face it, this place and this time is our mission field. It is our own generation starting right where we are. What we're looking for in a Church is some kind of *base-camp* community of the Spirit-movement which will encourage and resource us for this mission. What Alan and all of us need is a Church community that is obedient to Jesus Christ in his compassion for those still walking in the darkness of this disenchanted scene. That may be more easily said than discovered.

All that Alan needs to do in order to discover his mission field is to get into conversations with most of his own peers to realize how very much they are captives to that darkness.[19] They are products of a culture that invents its own truth (or its multiple truths). It determines its own code of behavior without the benefit of any of the historical cultural roots which the Christian community once provided. It creates *designer gods* to its own liking. Alan's generation is much more a product of the Information Age in all of its "without boundaries" or "it works for me" expressions—than any previous generation in modern history.

I, by contrast, am from a generation that grew up formed by all of the traditions of the great Biblical story. That was still present in the culture, even among those who did not identify with the Christian faith. The cultural influences of the Hebrew-Christian worldview were very apparent. That is no longer so. That, consequently, has left a huge vacuum in this present generation. In every human psyche there still resides some kind of an inarticulate longing for the "heart's true home" (whatever that might be). It is both sad and fascinating to watch totally secular and

---

[19] One thinks of Middleton and Walsh's *Truth Is Stranger Than It Used to Be* (Downers Grove, IL: Inter Varsity Press, 1995) as one of the superb and profoundly insightful explications of the cultural thought-patterns of the postmodern age. This is no minor variation in thinking, but a radical shift that most North American church folk have not even begun to take seriously.

detached young adults begin to look around and wonder what it is all about. Sometimes church institutions wake up to their missional calling and provide a welcoming place for persons such as these to come with all their doubts and cynicism and inquiry. But not often enough!

The church is struggling to understand itself in such a strange new land. We're caught up in that struggle.

It's A Tough Call

We are living as "children of Light" in this "strange new land." It can be a *tough call* to find our place in and among and with the people of God in some form of Church at any given place and time.[20] It is something we must always approach with humility and the grace of God. The answer to any question about the authenticity of a particular church, or Christian community, is more-than-likely both: "Yes, it almost is;" and "No, it's not quite." It *is* and it *isn't*—in varying degrees! But that doesn't in any way diminish God's calling to you and to me to be his practitioners of the very New Creation authenticity which we seek. Somebody has to be the flesh-and-blood demonstration of that authenticity to the flock of God.[21] I am convinced that such authentic living in the community is, by virtue of our baptism into the Body of Christ, a responsibility given to every one of us by God.

Can you handle that?

"It's a stretch."

It's a stretch because we keep on thinking primarily of larger and more impersonal church institutions. Let me hasten on to say that in such a calling every believer needs a *primary* or *smaller* community of persons with whom he or she can mutually converse, minister, encourage, and keep

---

[20] We need to acknowledge the place of Providence in our being in a particular church body. It may *not* be of our choosing. It may be an 'accident' or the 'only known option'. Globally most followers of Jesus Christ do not have the multiple choices of church community. They cannot 'church shop' or jump from one to another such as often afflicts North Americans.

[21] In I Peter 5:3 Peter tells the Elders that, among other things, they are to be models of God, or examples to the flock. Somebody has to demonstrate in flesh and blood what it means to be a follower of, or believer in Jesus Christ.

clear focus on their common calling by Christ, … even if it's just one or two others. Our Seven Signs of Authenticity need to be practiced in and among a *household* of others in Christ in which all have *names* and *faces* and *stories*. It needs a context in which all assume some accountability to specific *each others*. Sterile and impersonal *societal* relationships simply will not suffice. Just register that need in your data base. Such smaller primary groups have been, are, and will be one of the most formative and under-documented Spirit-agents in the long history of the Church!

Brace yourself, because I'm finally ready to respond to the pastor's inquiry of you about "joining" West Park Church. I've been attempting (delicately) to indicate that such church institutions as West Park are probably only *secondary* to the kind of *primary* group that I just proposed. I make that distinction because (to my mind) such church institutions have the capacity to be either *major distractions* to discipleship or (more hopefully) *wonderful encouragers* of such discipleship—or maybe both! They can be creators and encouragers of primary New Creation communities. They can provide resources and networks that provoke and call forth our signs of authenticity. Or, on the other hand, they may have nothing at all to do with them. Many exist only as some kind of enclave for comfortable spirituality, good but inconsequential programs, and other 'religious' activities that distract the participants from the mission of God.

I may be confusing you more than I'm helping you here.

Let me give you an illustration. It is interesting that in Communist China it was only when the Cultural Revolution took place, and when the Church was disenfranchised, persecuted, and dispossessed of its institutional property—that something took place which no one had planned. The Church went *underground*! The followers of Jesus (Catholic or Protestant or Independent or Pentecostal), out of necessity and for their survival, met in house churches. They became clandestine cells. What happened? The gospel 'took-off' uncontrollably and with quantum growth! What in the world happened? Well, when all that you have left to cling to is your calling by Jesus Christ, and to the power of God in your lives, … then you are compelled to focus on what it is that God has called the Church to be and do in the first place.[22]

---

[22] Missiologist (and friend) Howard Snyder has provocatively proposed that if we really want to know the vitality of our churches, then we need to sell the buildings, then we'll

Enchanted Community

It is probably (though arguably) true that (were it quantifiable) the largest expression of Christian community in the world today is in *house churches*.[23] They are versatile and they can exist flexibly, temporarily, and pragmatically, and so are able provide both the "one another" support and the community dimension for a season. Then, when circumstances change, they can cease to exist, move, or morph into another form of New Creation community. They are not encumbered with institutional baggage.

West Park Church is somewhat typical of many substantial older denominational Protestant congregations. Measure it by our *authenticity dialog bars* and it would probably do pretty well on some of the signs, and then blink out totally on others. But then, that could be said of most of the larger churches that I know. As for you, in a year or two you might land in some other nation where your only option would be, say, for a Roman Catholic, or an Orthodox institution, or maybe a Pentecostal assembly, or some local expression of Christian community (or maybe into a scene with no discernable Christian presence at all!). Those churches from other traditions would probably measure up not unlike West Park. They might, for instance, be pretty impressive on one or more of the signs, and then blank on others.

Disenchantment is, unfortunately, a perennial pathology for churches that have had institutional form for too long. Some have lots of 'form' and no Life. Others have real Spirit-Life while having, at the same time a rather ill-defined or casual form. Some will have no memory of the Church's past history or of its existence beyond their own assembly. That leaves them impoverished in many ways. Others will live in the past and be seemingly oblivious to their present mission.

Like I say, Alan, not always an easy call to make.

But what I want to push you toward is this: church history keeps turning up the fact that within so many existing church institutions, within so many church forms that may seem to be totally forgetful of their calling, … there frequently are those cells ("sleeper cells?") of true Life. In

---

see how much reality is present (cf. *Radical Renewal: The Problem of Wineskins* (Houston, TX, Touch Publications. 1996).

[23] I would refer you to: Wolfgang Simson, *Houses That Changed the World* (U.K.: OM Publishing/Paternoster, 1998); Jim Petersen, *Church Without Walls* (Colorado Springs, CO.: NavPress, 1992); Robert and Julia Banks, *The Church Comes Home* (Australia: Albatross Books, 1986).

unexpected places you will discover colonies or *pockets of authenticity* as persons, such as yourself, seeking to live out their calling faithfully with "one another." They do that in the midst of the somewhat inauthentic and forgetful church institutions. That is true of West Park Church! Many of the great episodes of *Enchanted* life in the history of the Church's mission have come out of such seemingly moribund institutions.

"Moribund?"

Apparently dead, OK? And sometimes when it all looks most unlikely, then those same "sleeper cells" will burst into a flame that invigorates again the larger unlikely church scene with authenticity. Such cells are made up of "one anothers" (like you) who have found each other and who have determined together to seek the glory of God, not where they *are not*, but where they *are*. They will have accepted their calling and incarnation in midst that very immediate and forgetful and inauthentic ecclesial wasteland—and *not* by seeking escape into some other place. It has been just such cells that have been my own primary source of encouragement over these past decades in many different ecclesiastical landscapes.

Alan, I am not even raising up here the possibility of such cells becoming the seed for planting a new church. That's a whole different subject. But it is no secret that healthy new churches come out of (and are also built in) such cells of Spirit-life.

"Does that mean that I and my three friends on campus could be experiencing more of an authentic New Creation community than lots of folk residing in formidable church institutions?"

Could be. But let me come back to you (or me, for that matter). Don't discount the role of the larger assemblies such as West Park Church. They can be and should be: 1) the context of contacts with the larger Christian community; 2) the forums for profound teaching of the Word of God; 3) the agencies of cooperation in missional outreach; 4) the forums for discussion on cultural challenges to the faith; 5) contexts of worship, adoration, prayer, and the so-called 'sacramental mysteries'; plus, 6) the rallying points for any (or all) of our Seven Signs of Authenticity. You only have to look at the story of two millennia of the Church in mission to realize this.[24]

---

[24] Which opens up the possibility that church institutions that are authentic will be demonstrating their missional sign/authenticity by spawning off new church communities

But for you it still begins with God at work in *you*! You can't live your life as a follower of Jesus Christ dependent on the someone else's obedience to Christ's word. It begins with you! I love Paul's word to the timid Timothy: "... and what you have heard from me among many witnesses, entrust to faithful men who will be able to teach others also."[25]

"Excuse me, but where did you come up with all this stuff? I mean, I'm getting a whole lot more than I bargained for. But now you've got me interested. All this stuff is obviously a subject that has been brewing in your tank for a long time. How did you get into this weird kind of thinking that you're unloading on me? There was obviously something brewing in you before I met you here in this coffee shop and punched your button those months ago. Sometime you've got to tell me that story."

I had to chuckle at that one. The problem that my generation has with guys like Alan (who is fifty years my junior) is that they don't like disembodied treatises. They want to know something that has flesh and blood *now*. I had been rambling around with Alan for months now, and it had to happen. It finally did. He wanted to know what influences and experiences had brought me to all of these concepts we had been talking about. My generation was good at theorizing and discussing abstract ideas, and never looking behind the mask of one another. I knew he had me impaled on a really good question, but one which I had never deliberately articulated for myself.

So I continued: You've got me on that one. That's a whole other discussion and it could take a long time. That's for another time.

I know you want me to tie all this up, and I do have at least one more piece that I hope we can process together before we sign off on this conversation.

"Only one. Yeah, right!"

(cell-based, experimental, often temporary), in order to reach non-Christians, met a need, or bring Light and Life into new areas.

[25] II Timothy 2:2

Journey Ten
Enchanted Community Begins With ...

To: bob.henderson@belbury.com
From: alan2@gitech.org
Date: Fri, 5 Dec 2003
Subject: So What? Where Now?

Bob: I know we've got to tie this thing up pretty soon. My schedule is getting sort of wild here at school. After all, we've been on this crazy trip now for months. On the one hand, I'm still stuck with my initial dilemma of what to do with the request from the pastor of West Park Church about joining his club. How does it fits with my sense of discipleship? Then on the other hand I'm tracking with you on the whole question of why the Church even exists in the first place—and frankly, it gets both more confusing but more exciting to me all the time.

Last weekend I escaped out to the Cistercian monastery just to find some quiet to have a personal retreat and digest all we have been discussing. Sitting there in the chapel, and looking around, listening to the monks chant the psalms, absorbing centuries of tradition, aware of their reverence for the Host on the altar—I guess it all reminded me that, notwithstanding the enormous cost in time and labor and money expended to build that place, it is still somehow a remarkable signifier of something so awesome and timeless. It reminded me of all of the conversations you and I have had about how much of the Church really is a mystery, so unexplainable, provisional and imperfect—yet it is still somehow an echo or a rumor of the glory of God in physical form.

One of the things I was thinking (again) was about those haunting descriptions we came up with about that original community. Do you remember that we described their disenchantment as: orphaned, suddenly alone, lost to their heart's True Home, intimates became strangers, silence replaced song, sadness eclipsed joy, darkness descended, hope faded, the magic and the enchantment ... but a memory, fear replaced trust, "you will be like God" they were told but it didn't happen. It was not supposed to be this way! Death, dissonance, "all creation groans, ... waiting ..."

Remember all that?

What brought all of that back to my mind was that there were so many people of my own age there looking, reflecting. My impression (from what I observed and heard in their muted conversations) was that these weren't necessarily the Catholic devout. I think they were just people very much like me, out there on some kind of a quest after something just beyond their grasp. And I was wondering how much of our discussions about the authentic New Creation community would resonate with them. Does that make sense to you? It whetted my desire even more to know just how I, and we, communicate Christ to such people. When Jesus builds his Church, do the 'orphaned' find community? Do they find that they're not 'alone' any more? Do they find that the Church is the company of others who have found again their 'heart's true Home'? Does the aura of *enchantment* return? Where would they look? What would they listen for? How would that 'something just beyond their grasp' communicate to them? That's pretty important for me to figure out at this point. Can we go there whenever we get together again? Alan.

To: Alan2@gitech.org
From: bob.henderson@belbury.com
Date: Sat, 6 Dec, 2003
Subject: We should go there!

Enchanted Community Begins With…

Alan, I love your questions. By all means, we should go there. We *must*, actually.

You've brought us all the way round to one of our earliest observations, which was that when that Adam and Eve, in their grasp for autonomy, rebelled and left God out of their equation … that the whole thing began to unravel for the very reason that it violated the very basis of God's *Shalom*. All of those descriptions you remembered describe what resulted when they estranged themselves from the God. What they didn't anticipate was that they would also become strangers (even enemies) to each other. Those two foundations of true human community were destroyed. So I think that it's not only legitimate but downright critical that we ask those questions about what those fellow-seekers will find in the Church.

By all means let's go there. You'll be taking off for the Christmas holidays shortly, so could we, maybe, agree on some time, like a Saturday in January to land somewhere and try to see if we're close to some satisfactory resolution of all these questions we've got floating around? Bob

---

To: bob.henderson@belbury.com
From: alan2@gitech.org
Date: Sun, 6 Dec 2003
Subject: Sounds like a plan

Bob, I am leaving for the holidays this week, but maybe we could set aside Saturday, January 10 for some time. If the weather is not too awful, maybe we could go back out to the monastery for the day. We could find a corner or take some walks, pray together – and maybe we can get some sense that we've done a good day's work after all these months. If the weather's going to be horrible, could we do it at your place? Have a wonderful Christmas. Alan.

A Day at the Monastery

The Saturday was, happily, one of those gorgeous and mild winter days that come to us occasionally in Georgia. By this time we had both become well acquainted with the guestmaster at the monastery and I had called ahead and asked his permission to spend the day there. In that we didn't need overnight accommodations he was happy to offer us the hospitality of the community. He even asked how he could assist in making our time more fruitful. So Alan and I landed there, checked in and had a cup of coffee and spent some time reporting to each other about Christmas activities.

Caught In An Irresistible Movement

We strolled outside into the bright winter sunshine in silence for a while. Then Alan dropped the question:

"OK. What's the plan? Where do we go with this? How do we corral all of these months of conversation with each other and bring it home to some practical conclusion?"

Here I was with this incredibly thoughtful, winsome, and gifted guy. He had (for whatever reasons) sought me out, and was trusting me with this huge question pertaining to his life. I was not about to rush into any superficial or distracting responses to such a critical inquiry. But he was right. It was time to tie some things together. Alan didn't need a theological treatise from me. He was looking for some understanding that would give him conviction in his *praxis* of the new life he had in Christ.

I thought about it, and finally said: OK. Let's bite the bullet and take a shot at it.

Let me tell you a story. The other evening four of us were sitting together in a steak house facing each other across the booth. We had decided on the spur of the moment to eat together. But there is more to it than that. Each of us were products of the transforming work of Christ. Several years ago the Spirit of God had brought the four of us together and had given us a very special bond of love for each other. We had spent time being formed by the Word of Christ in Bible study. We had, for several years, shared our pilgrimages. We had some sense of accountability to each other as we sought to live out or lives of obedience to the mission of God in our daily lives. We had been in a prayer discipline together. We had a remarkable degree of intimacy with each other in the Spirit.

Enchanted Community Begins With...

If you think about it, all of our "signs" about the *authenticity* of Church and New Creation were there in that booth. Anyone sitting in with us on that evening, and listening to our conversation, but who had never been through the *back of the wardrobe* (the Door into Christ) would not even have had a clue what it was all about.

What was going on? Was this foursome the Church? Was this an expression of being *called-out* by Jesus Christ into his New Creation? Was this a participation in the community in the Spirit?

"Well, ... was it?"

Hang on to that one.

Or another story. I know a guy who was cruising along brilliantly in his academic career, consumed by his fascination with knowledge and the exploration of new subjects, ... when inexplicably something intruded and made him aware of his incompleteness. Sound like someone we both know?

"Sounds familiar."

Alright, now that we know who we're talking about, ... *something* made you realize that there was a bigger picture. Face it: *something* (or *Someone*) provoked you to begin looking, and that *looking* somehow brought you irresistibly to a discovery, ... and then to embrace Jesus Christ as the answer to your quest. Whatever it was that happened to you, you experienced the "lights going on" in your mind and life. Newness, freedom, joy. But that wasn't all. That same mysterious *something* drew you inexplicably to three other guys from the campus community. All four of you had encountered Jesus Christ in different ways. That *something* bonded the four of you together. What was going on?

The Spirit-movement was going on, that's what was going on. And you were caught up in it.

The four of you guys all had the same new life in the Spirit—the Spirit of the Father and of the Son. You all had embraced Jesus Christ as the focus of your lives, as Savior, as Lord. You spent time together studying the scriptures, praying, laughing, processing your lives and responsibilities, ... and Jesus was present with you by his own Spirit. Because of that Presence among you, you all shared a strong passion to build bridges to your acquaintances who were still *outside* in the darkness of disenchantment. But now, take note: once again all of our *evidences of authenticity* are present in your foursome. How do you explain that?

Enchanted Community

"So, are me any my guys really the Church?"

Listen: if some one from outside of the Door (Jesus) were to sit in with either of these two gatherings (mine in the steak house or yours with your buddies), someone who was still in the 'dark', their first response might be: "These guys are really weird!" That might be (or probably is) true. But then you can just bet your life that behind that immediate cynical appraisal, they just might also be pondering: "These guys really do see something, hear something, know something that I don't. I wonder what it is."

Are we talking about *enchantment* here, or what?

That's not the end of it. The four of us in that booth at the steak house met each other at West Park Church. And we two couples overlap with other "pocket groups" of New Creation folk from West Park who are of like heart and mind. Something only explainable by the Spirit is going on that binds us to one another. In a similar way I have met with other groups (as have you) on your campus. I have met with a small group of international students studying scripture there, and we were instantly bonded and were one in the Spirit. We instantly bridged the huge cultural and ethnic differences because we were one in Christ. Explain that!

You've gotten caught up in a movement, in the irresistible Spirit-movement.

"Say what?"

It gets wilder still. Try multiplying these two stories by some huge exponential factor, and then multiply that times the two millennia of the Church's story. Factor-in all of the huge variety of ways in which the Spirit of Christ has been at work actually building the Church. Just look at it! It's totally awesome. We're talking about God's great *rescue-reconcile-and-recreate* movement. We're looking at God's design to magnify his own Glory by making all things new.[1] Think back to that earliest scene in Genesis when God spoke about "the seed of a woman" bruising the serpent's head. Look at the angelic messengers promising to the patriarch Abraham that in his seed should all the people groups (nations) of the world be blessed. Then listen as the prophets in the seventh century B.C. hold out the promise of an Anointed One, a Messiah, who would accomplish God's salvation. Stand in awe as Jesus of Nazareth comes into human history to

---

[1] Revelation 21:5

inaugurate this promised New Creation, this Dominion of God, ... and so to reconcile the world to God by the blood of his Cross.

Then there was his statement that caught your attention: "I will build my Church." He spoke that promise knowing full well all the vicious opposition they would face in the forces of darkness. Connect that affirmation to his enigmatic statement (made to his still non-comprehending followers) that they couldn't even begin to accomplish what he was giving them to do *without the Spirit.* Jesus would build his Church, and he would do it by the powerful working of his own divine Life within them. He would do it by the Spirit whom he would send upon them.

"Like, they really would be *enchanted*, right?"

You got it.

Add to that Jesus' interesting metaphor about the Spirit being like the *wind* that blows wherever it wants to. You can see where the wind has been but then you don't know where it comes from, or where it is going. When you read the account of all of that beginning to take place it begins to give you some clues to your question to me about the Church. Jesus launched his Spirit-movement in Jerusalem. Then it moved out to Samaria. Then into Asia Minor, Greece, and Rome, ... and so on out into the centuries that followed. It has moved to the far places of the world, right down to our present and to you and me.

So much can be learned by simply reading into the side streets and back alleys of church history—not only about all the aberrations and eccentricities but about the irresistibility of Christ's building his Church

The Church Is Still a Mystery

What's this all about? The Church is still a mystery. One person, then a group of persons, or an assembly of people, maybe a household, a gathering by the riverside, intentional communities, mission groups, colonies of exiles, small informal settings, large institutional settings ... *the Wind blows.* The Spirit moves irresistibly across boundaries and around barriers and into obscure settings. It refuses to be held captive by institutions or by restricting theological definitions. In its wake ... are communities of

New Creation individuals (like our own) which are the evidence. And Jesus Christ is building his Church.

Look at God's faithful folk who find their company of New Creation sojourners in such a vast variety of ways. Some engaged in the high drama of the worship and the icons of the Orthodox Church. Some are nurtured in the Eucharistic ritual of the Roman Mass, or in the worship traditions of the great diversity of God's folk both in highly formal settings, and others in innovative expressions. Some are formed into discipleship in the rambunctious and expectant spontaneity of Pentecostal assemblies. Add in to the mix such companies as your foursome on campus. But then you must also take into account house churches, or clandestine gatherings, which are somewhat out of sight. They may well make up the largest expression of the Church in the world today. Take them all seriously. They're all part of the mystery and the irresistibility of the Church as a Spirit-movement.

That is more important than you realize, Alan. Given the nature of our transient society and this shrinking world, ... any one of these could well be where you yourself will find fellow sojourners in God's New Creation. The Church is a world Church, and God's family gathers in Jesus' Name in all of those contexts. You never know where you may land in some as-yet-unknown destination of your career. You may be surprised to discover authentic and *enchanted* colonies of Salt and Light in any one of these many expressions in the world Church. After all, that's the role that West Park Church played in your life and mine!

That's where we are. Those are only the expressions of New Creation that are somewhat visible to us. But whatever you do, don't stop looking beyond those *in-process* communities. Don't stop looking to that *eschatological design* of God for his Truly Human community. Don't stop looking for his New Creation community now being built on Jesus Christ by the Spirit. Don't stop pursuing the *authenticity* of the *Truly Human community in the embrace of the Trinitarian Community*. The Church: the glory of God. Don't stop insisting on the Church being faithfully engaged in the Mission of God to bless all the nations—and to invite them again through the Christ the Door into their heart's true home. Don't forget that God designs to bless every ethnic and cultural group in the world, ... to seek and to rescue his lost children through his Dear Son. Don't stop! Don't forget!

Enchanted Community Begins With…

"Whoa! Let me process that for a few minutes."

So we kept strolling around, stopping occasionally to sit on a bench and take in the winter landscape. Finally Alan broke the silence:

"You know what I think? I remember all those off-hand adjectives you dropped on me when I first asked you that question about the Church, remember them? *Enigmatic, enchanted, confusing, mysterious, awesome, contradictory, uncontrollable, clandestine, impossible, laughable, and unpredictable.* I remember them. I asked you to write them down for me. I have your notes. I think you were serious, weren't you?"

Really? No! You caught me so off guard that I responded out of my gut. But maybe they were more inspired than either one of us knew. Now that you repeat them back to me, I sort of like them! Jesus really *is* building his Church. There are now, around the world, colonies of Hindu followers of Jesus, Islamic followers of Isa (Jesus), Messianic Jews, not to mention the Church's penetration into the most closed political systems of the world. It's awesome to watch. Every new generation is a new culture. All of the destructive pathologies of the darkness keep trying to quench the movement, but it keeps on breaking out in some new expression. It is a Movement of Hope, if it is anything at all.

God Moves In A Mysterious Way

A couple of centuries ago William Cowper wrote something about this mystery and this enchantment in a wonderful poem-hymn:

> *God moves in a mysterious way His wonders to perform: …*
> *Deep in unfathomable mines of never-failing skill,*
> *He treasures up His bright designs,*
> *and works His sovereign will.*[2]

I think Cowper captured something of the mystery and enchantment: "unfathomable mines of never-failing skill, … His bright designs …"

---

[2] William Cowper c 1774

All of that, and more, is what you've gotten caught up in. There is no way that the Church can be explained humanly. You can't capture it in a theological proposition[3] or contain it in an institution. You can try, but it won't work. It is a Spirit-movement. It is Missional movement. It is a Glory movement. And behind it all is Jesus Christ irresistibly building his Church just as he said that he would. Now you've gotten caught up in it in the mystery of it all.

Do you have any problem with that?

"No. Cool!

"Do you want to spell out your Spirit-missional-glory movement thing?"

I grabbed those out of the air. But they fit. The Spirit of the Father and the Son is the inexplicable power that is at work. Jesus said that the power of the Spirit is like the "wind" or like "leaven in a loaf" which works unmistakably but without being seen. So is the building of the Church. It is a work of the Spirit. Remember that the apostle referred to the Church as the "dwelling place of God by the Spirit."

As for Mission – the whole of human history is the story of God's great rescue mission. God's Mission focuses ultimately in Jesus Christ, who is the Great Rescuer. It is for such a Mission that the Church has been created. It is the community and the agent of the great Missional Heart of God. Human history is only the scaffolding—the building is the Church! Then, always, *always*, the Spirit and the Church's mission are the glory of God. The Church is to be a bright and shining witness to the wonder and glory and love and ultimacy of God. You wrap those all together and then you will catch something of the flavor of the movement. You could toss in some more if you wanted to, ... like, maybe a Joy movement, or a Love movement—just so long as it all focuses in God and his glory, and his mission carried out through Christ and by the Spirit. OK?

---

[3] I have in my notes that the Church is: institutionally anti-institutional, predictably unpredictable, definably undefinable, securely insecure, perfectly imperfect, eternally temporal – glory in the most unlikely vessels. Or maybe as F. R. Maltby stated it: "The [New Testament] church was absurdly happy, completely fearless, and constantly in trouble." (Quoted in W. Barclay, *The Letters to the Galatians and Ephesians* (Philadelphia, Westminster Press, 1958) p. 146.

Enchanted Community Begins With...

Authenticity?

"Time Out! Let's stop right there. You're really hung up on this 'authenticity' bit, ... and I think I'm tracking with you. But I don't think I've ever seen that word in scripture, and certainly not spelled out in any 'seven signs'. So where'd you come up with this?"

Good shot! And you're quite right. It's not in the Bible as such. But then again it is (is that *doublespeak* or what?). Try out the word *holiness*. I think that word comes close. It is an enormously prominent word in scripture. Unfortunately *holiness* doesn't get much 'press' in today's church. But since you've asked me about my "take" on the Church, I'm giving you the responses of my own discipleship. I'm not proposing any kind of rule or a theological formula. Is that OK with you?

"No problem."

As for my seven 'evidences' (or Signs of Authenticity that I'm sharing with you), they are really only the disciplines that I've distilled out of a lot of my own Bible study. Saint Patrick was said to have had his *Breastplate*, which was a set of his daily disciplines. As he laced up his tunic each day he prayed over each step as he figuratively "bound on to himself" a set of theological and Biblical propositions in order to keep himself well-balanced in his incredible leadership of founding the Church in Ireland. My seven Signs of Authenticity are like Patrick's breastplate. They are a set of disciplines that I have discovered to give me similar balance in my own life and role of Spirit-influence in the Church.

I use *authenticity* as a word very much akin to the Biblical word *holiness*. The two words signify something of the same reality. Holiness has to do with the flavor of our lives being 'in-*synch*' with the Life of God. As a consequence, we become those 'in-synch' with the *each others* with whom we share the Life of the Spirit within the household of faith. Holiness is our living-out of the life in God (or in Christ) which is ours by the Spirit. It is the Spirit-life of God inhabiting us both individually, and in our relations with others and in the human community. It is God glorifying Himself in us through our *praxis* of New Creation life (if that makes any sense). It's "Like father, like child." It's a consistency of life, or a *wholesome consistency*. It is beholding the glory of the Lord and so being transformed into the same image, from one degree of glory to another.[4]

---

[4] II Corinthians 3:18.

Let me put it another way. God is *consummately who He is*: God is *holy*. As we, then, are embraced by Him through Christ, and as we have his Spirit at work within us, ... we then become consummately *who we are created to be* in Him—we are made *holy*. That is what *true humanity* is all about. The life and character of God in us is what makes us to be authentic both individually and as a community. It creates us *holy*.

For instance, there is the beautiful and challenging word in Hebrews: "Strive for peace with everyone, and for *holiness without which no one will see the Lord*" (italics mine)? It's like: strive for authenticity in your New Creation life. Or maybe the creed could be paraphrased: We believe in the one, *authentic/holy*, catholic, and apostolic Church! How does that sound? And wherever that *authenticity* is evident, then the cynicism of those outside is silenced. Where it is present there is inevitably the return of song, and joy, and hope, and love—all those blessings which were lost when the human community left God out of the equation.

"I'm still tracking.

"So how does that authenticity exhibit itself in us and in the Church?"

My disciplines would say that I must, first of all, acknowledge that it is the Spirit of holiness[5] who has called me into Jesus Christ. It is the same Spirit who inhabits me with the true Life of God, that Life which I have only in and through Jesus Christ. That, in turn, means that we know *absolutely* that such a humanly incomprehensible New Life cannot take place apart from the Spirit's dynamic presence. We know that it is in the Spirit that we see and anticipate God's irresistible working far beyond anything that we could ever ask or imagine.

All of our other signs of authenticity are made possible and animated by the Spirit. It is the Spirit of the Father in me (and us) that exalts the Son, and the Spirit of the Son in me that exalts the Father. But the Father's glory is in Jesus Christ, so the Church's authenticity is always exhibited in a community that is Christ-focused. It can't be anything else and claim to be the Church. It all begins with you and me being so focused on our Lord Jesus Christ in all that we do and say.

And it is also the Spirit who has, in the mystery of it all, given us the Word of Christ and the witness of God's self-revelation in the many-

---

[5] Romans 1:4

splendored writings of contained in the Bible. If we are to worship in Spirit and in truth, then the dear Lord knows we need some standard of truth and knowledge—so, scripture. The apostles consequently put great emphasis on *knowing*, on the Word of Christ dwelling richly in the midst of the community—so that the Church doesn't lose its bearing or wander into something less or other than God's bright design.

"OK, OK. I get the connection. So the rest of your seven signs: prayer, mutual love, thinking and behavior, and God's mission—all of those are expressions of our connect, our authenticity, our in-synch with God, ... holiness, right?"

You got it.

It's also helps to me to turn the order of my list *upside-down* and to begin with the sign of our engagement in the Mission of God. It helps me to look back through that particular lense, and see how the other six signs are integral to God carrying out his missional design through the authentic Church. The two *praxis* signs (just previous to the mission sign) are especially critical in our age of cynicism. They're critical to your generation which is suspicious of words but which, at the same time, is looking for Life. There is a large component of cynicism about the church among your friends.

But cynicism about the church is answered only by authenticity of New Creation Life exhibited in the thinking and behavior of Jesus' followers. For your peers to be able to *see* a community that not only loves and cares for each other, as God in Christ loves and cares for us—but also to *see* a community whose behavior and thinking are redolent with the wonder and honesty and profundity and creativity and joy of God's New Creation ... is an enormously powerful testimony to *something Enchanted*!

The Church is authentic in direct proportion to its authenticity in something that looks and smells and thinks and lives like our seven signs. I think that's the "*holiness* without which no one will see the Lord" is all about.[6]

"I got that one, but we're not there yet.

"You've got to help me over another hump. Jesus calls us into this thing called 'the Church'. OK? He sends the Spirit to be the Creator of

---

[6] Hebrews 12:14

it in all of the mystery and irresistibility of the design. I got that. Then he draws me, he draws us, to himself and to each other. I can work with that. But it's a big jump to get from *that* ... to West Park Church! I mean all of the complex inner workings, the tame religious life of that scene just sort of blows me away. How does it fit, ... and where?"

Visible Expressions of the Church

Do you ever still get sucked back into the patterns of your former life, your life before you came to Christ?

"Probably at least once a day!"

Or do you ever get distracted into some agenda that for a time displaces your focus on what Jesus has called you to be and do?

"How did you know?"

Or maybe: Are you ever tempted to try to equivocate or dilute the demands of discipleship to make them fit some personal passion, or some cultural *zeitgeist*?

"*Zeitgeist*? Where are you going with this?"

Where I'm going is simply to say (that as we have already agreed) that the Church is totally and continually *in process*. It lives with the continuing reality of its own *merely human* proclivity to leave God out—and to become, thereby, a merely human religious society. It is always tempted to conform to the cultural *zeitgeists*. It happens! And the bigger and more traditional and more institutional it becomes, the more this seems to happen. Almost inevitably and inadvertently the focus tends to be shifted from the Mission of God toward the success and survival of the institution with its buildings, budget, staff, membership, status, ... and all that ecclesiastical stuff that, as you say, seems so "tame."

But let's don't go there yet.

I look at three major types or expressions (or manifestation) of this movement which we call the *Church*. Jesus calls his people together, in and by the Spirit, in order to live-out the "community of the New Creation." Let me try to spell that out in three church expressions: *Primary Churches*, *Church Assemblies*, and *Church Institutions*.

1.) The **Primary Church** is something like you and the other three guys on campus. Or it is like a table fellowship, or a house church. It has

Enchanted Community Begins With…

to be small: two or three or a dozen. It's like you and me over these recent months. It's intimate. Everybody in it has a *name* and a *face* and a *story*. It prays. The members hold each other in some degree of accountability for their new life in Christ. They read and study and discuss together the Word of Christ as they seek to incarnate the New Creation in their daily lives. They shares weaknesses and strengths, joys and sorrows.

    I see this *Primary Church* as about the only context in which our fifth sign about 'One Another Love' really being practicable. We cannot actually love each other as Christ loved us *in theory*, or in the abstract, or in some large and impersonal society. It is important for you and your guys at the university. For me such a primary church has always been the somewhat unplanned-for but (at the same time) the most formative part of my sojourn into discipleship. And for the sake of our conversation here, I have found just such a bunch of primary church expressions inhabiting West Park Church in the same way that you have found one in your four guys on campus! That is why the "house church" is such a huge phenomenon in the building of the Church by Jesus Christ around the world today (as well as over the centuries).

    I should add that such a single *Primary Church* may not be exclusive for us. Actually, as the Spirit moves in you and in others, you may find complementary and sometimes overlapping expressions such as mission groups, study groups, focus groups, neighborhood groups, professional groups—but one of them will usually have priority in your life. For instance, I have been part of a group of church leaders from across the nation who have met together annually for 28 years simply because we needed a support and confidentiality fellowship of other such leaders. That kind of intimacy was impossible in our local church settings, given the public roles of leadership that we occupied. At the same time, I have usually been in some small fellowship in the place where I lived. Such groups may be quite temporary, or they may be long-enduring. But they are all part of the Spirit movement in building the Church.

    Primary Church expressions are like (to use a mountain climbing metaphor) the Base Camps from which the adventurers find their resources and places of meeting before venturing out to tackle the 'ascent' of their daily mission as Salt and Light. It is also my own opinion that it is in the intimacy between the participants of such primary churches that a true pastor-teacher can function most effectively. It is where disciplemaking

Enchanted Community

takes place at its best. It is where we discover our true humanity in Christ and in the context of *one another.*

2.) As the Church grows, and as the *Primary Church* expressions clone themselves into more and more colonies (more Base Camps), there is a very natural and often very helpful meeting together in **Church Assemblies**—in larger gatherings—for mutual purposes. Persons in *Primary Churches* naturally want to meet and know others of Jesus' followers in their neighborhood, town or city, or professional and special interest contexts. They do this through larger assemblies, in local congregations, in congresses and conventions, as well as in conferences and associations. Such assemblies are most useful for mutual benefit through teaching and support, as well as for common causes in the Mission of God. They may be temporary (such as in conferences, or weekend retreats) or they may be more long-lasting and semi-permanent.

To continue our mountain climbing metaphor, *Assemblies* are like the "Staging Areas" where groups of climbers with their mutual goal are equipped, warned, made ready, reinforce each other, taught—becoming familiar with all those pieces necessary to engage for their move on to base camps. They are all anticipating and preparing for the unknown challenges and hazards before them.

We see *Assemblies* right away in the early Church. After thousands came to new life at the Pentecost outpouring, Luke writes of the multitude who had believed being together both in public (assemblies) and from house to house (primary churches). To have a larger forum where the apostolic teachings (the Word of Christ) could be taught to all by the apostles was only natural. Together they evidently confronted their growth pains, their mutual persecution by the authorities, the needs of indigent members, plus all kinds of mutual life requirements. Note, however, that they used public spaces, such as the porch of the temple, or a rented hall, or some such available gathering place. The infrastructure for all of this seems to have emerged along the way.

3.) **Church Institutions** are more problematic. Now we're talking about expressions of the church such as West Park Church (or St. Athanasius, or Holy Name, or Grace Bible, or whatever). In many ways these institutions could be an aberration—but they happened. For better or worse … we've got them! They are a later development in the Spirit movement. So long as the Church was a minority and a threat, and was even illegal, and so long as it was primarily a mission movement, the very idea of forming institutions, of putting down permanent roots, of creating all of the institutional accoutrements, was hardly even an issue.

I need to add, however, that *Church Institutions* are a normal development. The Church was growing and getting more complex and faced with more internal and external challenges. There was, almost inescapably, that normal desire for some definable form and some sense of inner order. But *Church Institutions* are where you need a good sense of humor. This is so because it is with them that the *mystery* and the *ambiguity* of the Church gets really 'thick'. It is a natural development to want a *place* and to want *security* and *permanence*—none of which Jesus ever promised by the way. The problem is that those natural human desires quite easily devolve into a desire for power and control and permanence, which in turn can easily quench the Spirit. They can also side-track the missional movement. They can side-track the authentic Church! Such desires can easily become a seduction away from the "pilgrims and strangers" essence of the Church in this present age.

When that happens, the Spirit is reduced to something like a merely human *esprit de corps*. The mission becomes institutional growth and success. The 'glory' becomes the church buildings, the church campus, or stained glass, or hoary tradition, or prestigious membership, ... but something quite less than the New Creation of God in the lives of the participants.

Just remember that you and I met each other in just such a setting. So it can't be all bad!

There *can be* a high degree of authenticity in *Church Institutions*... *when* they are formed in the consciousness of their role as more permanent 'Staging Areas' for the pilgrimage of God's people in the Mission of God. They *can be* marvelous equipping areas. They *can* provide resources. They *can be* wonderful places of teaching the Word of Christ. They *can* provide heartening occasions of worship and adoration. They *can be* Missional Communities and cooperative agencies to facilitate reaching those outside in the community and the world.

They *can be* ... but then they can also be a *total distraction* from all of that, and so become inwardly and institutionally idolatrous! Somewhere in the early centuries the church took a turn backward to the paradigms of both temple and priesthood. Jesus claimed to have transcended both of those in announcing his messianic New Creation. Somewhere over time, however, the grassroots meaning of the *incarnation* was obscured so that only certain places and certain persons became 'sacralized'. Buildings became like the temple. They were conceived as sacred places called "the House of God" or "the sanctuary." It was as though God were not the God of all creation, whose dwelling in the world was in and with his people by the Spirit wherever they were as that community called the Church.

Even worse, there was created a special class of *clergy* or *reverends* or *priests* in direct contradiction to the priestly role of every believer which is so clearly taught in the apostolic writings. Such a 'special class' relegates the huge majority of God's people (who are called by Jesus Christ and indwelt by the Spirit) to some secondary role. That is a *subversion* of the New Creation design, *in spades*! I've said too much already.

"I catch your drift. Go for it! But you're going to weird-out your clergy buddies."

I really don't want to say more. There is so much in so many *Church Institutions* that is nothing less than awesome. There are church leaders and pastors and teachers salted all through the fabric of these institutions, gifted persons recognized as such by their peers in the community, and who produce incredible fruits of authenticity and of New Creation Life.

The problem is that institutions tend to be too large to be true communities, … *unless*, as some savvy institutions are recognizing, they deliberately design their institutional life and their staffs not only to encourage, nurture and produce such communities (*primary churches*), but also to nurture within them something like our Seven Signs. That is, happily, actually happening in many of places. In such church institutions and with that design they are calling to leadership people with specific proven gifts: teaching pastors, small group pastors, mission pastors, prayer pastors, … those to be leaders with responsibility over those necessary areas. They are also receiving and forming *all of their participants* with that kind of a vision, and then equipping them for *authentic* New Creation living and thinking.

Sadly, such purposeful church institutions remain a minority. Most church institutions retain something far less focused.

"Do I want to 'join' such a critter?"

Enchanted Community Begins With…

Joining

Join? Probably! But never passively. Never mindlessly. Never without asking questions about authenticity.[7] Still, there is real merit in identifying yourself with the people of God where you live, and on a larger scale than just your *Primary Church*. But, at the same time, if you come to such an institution and then 'demand' that it be a blessing to you, you will at that point become a liability to the Mission of God.[8] On the other hand if you identify yourself with others and engage with them in *encouragement*, in *ministry* to one another, in *obedience* to Christ, in *seeking authenticity* with them—then *you* will become an enormous blessing to the community of God's people. Jesus Christ will be glorified in you, even if you are in that particular place for only a brief time in your transient life.

"My brain is fried."

Mine too.

Reflection Time

"Bob, I think I need some time to process all of this by myself. Is that OK with you?"

We agreed. It was time for lunch in the refectory, and so we both joined the others in silence and ate while listening to a quiet recording of Gregorian chants. After lunch Alan wandered off by himself toward the chapel. Fr. Francis (bless him!) stashed me away in a quiet conference room, asked if I wanted some tea (which I did) and left me to myself.

---

[7] 'Joining' is never a word or concept used by scripture, so it is open to much trivialization and abuse. In scripture the followers of Jesus are taught that they need to be together in a community of believers in order to fulfill the calling into New Creation. It is never a formal identification with an organization. The sign of identification was public profession and baptism. The brothers and sisters had names and faces and stories and a shared accountability to each other in the mission of God.

[8] I refer my readers to Dietrich Bonhoeffer's very poignant study of Christian community in his book *Life Together*. He wrote this out of the context of the "underground church" in Nazi Germany in the 1930s. It was, to my knowledge, one of the first significant studies of the nature of the Communion of the Saints to emerge after a long dry spell of looking at the church through more impersonal eyes. In that volume he has strong words of those who come making demands and looking for the perfect community.

Enchanted Community

If Alan needed time to himself and with the Spirit of the Lord, I even more. I was overwhelmed with the consequences of what I might be doing in the life of this remarkable young friend that God had dropped into my life, ... and where I had taken him. Here I was in the "late afternoon" of my life, and he was in the "bright mid-morning" of his. He was new to it all: pragmatic, honest, slightly cynical, and a bit idealistic—as were most of his peers. But he was irresistibly caught up in what God is doing in the world. He had jolted me out of my non-expectant and almost-jaded (maybe even calloused) routines of Christian living, and brought me face to face with the *Enchanted* world of the Age to Come. He had forced me to confront the questions of *why* the Church is, and *what* it has to do with the good news of God in Jesus Christ. I had never had to confront those so starkly before. Alan was God's gift. I wanted to be God's gift to him.

Dear Lord, keep me from becoming a stumbling block to my brother. Come Holy Spirit!

(To be continued ...)

Stopping Place
Enchanted Aliens Between the Ages

It was mid-afternoon when Alan found me again. The two of us found a cup of coffee and returned to the quiet room Fr. Francis had provided for me. Alan sat for a while, not saying anything, just sipping his coffee and looking out the window at the winter scene in the monastery garden. Here we were where we had begun: "the Church over a cup of coffee." The irresistible Spirit had called us the two of us to Christ, and then had called us into one another's lives, and into one of those mysteries of the Church.

Well, where are we?

"Pretty sobering, isn't it?"

An understatement. But then again, I would not be surprised but what *enchanted* may be the more appropriate description. I don't want to lose that one.

"I think I'm beginning to catch something of the awesome scope of what God is up to in the world. It's intimidating to try to figure out where and how I fit."

You're not alone. While you were away, I was sitting here lost in thought, and my eyes landed on that (I pointed to the Madonna and Child on the wall). Talk about being intimidated and alone. She's my model, and what a model she is of what we are talking about.

"Mary? How so?"

Just think about it. She's the 'Christ-bearer' by God's design. And here we are, you and I. Over these past months we've been taking a stab at delving into (or struggling with) the mystery of the Church. We've been discussing how (in some way) to maintain the integrity of our discipleship, and how to have authenticity in our relating to others within the New Creation community. In a very real sense we also are 'Christ-bearers' at this moment. I have proposed that you and I have been caught-up irresistibly in the Spirit's movement of calling-out, and assembling, such a community. I think we've both got to confess that we've been, maybe, just a bit more than ambivalent about so much of the 'church stuff' that we get caught up in. It can at times seem so unrelated that same Spirit-movement.

But just think of Mary. Speaking of something being totally awesome. There she was, probably in her early teens, unmarried, and then being told by that unearthly messenger that she was going to be pregnant by the Holy Spirit, by the power of the Most High. That would be sort of hard to digest. She was engaged to a man. She was still a virgin. So talk about getting caught up in the same irresistible Spirit-movement—God's great Plan of Salvation! Not exactly what she had planned for that day, would you say? She couldn't possibly have conceived entering into an *enchanted encounter* with that messenger from the Holy God when she woke-up that morning.

But it doesn't stop there. Just think about the setting. She evidently lived in a quite pious Jewish community, where the Torah was observed, where scriptures were known, and where neighbors knew all the gossip, and where you could be stoned to death for adultery. It was in that context that the angelic messenger broke the startling word to her that she had found favor with her Holy God, and that God was with her, and that she was to become pregnant by the Holy Spirit in order to bear God's anointed Son, the long-awaited Messiah. Her own son would sit on the throne of his ancestor David, and of her son's kingdom there would be no end.

Now tell me: just how do you communicate that to your husband-to-be, or even more to your parents and your neighbors?

Just compute what that meant for her.

But for our purposes (as we look at our calling) look at how she responds. After asking a few questions of the messenger to be sure she was hearing him correctly, and after being told that nothing was impossible with God—with all faith and simplicity she responds: "Behold, I am the servant of the Lord; let it be to me according to your word."

Talk about faithfulness!

Then what does she do with all of that in the days and months that followed? She lived-out that calling quietly and faithfully and out-of-sight in her ordinary daily routines.

And you and I think we're dealing with a complicated scene!

Everything about her life and about the context of her life was non-ideal. She lived in a community dominated by a somewhat decadent Jewish religion. Her homeland was occupied by a foreign army. They lived with marginal economic subsistence, with cultural confusion caused by multiple foreign occupations, and with local misunderstandings. All of that composed the social and cultural setting of the incarnation of God in the womb of that faithful peasant girl. According to our gospel accounts, Mary frequently didn't even understand what was happening to her or with her son herself. Still she faithfully bore and nurtured Jesus. She evidently did this so faithfully that when he was twelve years old he was sufficiently familiar with scriptures to be able to enter into debate with the scholars in the Temple.

That amazing legacy inherited from his mother is obvious in Jesus. When faced with his own ultimate challenge of faith in the cosmic clash of darkness and Light before the Cross, he could respond: "Father, if you are willing, remove this cup from me. Nevertheless, not my will, but yours be done." The irresistible Design of God, the inauguration of God's New Creation, the necessary and ultimate act of reconciliation—the Cross on which Jesus chose to pay the awful price, to give his life, to open the Door for us into the Reign of God. That is the Spirit-anointed son of the faithful Mary.

Mary's faithfulness to me is mind-boggling. Just think of it: "I am your servant. Be it unto me according to your word." She was with Jesus from the beginning of his life, then to the Cross, and then she was there on Easter morning. She never pleaded any human inability or ignorance or unworthiness—she was consummately faithful. From that moment

Mary accepted God's design for her and in her and for the rest of her life she was consumed with the results of that act of faithfulness.

That's why she's my model. That's why she speaks to me.

"The point being ...?

The point being that it is that kind of faithfulness in our own far-from-ideal context that I want for you and me at this juncture in the history of God's mission. It is that kind of faithfulness that I want for us in this our own 'moment' among the people of God in his Church. That is where we are. For two millennia Jesus has been building the community of his New Creation. Most of the time that true building has been done quietly and out of sight like leaven permeating a loaf of dough. Most of it has been in the most difficult and unlikely contexts.

For two millennia the Spirit has been calling ordinary folks just like you and me to enter into it through Christ. For two millennia, irresistibly, even when the Light sometimes burned very dimly, the Wind of the Spirit kept blowing, and the Leaven of New Creation kept infiltrating the whole. That's the *mystery* of the Church. That's the *mystery* which is why your metaphors of the "back of the wardrobe" or of "Gate 9 ¾" (from the children's stories) are so *apropos* to that mystery.

Now this is our moment to respond in faithfulness to the Wind.

It's our moment to be the Light and Leaven.

It's the only opportunity for such faithful obedience that we'll ever have.

The Church, after all, is what human history is really about. The Church is the *eschatological* (that word again!) community. Human history is only the temporary scaffolding around the Church that Jesus is building. The real the building is his Church. When the building of his Church is complete, then the scaffolding of human history comes down![1] If we cannot relate our lives to that mission of God, then (as someone said) our lives are irrelevant to history.[2]

You and I have to be faithful Spirit-people. We are called to be *enchanted*-people in our place and in our ordinary daily lives here between

---

[1] This helpful (to me) figure of scaffolding and building is not original with me. I first heard it in a sermon by the late Peter Eldersveld, who was a radio preacher many years ago.

[2] I attribute this to friend and missiologist Robert Coleman, though I cannot retrieve the written source.

the ages. We have to be such people—not where we're *not*—but where we *are*. We become Light and Life where we are, and with what's at hand. We become the dwelling place of God right in the midst of all of the "stink and stuff," all the non-ideal social, political, economic, religious, and cultural realities of this present moment of our lives.

"So, like, I'm to respond to God with the same faithfulness as Mary: 'I am your servant. Be it unto me according to your word.' I am also to be a Christ-bearer and God's authentic New Creation person in the Church as well as in my daily ministry as Salt and Light where I live and work. That means that I am to be a Christ-bearer in how I live and think and exhibit the Spirit-Life that is in me.

"Is that it? Is that what you're saying? Is that why Mary is your model?"

You got it.

"That sounds almost too neat and simple."

Anything but. The 'vision' is the easy part. It's the *praxis*, the living of it, that gets you into trouble. The Spirit-community is anything *but* harmless, anything but non-controversial, or 'spiritual'. More likely, if it is faithful, the Church is going to be an alternative (and quite counter-cultural) community of aliens and exiles. It almost naturally brings with it suffering and conflict.

"Spell that out."

Connect the dots. This age is described as an "age of darkness."[3] It is a world under the dominion of "the prince of the power of the air."[4] We live in a world in rebellion against its Creator. Jesus came into this scene to inaugurate the Dominion of God and of Light.

"That means that Jesus was a subversive."

You got that right! The reason Jesus came was to destroy the works of the devil.[5] That means that there are two antithetical dominions present on this scene here and now between the ages: one is the Dominion of God, and the other is the dominion of Satan—or these are sometimes referred to as the "age to come" over against "this age." That puts those of us who

---

[3] Colossians 1:13. Plus "darkness" is a frequent description of the day in which we live, and which is passing away because of the doming of the Light in the Dominion of our Lord Jesus Christ.
[4] Ephesians 2:2
[5] I John 3:8

are followers of Jesus Christ in a continual "missionary confrontation"[6] with "this age." We live between the ages.

That makes us the recipients of the antipathy (if not the hostility) of all that is part of that dominion of darkness.

"That would make us subversive too."

No way around it. Either you succumb to being conformed to this world, or you are a subversive. Do the math. As we walk in the Light, we unavoidably expose what is inauthentic and part of the darkness. We expose, as well, the hollowness of the disenchanted structures and the powers of our present scene. Jesus never veiled the reality of that hostile reaction of the world. Not only did he candidly warn us that if the world had hated him, then we should not to be surprised that the same world would also hate us. As if that weren't enough, he made a critical part of his calling to us that we should take up our cross and follow him into a death to all the other allegiances and loyalties alien to his New Creation.

"Does that really happen?"

Count on it!

As we are faithful to Christ's calling, to the authentic living and thinking of his New Creation—then the Salt and Light which becomes displayed in us will inevitably expose the inauthenticity that is present in life and society—where God is "left out of the equation" (even in the church). The death and darkness of this present age are not neutral. They are malignant and not at all passive.

The cultural structures of darkness don't take lightly or politely to that exposure. They will do everything they can to *co-opt the Church* and to conform it to their own agendas. When they can't do that, then they will seek to demean it or destroy it in a variety of sophisticated ways. There is an ongoing demonic attempt to erode the New Creation community by forgetfulness, distorted priorities, diluting it message, or turning its focus inward and becoming forgetful of its missional design. When that happens, then the church reverts to darkness, or disenchantment.

---

[6] Cf. Lesslie Newbigin. *Foolishness to the Greeks* (Grand Rapids, MI.: Wm. B. Eerdmans, 1986). 132 in loc. Newbigin plays on this missionary encounter, or missionary confrontation principle in both this work, and in his larger *The Gospel in a Pluralist Society.* (Grand Rapids, MI. Wm. B. Eerdmans, 1989). Both are highly commended to my readers.

The contextual hostility is energized. It may be quite sophisticated or it may be brutal. That is what is taught so colorfully and graphically in the last book of the Bible (which just may be the main purpose of that book!). In that Revelation the Lamb and the Beast are always in conflict. That personification of darkness is portrayed as the Beast, and knows that its days are numbered. It knows that its fate has been sealed on the Cross. But in this present age that adversary is given liberty to make war on the people of the Lamb. So it is no surprise that one of Satan's names is Apollyon—the the *destroyer*.

Suffering is part of our calling. You can get hurt being obedient to Jesus.

"So we've gone from 'too neat' to 'too ominous' in a heartbeat."

Well, let's just say it's 'not safe' for us to be faithful and authentic in New Creation life and thinking.

Subversion

Face it! We're not Utopians. We're not looking for some idyllic, sweet, happily-ever-after, and totally unreal church. Quite the contrary. If anything, we are the ultimate realists. After all, God's dominion (New Creation) which was inaugurated in Jesus Christ is (to be honest) *subversive* in its very essence. That's what Salt and Light are all about. That's what the Spirit produces in us. That's the *Enchantment* of the New Creation community.

The pressure is always on us to compromise that, to redefine it so that it conforms more comfortably to the plausibility structures of our locale. The temptation is to make it more popular and less confrontational.[7] When we succumb to that temptation, not only do we deny our integrity, but we in effect quench the Spirit. We become saltless salt or hidden light. Light

---

[7] I sometimes worry about the term "seeker-sensitive" which churches use in their evangelistic attempts—I worry whether that is an attempt to make the gospel more digestible under the guise of evangelism while it actually may cloak all kinds of compromises that truncate the gospel and fail to witness to the demands of the gospel. Of course it may be legitimate if it indicates a true sensitivity to the spiritual hungerings of the un-churched and focuses on a way to bridge the gulf that divides those truly seeking from the Water of Life.

and Life, of necessity, stand in deliberate confrontation with the darkness and death of this present culture.

"Then you're saying that authentic followers of Jesus are some kind of weird-o 'radicals'?"

Not a bad definition—but we're 'sweet' radicals.

"Sweet?"

There's not a shred of doubt about it. If you are formed by the Word of Christ, you are in that very process being recreated into God's true humanity. You have forsaken the rebellion and autonomy, which reduces humanity to something much less than God intended. The history of the Church confirms that. It is when God's people give themselves over to obedience, it is when they engage the cultural context in which they live with the dynamics and principles of the New Creation, that is when they are transformational. They return to their true 'roots' (i.e. their *radix*) in their Creator-God. Hence, they are *radicals*! They are also those through whom God's Living Water flows ... and that water of Life is *sweet*!

But, ... when that happens, then sooner or later there comes a counterattack of the *darkness* in one form or another. It doesn't mean, however, that we become nasty or adversarial or contentious. Those kinds of responses are *bitter* and cannot come from the Spirit. That's not the divine nature in us. Not at all. We are, after all, being transformed into the image and likeness of God. That means that we love our enemies and do good to those who demean us because of the image of God in us. We live-out the principled strength and sweetness of our Lord Jesus Christ as people of the Light. We live out the Sermon on the Mount. We become part of Jesus' own search-and-rescue mission.

It's easy to do all the "Jesus talk" stuff. It's safe to be consumed with religion and religious activities. There's no problem in doing all of that, while at the same time being essentially ineffective in any redemptive engagement with the 'dominant social order' (the dominant economic, political, global, religious influences, especially the dominant 'worldview' accepted by the influence-makers *du jour*).

When that kind of detachment takes place, when God's love for the world is eclipsed by comfortable programs inside the church institutions, ... then the Spirit is quenched in that particular scene. The Light is hidden. The Salt is useless. When that happens, then that particular church expression becomes irrelevant (if not inimical) to the mission of

God. When that happens the irresistible Spirit-movement will create, in its place, other faithful colonies of New Creation to be those transformational agents of that same Spirit.

Do You Have Some Dreams For Me and My Bunch?

"OK, Bob. So we've got Mary as our model. And we know it's not safe. But where do I, where do we, begin with all this stuff? Give me some handles. Give me some dreams. No offense, but you're an old guy, you're on the way out. But I'm just starting. If you could dream dreams for me and my bunch, or if you could bequeath some helpful stuff to us, what would it be?"

I laughed at his honesty and could only reply: "You didn't have to be so blunt about it! But alright."

Let me interject something here. I do have dreams for you and for your generation. But that could be for another day. Whatever dreams I have, or could share, begin precisely where you *are*, and they definitely do not begin where you're **not**. And the present place and time in which you and your generation live is unbelievable. I really envy you. My imagination makes me have a thrilling and unbounded expectation for you because of what is unfolding around you. Your generation is a phenomenon that has never happened before, and I am enormously hopeful about its potential in the Mission of God.

"How so?"

Just think of it: yours is the first generation whose lives are totally unbounded by geography or traditional barriers—it is totally global. You travel, you have access to the Church in every nation. Your campus neighborhood is international. Just last Sunday there were followers of Jesus with us at West Park Church (that I know of) from Iran, India, China, Kenya, Sierra Leone, Lesotho and who knows where else. Plus, the internet gives access and connects you instantly across all kinds of boundaries and opens up resources not conceived even a very few years ago. Just think of what that means in being able to model a Church that is composed of persons reconciled, living and loving in community from every tongue and ethnic group and nationality. Incredible! That's an awesomely powerful testimony to God's design in Christ.

Plus, your generational bunch has a pragmatic *fix-it* approach to life and problems that bodes an interesting future for the church—which will be undoubtedly different from older and more traditional churches. I like that! You are not captive to provincial boundaries such as denominations or empty traditions. At the same time your generation seems to have an unusual appreciation for (even a longing for) the viable and venerable heritage of the Church's past, and for its treasures and for the lessons of its history as a world Christian movement.

Add to that that you have been formed by the Information Age. You have more resources at your fingertips—and more Biblical and Christian resources—than any generation before. You go on the web and have access to more good stuff to equip you for Christian thinking than the greatest Christian thinkers of past generations ever dreamed of. That means that you need a lot of *discernment*, and a lot of intention to access it, but it also means that it's there and available for you.

I knew that in one sense this nearly year-long friendship and conversation would never have a conclusion. There would always be one more side-road to go down. There would always be one more question to chase. I also knew that we had to put a concluding marker at some point and come to a stopping point. We were almost there. I also knew that the implications of however I answered his request, along with his trust in me were pretty intimidating. But the Spirit is given to provide wisdom at such moments, and I prayed in my heart and responded …

Alan, we could get into all kinds of dreams and agendas that I might have for you and your generation, but that would get us into the *what* of the Church, and I have been trying to direct your focus, rather, to the *why* of the Church. I am persuaded that if you and I know the *why* of God's design for the truly human community, then as you are being formed by such disciplines as the seven signs of authenticity that we came up with—that you will be able to be transformational agents of the Spirit's working in the church where you find yourself.

Any dreams I could share would always come out of that which we've been processing, namely, that the Church, its essence and its mission flow right out of the *missionary dialogue of the Trinity*. The would express my conviction that the Church is to be the provisional demonstration of *true human community as God intended it to be.* The Church is to live both in and out of its communion with the Trinitarian community in such a practical way that its inner-life and its character are by the Spirit *in-synch* with God's life which dwells in and among them. That is what makes the Church to be "the dwelling place of God by the Holy Spirit."

My dreams would also be formed in many ways by the hope that your generation would be alert to the pit-falls of that have subverted the church too often.

"Such as …?

Don't tempt me. But just for maybe some future conversations:

- That you not forget that the Church exists for those outside of itself. We are part of God's "search and rescue mission" and are to have his sensitivity and compassion and understanding of those on our doorstep or around the world who are still outside of his saving embrace and so lost to their heart's true home.
- That you remember that the Church is to always remain flexible and mobile and versatile and conscious of its missionary essence. Any form that it takes-on must never detract it from that for which Jesus is calling it as a demonstration of New Creation and hence as a sign of the New Creation.
- That the Church be delivered from its *captivity to the clergy.* What I mean by that is that the Church is *all of God's people* dynamically engaged in the ministry of their daily life and work, and that there is not some special category of 'super-Christians' who are the only ones called into 'full-time Christian service'. This misunderstanding has been a pathology that needs to be dealt with. The Church needs to be returned to the people of God, who all have gifts and ministries by the Spirit.
- That (along with that deliverance) the Church would reclaim the Biblical design of a community in which every member has a contribution to the others in a community of mutual ministry, and of interactive giftedness. The Spirit of God knows what are the needs of the people of God in the community of God, and so gives to individuals the anointing to express their *one another love* in practical ways. Some are encouragers, others helpers, some are gifted to communicate the gospel to outsiders, others gifted

to equip those inside into maturity in Christ. Some become the initiators of new church communities. Some have administrative skills, and others have financial means sufficient to meet the needs of the community. All are gifted. All are interactive and interanimating and mutually upbuilding. No one is passive. I dream of a Church that understands this and practices it. Again, the happens mostly in small, household-size groups and not in large impersonal institutions.

- And, finally, I would dream of the Church reclaiming its formation by a *holistic* understanding of the gospel—an understanding that is transformational in its understanding and practice of the radical nature of God's New Creation in every area of life. I dream this so that the world outside the Church can see *visibly* those whose behavior in that community, and whose thinking, are redemptive and creative and joyous and imaginative and artistic and caring and profound—*enchanted*. This is not some subjective 'spirituality' but rather a whole wonderfully counter-cultural way of living and thinking. I think that would be awesome (and is so rare on the contemporary scene).

"Good dreams. Thanks. I love it. But that raises another question for me. Is it an OK thing to actually seek some place of leadership and influence in such a community? Or is that a no-no?"

It would probably depend on your motives and on your genuine humility in seeking some such a role. Would it bring glory to Jesus Christ? And would the desire flow out of that desire to obey him? Paul told his young Timothy that those who seek to be overseers seek a good thing.[8] From that I have to assume that it is not at all improper for a person such as yourself to seek a place of leadership in the community. It is not out-of-line to desire to become the 'shaper' of New Creation community. It is not improper to seek to influence the community toward faithfulness and authenticity. That influence begins with your prayer life. It is *only* proper, however, as you seek such a role with all the *self-effacing humility*, and the love of Christ. It is *only* proper as the servant-mode of Jesus is authentic in you. It must *never* be a grab for power.

---

[8] I Timothy 3:1

Having said that, don't ever sell yourself short in your capacity to be a wonderful New Creation influence on other individuals, and to encourage the whole community as you yourself mature into the image of Jesus Christ. Leadership gifts such as overseers, elders, or deacons (for instance) are also Spirit gifts. The harmony and mutual caring and interanimation of such a community is in itself a sign to the outsiders.

There are unquestionably a whole lot of other pieces involved in such reclaiming of the Church's *authenticity*, but all may come under the heading of *reclaiming of our call to discipleship and to obedience*. Such obedience will put the 'lie' to the idea that any of us is ever called to 'passive membership' in the Church. It will label as *inauthentic* the understanding of 'membership' in which persons are unaccountable and non-responsible for their stewardship of God's New Creation in Christ. What *discipleship* involves is a *radical conversion* to God's New Creation in Christ. Tragically, such conversion is hardly ever mentioned in all too many of the institutional churches of my experience.

Alan, such *refounding* of authenticity in the Church seldom takes place from any top-down initiative, even from the best-intentioned ecclesiastical officialdom. It is not a *program* that can be packaged and bought, and then put into practice in a community. It will only take place, as Jesus promised, where two or three or more '*one anothers*' gather in Jesus' Name. It happens where he is present by the Spirit transforming them into *true humanity*, and into *true human community*. It happens where we are embraced again into the community of the Father, Son, and Holy Spirit. When we are together in such a Spirit-community, whether over a cup of coffee (such as you and I right now), or in a household, or an intentional small group—there the Spirit produces the *enchantment*, the joy, the vision, the hope, the conversation, the song, the clarity—yes, the *authenticity* of God's design. And when that smaller group (you and I and others) takes its place in the larger assemblies, in church institutions (such as West Park), then it brings with it that New Creation authenticity. We become Light and Life at the grassroots. We become the Spirit-Presence in that gathering.

Not a bad vision, is it?

"Awesome."

Hey! It's getting late, but maybe a couple of stories out of my own sojourn these past couple of years will add something important to this conversation.

A Conference

I was enormously moved several years ago to be in an assembly of, maybe, a thousand, or eleven hundred, followers of Jesus out of the academic community. They were mostly persons such as you. They were graduate students and faculty invited by a wonderful Christian organization to spend several days under the theme: "Following Christ—Shaping the World." What a vision! There was something intentionally missional and formative about the very atmosphere. Everyone who was there came with that missional purpose and with that sense of the stewardship of the Spirit's presence in their lives and in all the disciplines they represented: natural sciences, physical sciences, humanities, religious studies, environment, arts, media and many more.

For those several days all of those participants were in an intense engagement with others who understood themselves as God's people to be entrusted with their particular callings as transformational agents. Scriptures were taught at a profound level, such as was fitting for such intellectual gifts as were gathered there. Worship times were sensitive and Spirit-anointed and deeply moving. Prayer was encouraged, and it was not unusual to see groups sitting on the floor in the large ballroom praying fervently with and for one another.

It was thrilling to contemplate that those men and women would go back to campus mission fields around the world with renewed vision and encouragement to be both excellent and faithful in their callings. It was only a four day assembly. But, … *it was the Church for those four days!* It was transformational. It was encouraging. It was a New Creation community in a hotel ballroom. It was the Church over meals, or over a cup of coffee, or over a pint. It was authentic. The glory of Father, Son and Holy Spirit was present. I was personally transformed by it and its influence on me lingers.

A Parish Church

Or try on the story of my brief engagement with an awakened Anglican parish in Oxford, England. In recent years there has been a remarkable flow of authentic Life and Light out of a very old parish church in the middle of the city of Oxford. The rector emeritus told me that St. Ebbe's was actually founded as a preaching point in the seventh or eighth century. There has been a building on that site since the eleventh century. One would hardly question that, for many of the generations or even centuries that this parish church has been in existence, it probably was routinely performing the rites, inhabiting the religious death of moribund and traditional (yes, *disenchanted*) ecclesial life. For generations it was probably anything but an expression of authentic New Creation community. I don't mean to be judgmental—I just can't imagine anything other than that.

But somewhere in recent years there were evidently some who came alive in Christ, and some who took their places in that scene to be 'shapers', to be intercessors, to be authentic New Creation persons, and to be a colony of authentic Light and Life. The result has been (however it happened) that St. Ebbe's is presently a wonderfully vibrant and encouraging witness to the good news of God in Jesus Christ. Outwardly it is a church institution housed in a typical old gray stone building, stained with the grime of the city and unimpressive. But what gathers there is an authentic assembly of God's people who are very intentional about their engagement in the mission of God to that great university city. That intention and *enchantment* are present from the grassroots right up to the rector.

Somebody was faithful. Somebody was patient and longsuffering. Somebody was undoubtedly frustrated more than once. Somebody had a vision of transformation. Somebody saw the strategic missionary location of that ancient parish in downtown Oxford. The result has been a demonstration of transformed human community, and transformed human lives that is like a stream of Living Water into that cultural center. Jesus Christ is exalted.

Such is the mystery of the Church. Such is the mystery of *Enchantment*. Such is the irresistible movement of the Spirit.

Stopping Place

By now it was late afternoon, and we had both agreed to be finished by about this time. We had covered a lot of ground in the many months of our quest to understand the mystery of the Church. I felt compelled to add one final piece, and that was about the glory of God in Christ. The glory of God is made known to us in his Son, Jesus. As Jesus lives in us by his Spirit, even so does the glory of God inhabit those of us who are the Church. I have a very strong conviction that when Paul talks about God's power at work in us manifesting God's *glory in the Church and in Christ Jesus*—that it only follows.[9] Jesus Christ is the first-fruits of the New Creation, and so the Church is the community of that New Creation. By the Spirit dwelling in both individual followers and in the community of followers, they bring glory to the Father. My word, then, to Alan: *Focus on the glory of Christ in the Church, … and the authenticity and the enchantment will surely follow.*

He stood looking at me thoughtfully for several minutes. Then his response (his quiet reflection now morphing into a mischievous glint in his eye): "One thing I can say about you old guys, you sure do use a lot of talk, … but thanks.

"Enchanted? Eschatological? Irresistible movement of the Spirit? Perichoresis? Yeah, right!

"I think I can get into it. And that 'Missionary dialogue of the Trinity' piece – that puts a lot of things into place also. Seven Signs of Authenticity? Not bad! Sounds sort of challenging doesn't it?

"Yeah, I can get into that. I like it. It helps me see through my misgivings. Thanks."

So we stopped by the desk and thanked the brother for the hospitality of the day, left our contribution to the costs of the guest house and wandered out to the car park reminiscing a bit about our months of reflection. Alan reminded me that we were probably just being added to

---

[9] Ephesians 3:20-21

an innumerable company of fellow aliens and exiles over two millennia grappling with the same mystery of the Church. When we got to the car he couldn't resist one last shot (which I deserved):

"Yours has got to be the longest, most circuitous damned answer I ever got to simple question!" Then he laughed a belly laugh, and added: "I love it!" He grabbed me and hugged me, we looked at each other for a few seconds in mutual appreciation, got in our cars and left for home.

Epilogue

"You have not come to what may be touched ...
[**translate**: to a merely human church community ...]
But you have come to Mount Zion
[**translate**: to the Enchanted and eschatological community of God's New Creation]
and to the city of the living God,
the heavenly Jerusalem,
and to innumerable angels in festal gathering,
and to the assembly of the firstborn
who are enrolled in heaven,
and to God, the judge of all,
and to the spirits of the righteous made perfect,
and to Jesus,
the mediator of a new covenant,
and to the sprinkled blood ...
Therefore let us be grateful for receiving a kingdom
that cannot be shaken,
and thus offer to God acceptable worship,
with reverence and awe,
for our God is a consuming fire."
(Hebrews 12:18, 22-24, 28-29)

www.ingramcontent.com/pod-product-compliance
Lightning Source LLC
Chambersburg PA
CBHW070312230426
43663CB00011B/2099